THE
AMERICAN
MUSICAL
THEATER

OTHER BOOKS BY LEHMAN ENGEL

This Bright Day

Getting Started in the Theater

Words with Music

*Planning and Producing
the Musical Show*

The American Musical Theater

REVISED EDITION

by Lehman Engel

Macmillan Publishing Co., Inc.

NEW YORK

Macmillan Publishing Co., Inc.
866 Third Avenue, New York, N.Y. 10022
Collier Macmillan Canada, Ltd.

Library of Congress Cataloging in Publication Data

Engel, Lehman, 1910–
    The American musical theater.

    Discography: p.
    Bibliography: p.
    Includes index.
        1. Musical revue, comedy, etc.—United States.
I. Title.
ML1711.E5   1975   782.8'1'0973   74-31255
ISBN 0-02-536080-9

First Printing 1975

Printed in the United States of America

TO
THE MEMORY OF
E.L.
WITH GRATITUDE

CONTENTS

INTRODUCTION

by Brooks Atkinson

For years Lehman Engel has been looking at musical dramas from a point of strategic advantage. He has been standing at the conductor's desk in the orchestra pit, waving his arms at the instrumentalists, looking apprehensively at the singers. Success trapped him into looking at *Fanny* for two years, at *Call Me Mister* for almost two years, and at *Take Me Along* and *Wonderful Town* for about one year each.

As a consistent theatergoer, I have many memories of gazing at the back of Mr. Engel's head and seeing his white shirt cuffs giving the beat. I have also seen him grow steadily more imposing from the fine dinners he consumes in some of New York's epicurean restaurants before he dashes off to the theater.

Since he is a man of exuberance and gaiety, many of his friends have wondered how he could stand the monotony of looking at and listening to the same show month after month. Now we know. He has been studying their craftsmanship. He has been thinking about their theatrical values. With all this experience (much of it concerned with music outside the theater) he has written an important book about the musical stage. It contains the artistic judgments of a serious musician; it also contains the practical knowledge of an experienced professional who is impatient with the muddle of amateurs. If this makes him sound crotchety, let me add that the book also contains the enthusiasm of a man who loves what he is doing.

Since the book deals with matters that I have been acquainted with for years, it naturally fascinates me. But it has also instructed me. It contains the workaday information that only an alert professional can supply. When a show succeeds, it captivates an ordinary theatergoer so thoroughly that he is unaware of the craftsmanship. Mr. Engel enjoys a fine musical as much as the most uninstructed theatergoer does. But he is always aware of the structure of the play. His mind disciplines his emotions.

As an art form, the musical stage is entitled to serious consideration. The musical stage is pure theater. I have sometimes wondered whether it is not a more genuine and comprehensive form of theater than the spoken drama. In essence, theater is poetry, and the musical stage has the spontaneity of poetry. It is the most effective method for creating imaginative drama. It has a centrifugal style. You might logically expect that the performing art that presents the audience with live actors would be the most realistic. It is not. The film, which presents the audience with photographs of live actors, is the best medium for realistic drama. The stage cannot compete with the screen here.

On the screen, however, musical dramas and musical comedies look thin, flat, bloodless, and contrived. The virtuosity of camera angles is merely a desperate attempt to rescue them from dullness. The stage is the medium that can add a dimension to life. It can captivate a theatergoer into believing that in *Carousel,* for example, Billy really goes to heaven and observes the earthly career of his fifteen-year-old daughter. On the modern stage, a soliloquy is difficult if not impossible to act without making a theatergoer self-conscious. But on the musical stage, most songs—perhaps all songs—are soliloquies. Is there anything more eloquent in the modern theater than Billy's long soliloquy in *Carousel* after Julie has told him that he is going to be a father? Without that rambling soliloquy it would be impossible to express the gentleness of spirit that lies under the rude exterior of this difficult character. Since both the music and the lyrics are exalting, they give the audience an intense emotional experience.

Although Mr. Engel is an old hand in the musical theater, I

am glad to note that he is one of the believers and can lose himself in the glow of musical occasions. Commenting on the music-lyric treatment of "One Hand, One Heart" in *West Side Story,* he says it "is nearly unbearable because of its simplicity and impossibility." For the musical stage is phantasmagoria. Like poetry, it deals in myth. It incantates the theater. By the richness of its medium, which blends music, dance, verse, costume, scenery, and orchestra, the musical drama makes complete use of the theater. It is the one element of poetry left in a form of literature that was all poetry originally; and it is worth the serious discussion that Mr. Engel has brought to it in this book.

To me it is gratifying to have a personal impression validated by an expert. Mr. Engel says that a good book or libretto is the cornerstone of a successful musical show. He says the book or libretto must operate from a set of dramatic principles. For all the elements of the show—music, dancing, acting, décor—hang on some plausible resolution of the conflict between the characters; and (this is his most original observation on this subject) the characters must be so clearly defined that the dramatic conflict "sets up a *need* in the audience to see a genuine resolution of their differences." If the show is to succeed, the audience must believe in the theme. Passive entertainment is not enough.

And this surely explains the inadequacy of the traditional, perfunctory musical comedies that seemed to the public to be generally satisfactory until *Show Boat* came along in 1927. The identifiable characters from Edna Ferber's novel put Jerome Kern's glorious music and Oscar Hammerstein II's poignant lyrics into dramatic perspective. Before 1927, journeyman books with stereotyped characters—the romantic pair, the comic pair—had seemed to be good enough, and some memorable songs came out of them—"Fascinating Rhythm" from *Lady, Be Good,* for example, and "Tea for Two" from *No, No, Nanette.* After *Show Boat* had transmuted the musical stage into a form of idyllic drama, the day of the mechanical musical comedy was finished.

It was a long time before the lesson was learned. In 1933

xi

Roberta brought an intolerable, trashy book to a score by Jerome Kern that included "Smoke Gets in Your Eyes," "Yesterday," and "The Touch of Your Hand," and failed. Good music cannot be appreciated in a silly book show, and cannot attract a public. In 1933 *Very Warm For May* brought another intolerable book to a Kern score that included "All the Things You Are," and again the production failed.

In 1931 *Of Thee I Sing* introduced intelligence to the musical stage, and in 1935 *Porgy and Bess* raised the level of the musical stage about as high as it can go. But the '30's were still in the grip of the past. The fifteen musicals that Mr. Engel has chosen as the great ones come from the golden period between 1940 (*Pal Joey*) and 1957 (*West Side Story*), when talented writers and composers had enough vision to approach the musical stage as if it were a form of literature. Richard Rodgers and Oscar Hammerstein II were at once the most workmanlike and the most inspired. Mr. Engel would probably have included *Fiddler on the Roof* * in the category of immortal works if it had been produced earlier. I would include *Man of La Mancha,* but he would not. But we agree that the days of consistent high endeavor on the musical stage are over and that the Broadway stage has reverted to the kind of hackwork which was acceptable until *Show Boat* broke the mold. *Hello, Dolly!, Funny Girl, Sweet Charity,* and *Mame* run on year after year like robots. They lack everything that made the American musical stage great in the '40's and '50's. It is a measure of what we have lost that audiences are again satisfied with trash.

Although I share Mr. Engel's enthusiasm for literate musicals by writers and composers who are genuinely gifted, I regret the loss of the buffoons. They have gone into the discard. There was no place in the adult musical plays for the extravagant clowning of the late Bert Lahr although his superb comic mummery did not delight enough theatergoers in 1964 to make a success of *Foxy.* He was the last of the royal line. The shows in which Bobby Clark, Ed Wynn, Willie Howard, and W. C. Fields used to appear could not compare artistically with *Oklahoma!* or

* *Fiddler* is now included.

Annie Get Your Gun. In point of fact, the clowns generally appeared in revues, which have become victims of technological obsolescence since America became swamped in television.

By abandoning the buffoons, the musical stage has lost one of its most legitimate assets. They belonged to the musical stage because they, too, were larger than life and inhabited a fantasy world. They were as legitimate as the music, dancing, and décor. I never reached the stage of maturity when I doubted that Bobby Clark chasing a prop lion in a *Music Box Revue* or W. C. Fields grandiloquently playing pool with a crooked cue or Willie Howard looking with surprise and delight down the neck of the contralto with whom he was singing grand opera in a concert version or Groucho Marx loping around the stage in a crumpled morning coat were great theater. I regret the loss of the clowns.

As a professional musician, Mr. Engel is able to discuss one touchy subject without condescension—the relation that exists between grand opera and the finest of the Broadway musical plays. Of the fifteen plays he has selected as the best, he regards six as opera—*Carousel, The King and I, Brigadoon, My Fair Lady, West Side Story,* and *A Little Night Music.* Everyone has always accepted *Porgy and Bess* as opera if only because George Gershwin deliberately wrote it in that medium. To me, grand opera is a synonym for boredom. In the first place, most of the libretti are about as witless as the libretti of the musical comedies that Broadway has outgrown. In the second place, the stage work on Broadway is vastly superior to the staging and acting at the Metropolitan Opera House. In 1950 that fact was vividly illustrated. Broadway staged a brilliant performance of Leonard Bernstein's *Candide* (book by Lillian Hellman) at the same time that the Met was staging a loose, facetious, sophomoric production of Offenbach's *La Périchole.* Since patrons of the Met go to hear and not to see, they do not object to the clumsiness of the staging and the dreariness of the acting there. But I do. I have been trained to the standards of Broadway, which are high. The only grand opera I ever saw that thoroughly enraptured me was a performance of *The Rake's Progress* in Stockholm. It had been staged by Ingmar Bergman, a theater man. Grand opera does not have to be stupid; it can be acted and directed with skill and taste.

"True American opera—which I feel already flourishes—has descended from Broadway," Mr. Engel remarks. (I enjoy his verb "descends"; it suggests that the path of the opera house leads to the grave.) To continue quoting from Mr. Engel: "It is this American musical tradition which speaks to us truly and reflects who we are." In other words, we recognize the people in *Porgy and Bess* and *My Fair Lady* because the composers and writers are working without pose in a brisk, modern style. Unfortunately, the musical stage lacks singers in any way comparable to the great voices at the Met. Although the composing for the musical stage is often versatile and creative, the singing is elementary. Since many of the scores are eloquent, it is a pity that they cannot all be sung by people with voices as stirring as Ezio Pinza's was in *South Pacific* and John Raitt's in *Carousel*. But the material for these plays is operatic, as Mr. Engel declares. The fact that it is enjoyable should not be held against it.

Thanks to Mr. Engel's alertness and industry, we now have a penetrating and comprehensive book that gives everything its proper name and makes enlightened judgments. After more than thirty years of break-in tours on the road and conducting night after night on Broadway, to say nothing of writing music, conducting choirs, and teaching, Mr. Engel knows more about the American musical theater than anyone else. He is enthralled by the beauty of its finest music. But he does not regard the dilemmas of show business as beneath his dignity. It is all here, including the hysteria of the preliminary tours in New Haven, Boston, and Philadelphia.

After all these years of looking at the back of Mr. Engel's head in the theater, now I know what goes on inside it. Some brilliant thinking goes on there. He has put it down with force and candor in a book commensurate with the importance of the musical stage.

AUTHOR'S PREFACE

This preface is not intended to be autobiographical, but I believe it necessary to explain how and why I came to write this book and—such as they are—what qualifications I have for doing so.

I began as a composer of serious music; my studies naturally made me aware of the inner workings of music—an awareness that, once awakened, extended to all music.

My first professional work (I was twenty-one) was done in collaboration with Martha Graham, the great American dancer who stimulated in me an interest in things theatrical. My association with her inspired more original and imaginative efforts than I might ever have undertaken without her.

In 1934—through director Melvyn Douglas—I had my first job in the Broadway theater: composing (overnight) and conducting a considerable amount of incidental music for Sean O'Casey's play, *Within the Gates*. And because I was immediately "type cast," my career for a time became exclusively that of composer of incidental music. The O'Casey play was followed by many others, including *Murder in the Cathedral, Shoemaker's Holiday, Hamlet,* and *Macbeth*. I came then to be far more intimate with many of the world's great plays than I might otherwise have been.

Moreover, I also came to know, and had the opportunity to learn from, such directors as Margaret Webster, Orson Welles, Elia Kazan—and, later, Robert Lewis, Joshua Logan, Jerome Robbins, Michael Kidd, Jack Cole, Eva Le Gallienne, Mary Hunter, Lee Strasberg, George Abbott, Garson Kanin, Abe Burrows, Walter Kerr, Arthur Laurents, Peter Glenville, and many more.

During the Depression years, I worked in both the Federal Music and Federal Theater Projects. Though I continued to work in all sorts of theatrical projects, my primary involvement at this time was in the Music Project, with the creation of a vocal ensemble called The Madrigal Singers. Since I had not been formally schooled in Renaissance music, my approach to it was highly personal, and I had to learn how to communicate to large audiences the excitement, poetry, and drama that it held for me. This experience also taught me a great deal about style.

Then, in 1937, I conducted my first musical show. This was *Johnny Johnson*, Kurt Weill's first Broadway musical, produced by the enormously vital Group Theater. Type cast anew, I was engaged to conduct many shows—in all, as of today, I have written for and/or conducted 170 of them—and thus through the years was privileged to be associated with Harold Rome, Maxwell Anderson, S. N. Behrman, Marc Blitzstein, Moss Hart, Arthur Kober, Harry Warren, Laurence and Lee, Jerome Weidman, Leonard Bernstein, Jule Styne, Harold Arlen, Chodorov and Fields, Comden and Green, Saroyan, George Abbott, Bob Merrill, Gian-Carlo Menotti, Aaron Copland, Virgil Thomson, and others.

Serving in the Navy during World War II, I spent two years conducting band and orchestra programs and later was put in charge of music for Navy films—composing and conducting—and in another way exploring the problems of communicating with an audience. After the war, Goddard Lieberson, now Vice President of CBS, produced a large number of show recordings, never before made, with me as conductor. These recordings were followed by others for RCA Victor, and occasionally for Decca and Capitol.

In 1959, almost by accident, I began to conduct a musical-theater workshop for composers, lyricists, and playwrights, sponsored by Broadcast Music, Inc. The workshop has expanded and continued with the continuing generous support of its original sponsor, and today includes classes in Los Angeles and Toronto. The opportunity these classes have afforded many highly talented theater neophytes to develop their skills has, I feel, been of some benefit; I know that I learned much from the workshop members.

Finally, I was engaged as advisor to Columbia Pictures-Screen Gems. And in this capacity I read a staggering number of librettos and listened to an incalculable number of scores.

The workshops, lectures to playwrights, college audiences, women's clubs, etc., around the country; the reading of librettos sent from every corner of America; the listening to auditions of new shows; the studying, composing, and conducting—all have come into focus: what is the meaning of musical theater?

That enormous talent is to be found on every hand in America there is no question. Too often this talent gets caught up in a huge maelstrom of activity leading nowhere. Too often the time and energy and spirit of the gifted are dissipated for want of an awareness of what our musical theater really is, or what its best traditions have signified. I have seen playwrights, for instance, who normally write excellent plays plunge into the writing of librettos without so much as a pause to recognize that they are now working in quite another genre, with its own demands, requiring the mastery of a different craft.

Often, too, composers and lyricists who write truly excellent songs have shown, in writing for the musical theater, a failure to understand that music and lyrics meant to further the progress of a drama, in many ways need to be different from independent songs.

Certainly no composer would attempt to write a symphony without considerable technical background. Nor would a playwright attempt to create a play without knowledge based on an intimate acquaintance with the works of the important dramatists of all periods. But—whether because it appears to be a simple thing to do, or in response to the often chimerical lure of instant glamor, wealth, or whatnot—everybody in America, it seems, has suddenly written a musical!

Unfortunately, I have read nearly all of these works, and it seems clear that out of thousands of writers and composers only a very few have ever imagined that there is a precise skill involved in the creation of a fine show. Only a very few, that is, have given evidence of a recognition that there is one way in which they can acquire the essential knowledge, namely, from a study of the best and the worst shows that, taken together, have become a vast literature in our country.

It is this distillation that has become the chief interest of my life: to examine, to attempt certain conclusions about, and to help impart what I believe exists as a body of basic principles in the art of musical theater.

In the formative days of American musical theater, talented writers in the process of discovering themselves and new paths had ample opportunity (which will be described later in this book) to learn in the only way then possible to them: trial and error. Today the opportunities for learning by doing are far fewer, and failure is too costly both in dollars and careers. Also today—unlike thirty years ago—models do exist. They are there to be studied. If mistakes are more disastrous than they used to be, they are also more easily avoidable.

Most of what "works" today in our theater offers itself for valuable study. Unfortunately time (and the perspective that it can bring) is needed in making any final appraisal of any work of art.

But even without the benefit of time, there must be standards—some way, no matter how vague, of assessing the quality of any new work. Otherwise we are left merely with the criteria of passing popularity and fame (and, of course, the money that they bring). If these were to be the sole credentials of a theater work, then our models would have to include any and every form of entertainment that is privileged to hang out an SRO sign. Although I do believe that the very best shows have all been successful, and that, moreover, no fully excellent show has ever failed, it is also true that a great many shabby, cheap, derivative formula shows have, and will from time to time continue to titillate the not always discriminating public.

It would be a gross impertinence on my part (or anyone else's, for that matter) to contend that I even begin to know all of the things that make a musical show work. I do no claim anything so extravagant. Whatever it is that I *do* know has been painstakingly extracted from those shows that, in my opinion, work the best (and also from many others that did *not* work).

Being so deeply concerned with the future of the American musical theater, I am appalled by a disregard for the things that I am convinced are the workable principles of musical-theater writing. I do not mean to imply that there is any formula at all. The principles I speak of are not rules; they are derived from the work of our best practitioners. It is quite possible and perhaps even desirable for a talented writer who fully understands the principles to depart from them provided he is *aware* of his departure and has knowingly substituted some other workable element to replace what he rejects from the past. This practice is the very history of all of the arts. But the "new" has been authentically new only when it has consciously descended from a knowledge of everything good that has preceded it. In musical theater, the principles are often unrecognized and therefore ignored.

I do not care about A's career or B's, but about the growth and health of our musical theater; and, to paraphrase John Donne, any misfortune that befalls it affects every other person working within it.

Any claims that I would make for this book, then, are not claims for myself or my own judgment. Someone *had* to try to extract and collate the lessons to be found in our impressive body of literature, and that is what I have attempted to do. Walt Whitman said, "All truths wait in all things." To these truths, some of which I believe I have found, I have added nothing of my own.

What I hope for, then, is that this study might lead to some curtailment of much current waste of talent, time, opportunity, and money; it might also lead to disagreements, which could be healthy.

It would be impossible for me to conclude this introduction without expressing my thanks to people without whom I could not have written this book. First of all, my greatest indebtedness is to the composers, lyricists, playwrights, and directors whose work has provided me with the necessary material and stimulus. The privilege of knowing so many of them personally and of working with them has helped to widen my understanding of the problems they have had to face, and the solutions they have found. The people in this category are too numerous to mention; in fact, they constitute by now nearly everyone working in musical theater.

In addition, I wish to thank Robert Sour, past President of Broadcast Music, Inc., and Edward Cramer, his successor, who have made it possible for me to conduct my workshops freely and without reference to the affiliations of the participants; the men and women who have made them up, have through the years provided me with invaluable insights into the artistic dilemmas that plague all creative people.

I want to thank Marvin Schofer—a former workshop member—for his research, and Midge Podhoretz for her patient and understanding editing.

1

Prelude

The American musical theater can be traced to origins in the 18th century. In the 1790's, theaters and public stages in New York City were offering much more in the way of musical entertainment than of regular drama. John Gay's *The Beggar's Opera* had been seen as early as 1751. By that time music societies were already flourishing in many cities, and their concerts were well attended. These performances often took place in the theater, which was thriving despite moral prejudices against it.

Besides concerts there were circuses, puppet shows, shadow plays, ballad operas, plays with olios (songs, dances, acrobatic acts, etc.), but seldom any kind of theater without some kind of music.

Nearly all music in our theaters until about the start of the 19th century (and in most cases even for decades afterward) was foreign born. Lyricists adapted songs—often well-known ones from every corner of Europe—to new, colloquial texts. While these practices were usual and important, they can scarcely be called "American."

By 1796 the musical theater could boast an indigenously American production. Based on the story of William Tell, with a libretto by one William Dunlop and music by Benjamin Carr (credited in some quarters as the composer of "Yankee Doodle"), this musical was entitled *The Archers, or Mountaineers of Switzerland;* its success was immediate. Neither this theater nor any other at this time, however, was in any genuine sense a precursor of our own. It was to be more than a century before the main influence which fed American musical theater as we know it today—that is, the tradition of European operetta—took root in American soil.

Throughout the 19th century, productions fall into four categories: pantomimes, variety shows or vaudevilles, minstrel shows, and extravaganzas. Each of these contributed some element to that later amalgam that would come to be called the revue.

Pantomime, a French import derived from the 16th-century Italian *commedia dell'arte,* came to be put on as a kind of "curtain raiser," and generally constituted the first third or half of an evening's bill. Sometimes, to compete with the increasingly popular extravaganzas, pantomimes were expanded in length and elaborateness, using trick scenic effects and newly devised stage machinery. Pantomime, however, had disappeared by 1880.

Extravaganza, also a French importation, consisted of dance numbers featuring the female form, brilliantly costumed and surrounded by a sumptuous production, novel scenic devices, unusual lighting, plus melodramatic musical scenes—and American impresarios of the 1860's struggled to outdo one another in the lavishness of their offerings. These extravaganzas naturally enjoyed high public acclaim. The most successful of them, *The Black Crook,* opened in 1866. The production of *The Black Crook* achieved an unprecedented success by accident. Two producers, Henry Jarrett and Harry Palmer, had imported a ballet company from Paris, but before the show's opening, the theater it was to occupy burned down. In the meantime another producer, William Wheatley, had announced *"The Black Crook*—a melodrama without music." The ballet producers—with a company of dancers minus a theater—conceived the idea of joining forces with the play producer and converting his melodrama into a musical spectacle. To meet the production demands of this hybrid, the stage of Niblo's Garden had to be remade. The scenery and lighting were elaborate. More than 100 ballet dancers, all exhibiting their legs—or, as they were then referred to, limbs—in tights, were employed. The opening performance lasted five-and-a-half hours. The newspapers were unimpressed by the melodrama, but enthralled by the spectacle, particularly the female beauty; and *The Black Crook* was flocked to by a public whose anticipation was further heightened by attacks on the show from outraged clergymen.

The growth of the American musical theater followed the development of American cultural consciousness and national maturity. Larger questions aside—whatever in the surrounding society was no longer satisfied by such entertainments as the pantomime and minstrel show (a few of the latter continued to tour as late as 1920)—the demise of these two forms was hastened by the growth of the variety show, or vaudeville.

The variety show was a borrowing from England but very quickly underwent a major local adaptation. It was taken from the music-hall stage and brought for a time into the saloon—with a marked effect on its spirit and tone. The saloons in which these first variety shows appeared catered almost exclusively to well-to-do male customers. Song and dance acts on small stages competed with "waiter-girls," who were the best-advertised part of the setup. Finally it became desirable for impresarios to protect their clientele from police annoyance, and Tony Pastor, the shrewdest of New York's saloon operators, became the first to open a music hall in which the show was the sole point of interest. Women and even children could now attend without fear of being scandalized. Other producers followed Pastor's example. By the turn of the present century, variety shows had divided themselves into two related but quite distinct genres, vaudeville and burlesque: the one growing primarily out of variety acts, and the other, out of the blandishments of the "waiter-girls."

Minstrel shows constituted the one form that was directly related to American life: songs and dances, sketches and jokes, scenery, and costumes based on what was popularly imagined to represent southern Negro folklore. These shows, as such, seem to have grown out of an act first presented in 1828 by

3

Thomas Dartmouth Rice. Rice, in blackface, sang "Jim Crow," "Clare de Kitchen," and other songs from a fast-growing collection of synthetic comic and/or sad material about Negro life. In 1843 the Virginia Minstrels, headed by Daniel Emmett, the composer of "Dixie," gave what is credited as the first performance of a full-blown minstrel show. Almost immediately, other troupes appeared on the scene, chief among which was Christy's Minstrels. Stephen Foster wrote some of his most celebrated songs for Christy.

The minstrel show quickly achieved a standard format. Divided into three parts, it usually began with a parade of gaudily costumed blackfaced men who, after settling in chairs placed in a semicircle, engaged in a series of jokes, specifically between the "end men" and interlocutor. These were interspersed with solo songs backed by ensemble humming, duets, and so on. Part II was a kind of vaudeville that displayed whatever individual talents the company boasted. Part III frequently consisted of a parody on a play or opera, or was a kind of sentimental operetta based on southern Negro life on the plantation, at the levee, or at home. Needless to say, the minstrel troupes were composed of white men made up with burnt cork. (It is interesting to note that in 1898 a musical show, entitled *Clorindy, or The Origin of the Cake Walk,* was produced on Broadway with an all-Negro cast, which also included women.)

By 1900 there was a wide range of production in the theater—some of it new, some passing out of fashion, but all leaving influences on what was to come. Furthermore, each new discovery of style or combination of elements tended to weaken the demarcation between one genre and another. All of them employed girls, music, comedy, and dancing.

Moreover, genuinely native forces were at work. In 1874 Edward E. Rice, an amateur musician who worked in the office of the Cunard Steamship Company, composed a "girlie" show based, unlikely as it seems, on Longfellow's *Evangeline*—one of the first full-scale productions on a uniquely American theme. Between 1877 and 1885, the shows of Harrigan and Hart began successfully to fulfill the desire of audiences for less emphasis on girls and elaborate productions and more on homey comedy.

At this time also, John Philip Sousa and Reginald De Koven in different ways gave expression to a new assertion of national consciousness. And in 1901 began the productions of the man who perhaps more than any other was to make explicit a new assertion of Americanism in this theatrical new-found-land: George M. Cohan.

2

Breakaway

America in the late decades of the 19th century was a land of rapidly expanding frontiers, rapidly amassed fortunes—unstintingly displayed—and rapid accessions to power. The kind of fumbling entertainment it could claim peculiarly its own was gaudy, extravagant, makeshift, and formless.

For more sophisticated musical entertainment, the American theater was dependent on Europe—specifically, on the operettas of Vienna or Paris or London. (It is interesting to note that, on the basis of a numerical count, audience taste seemed to be about equally divided between the "serious" and the "popular": records show that between 1855 and 1900 the New York theater offered 83 operettas—most of which were European—and 72 musicals—mostly homegrown.) While the importations—largely operettas—were given productions in New York similar to those of their European originals, the new shows reflected the contemporary American tastes for broad comedy, dancing, spectacle, less sophisticated music, and subject matter that oscillated between homey local themes (*Pop,* 1883) and bizarre or picturesque places and people (*The Geisha,* 1896)—both equally popular.

In addition to the borrowings from European material, new

shows were affected by the immigration of young European composers trained in the traditions of the old world and eager for success in the new. Such men as Victor Herbert, Rudolf Friml, and Sigmund Romberg took up residence in this country and remained to offer those who were younger, and generations yet unborn, a rich legacy.

The first of the three to arrive, and in some ways the most influential, was Victor Herbert. Born in Dublin in 1859 and educated in Stuttgart and Vienna, Herbert came to America in 1886 to play cello in the orchestra of the Metropolitan Opera House, where his wife had been engaged to sing. Like an earlier opera cellist, Jacques Offenbach, he was primarily committed to composition. After eight years in the New York theater, he achieved his first production, *Prince Ananias,* which was followed by *Babes in Toyland, Mademoiselle Modiste, Naughty Marietta,* among about thirty-nine others. His popularity came to be enormous. Although his avowed purpose was to further Viennese operetta, he unconsciously succeeded in creating a style that represented the first significant step away from the European models. His melodies were simpler, more easily remembered, and easier to perform. His harmonic sense was less sophisticated, and although he was a highly skilled musician, he chose to shed musical complexities, which had been the hallmark of the Europeans (who were merely one step away from grand opera), and gave us clear, attractive, transparent, simple loveliness. In all of these qualities he was rapidly retreating from his progenitors and establishing himself as an ancestor of what he himself could not have dreamed!

Rudolf Friml, born in Bohemia, studied composition with Dvořák and came to America in 1901 at the age of twenty-two, achieving his first Broadway success in 1912 as the composer of *The Firefly.*

This was Friml's first Broadway show (he had been a "serious" composer until that time); he wrote the score in about a month and it was a great hit. Still heard today are "Giannina Mia," "When a Maiden Comes Knocking at Your Heart," and "Sympathy."

Sigmund Romberg, born in Hungary in 1887 and also spell-

7

bound by the operettas of Johann Strauss and Franz Lehár, came to the United States at twenty-two. By 1914—five years after his arrival—he, too, began composing Broadway musicals.

Meanwhile, their efforts were facing competition from the continuing popularity of European operetta. Lehár's *The Merry Widow* rang up 416 performances in 1907, Straus's *The Chocolate Soldier,* 296 performances in 1911, *The Count of Luxembourg* by Lehár, 120 performances in 1912.

World War I, however, brought further importation from Europe to an abrupt end. The four-year cataclysm helped to crystallize America's confidence in her own culture. Whether in a practical or in a deeper, spiritual sense, the war brought a crucial period of independence to the American theater. Victor Herbert had already produced thirty-one shows, Jerome Kern, an American, six, and Rudolf Friml, two. And it was in 1914 that Sigmund Romberg began his highly productive career.

The music of these men had already begun to assume a style that marked it as "non-European." In the operettas of Lehár, Johann Strauss, Kalmàn, and Oskar Straus, one still finds the spirit and technical demands of grand opera. In America, this was no longer to be the case; the new musical, like the society for which it was composed, was to achieve a far greater informality than the old, and a greater simplicity.

Indigenous influences were also beginning to make themselves felt in the music itself. Ragtime became the rage. In 1911 Irving Berlin had a huge success with "Alexander's Ragtime Band," and soon after, he followed up this one song with an entire theater score in the ragtime idiom.

Another change was gradually taking place in the musical form of the songs being written. American composers had originally followed the two-part, or AB, song form characteristic of the Viennese school. In *The Merry Widow,* for instance, "Maxims," "Villa," and the famous "Waltz" are in two-part form. Each of these parts contains antecedent and consequent phrases and nearly always in precise 8-bar blocks.

By 1914 the AB form was in the process of developing into what today seems such standard practice—AABA—that we

8

hardly remember the time when it was not the only one. This structure—which was to become the formal basis of American popular songs—enjoyed its first and most important exploitation in our theater music. A psychological improvement over its AB predecessor, the AABA form creates in the listener a feeling of satisfaction by rounding out the whole with a return to the original thematic material. The main A theme, exploited as it is three times, impresses itself more on the memory. The B section—called a release—is in actuality a relief. It provides a necessary contrast to the three A's, normally departs from the main theme in key, mode, and mood, and often displays rhythmic and melodic variance.

Besides the development of musical form, the librettos of musical shows were also undergoing changes. The traditional absurdity of musical books, with their broad comedy, pasteboard characters, and mythical settings, was driving the new, educated generation of Americans out of the musical theater. Librettists were also becoming increasingly aware of the need for more plausible plots, identifiable characters and settings—in short, for something more nearly approaching the life around them.

Unquestionably the largest contribution to our developing musical theater at this time was made by Jerome Kern. As always in the case of effective revolutionaries, Kern was brought up within the mainstream of the very environment he would subsequently help to change.

Born in New York in 1885, Kern as a very young man went abroad to study music on the Continent, and then worked briefly in London as a composer of songs that occupied unimportant positions in the shows of other composers. When he returned to New York at the age of nineteen, he again gravitated to music jobs related to theater. He became a song-plugger, a music salesman, and finally a rehearsal pianist, a position that provided contacts with performers and eventually—through them—the chance once more to interpolate some of his own songs in other composers' shows. After eight years, in 1912, he was assigned the writing of a complete score. When this first solo venture failed, Kern continued to provide songs for the scores of others. The first notable one was "They Didn't Believe Me" for the 1914 production of *The Girl From Utah.*

During this period, Kern met Guy Bolton, the English librettist, and together in 1915 they created a show for the tiny Princess Theater (seating capacity, 299). Although this first show was unsuccessful, a second, produced that same year, *Very Good Eddie,* was a smash. In this and in five succeeding Princess shows, in which Kern and Bolton were joined by P. G. Wodehouse as lyricist, Kern put into practice ideas that were radical for the time: the songs and lyrics were integrated into the action; comedy grew out of character and situation; the books had "reasonable" and contemporary plots and characters; and the language was everyday.

The simplicity of these Princess productions (competing with the lavish revues and extravaganzas of the time), the "everydayness" of the books (in sharp contrast with operetta fairy-tale-ishness), and the integration of all of the theatrical elements, constituted the first important breakaway from the conventions into which our musical theater had been born and was still steeped. They also influenced significantly two teen-agers who idolized Kern—George Gershwin and Richard Rodgers.

After *Oh, Lady! Lady!,* written with Bolton and Wodehouse in 1918, Kern returned to the big, old-fashioned commercial theater. He had spent three productive years creating a new form for musicals, pointing a finger straight ahead to the future; but even with success, the margin of profit in a theater accommodating an audience of 299 had to have been minuscule. And so when Ziegfeld and Dillingham and the other Broadway "greats" offered him shows, he went along with them, and at least for a time (eight years), he worked more profitably for producers who could not have cared less about his artistic point of view. During this period, he composed scores for fifteen shows—many of them big hits—and worked in collaboration with Otto Harbach, Oscar Hammerstein II, Howard Dietz, and B. G. DeSylva, among others. But in 1927, with Oscar Hammerstein II, he wrote *Show Boat,* based on the novel by Edna Ferber. *Show Boat* raised the Negro problem, dispensed with the conventional pretty-girl chorus, and was unhappy in tone, but it was a big hit. Florenz Ziegfeld, to everyone's amazement, produced it.

In *Show Boat*, and in three small "plays with music" that followed—*The Cat and the Fiddle, Roberta, Very Warm for May*—and in the more opulent *Music in the Air*, Kern's use of music was advanced. The long song verses had disappeared; in some cases, they had been eliminated altogether. The songs themselves were fewer, and they were integrated into dialogue scenes, reprised in part where doing so aided the dramatic action, and often were either left incomplete within a scene or developed more fully than formerly. Despite the fact that the songs were integrated into, and created to serve, the action, they were also able to stand alone. An impressive number of songs from these shows are standard today:

"Smoke Gets in Your Eyes"

"I've Told Every Little Star"

"The Song Is You"

"Yesterdays"

"Ol' Man River"

"Can't Help Lovin' That Man"

"Bill"

"Why Do I Love You?"

"Till the Clouds Roll By"

"She Didn't Say 'Yes' "

"The Night Was Made For Love"

Show Boat can be said to represent the consolidation of those innovations toward which Kern had been working for nearly two decades. About the time of *Show Boat*, a general, if unorganized, move in the direction of integrated musicals, with fresh music and lyrics and books that could involve audiences, was becoming discernible in the work of others. This trend could be found in the shows of Gershwin and Youmans and in the subsequent works of Rodgers and Hart, Berlin, Porter, and Schwartz and Dietz.

While a new era was being ushered in, the earlier tradition was not yet exhausted. The climax of the American operetta had only just been reached one, two, and three years before *Show Boat.* Although Herbert and Cohan were fading away, Romberg at this time surpassed himself with *The Student Prince* and *The Desert Song,* and Friml had reached his apex in *Rose Marie* and *The Vagabond King.* These operettas comprise the very highest achievement of the transplanted European heritage. The music excelled that of earlier operetta created in this country, and the books, although too easily traceable to Viennese models, were nevertheless less complicated, with plots and characters more humanly identifiable. With the exception of *Rose Marie,* set in Canada, all of the works of this period are mythological in feeling and, of course, intensely romantic: Heidelberg—a prince in love with a barmaid; Morocco—a disguised Robin Hood abducting the girl he loves; medieval France—a poet who is king for a day.

These shows, archaic as their books seem today, have to be viewed in the light of what had preceded them. Their romanticism was itself a reaction against a gathering swing toward prosiness. Friml had once said in an interview, "I can't write music unless there are romance, glamour, and heroes." But in the shadow of World War I, American composers and librettists discovered the world of their own time and gave it expression. Kern, for instance, focused on football in *Leave It to Jane; Very Good Eddie* dealt with a confused honeymoon. Romberg himself, ten years before his great operetta explosion, had composed such locally referring shows as *Hands Up, Maid in America,* and *Ruggles of Red Gap.* Herbert celebrated America with *Naughty Marietta, When Sweet Sixteen,* and *Sweethearts,* and Cohan contributed *Hello, Broadway* and *The Little Millionaire.* By 1925, with lavish revue, extravaganza, and local comedy all at the height of their popularity—and, on the other side, the new generation beginning to find its own new way with small shows in small theaters—the older generation reverted to what it knew and loved and, in a kind of figurative death-throe, "sang its last, then sang no more."

The end of the '20's, then, was a kind of turning point, with *Show Boat* a crucial link between past and future. Its score and lyrics are among the best ever written in our theater, but it nevertheless suffers from the serious weaknesses of the period in which it was written. The characters are two-dimensional, the proportions are outrageous, the plot development is predictable and corny, and the ending is unbearably sweet.

Magnolia is a dear girl. Ravenal is a romantic gambler, certain to win the girl and equally certain to lose his luck and become an albatross around the neck of his beloved. She is good; he is likeable and sympathetic, but weak. Magnolia's father, Captain Andy, is a darling with a shrew for a wife. Not a single detail departs from formula.

Julie, the ill-starred part-Negro singer, is rather more interesting, but possibly only because she is so shadowy. In Act I she appears briefly in Scenes 2 and 4, sings "Can't Help Lovin' That Man," and disappears. She reappears in Act II, Scene 3, when she sings the great "Bill," then vanishes forever.

The only original character in the show is the Negro, Joe, who sings "Ol' Man River," and what makes him particularly interesting are the lyrics in this one song, which he reprises three times. He is made to see the world from a distance—perhaps Godlike—and therefore whole. He states the sharp difference between Negroes and white people, and he states it not so much as a complaint but as a reality, as, say, the characters at the end of Chekhov's *The Cherry Orchard:* what is, is. The problem is thrown into the laps of the audience. Perhaps they will do something about it. . . .

In "Ol' Man River," Joe sings simply and sadly:

> Dere's an ol' man called de Mississippi
> Dat's de ol' man dat I'd like to be;
> What does he care if de world's got troubles?
> What does he care if de land ain't free?

later introduces his and his people's condition:

> You an' me, we sweat an' strain,
> Body all achin' an' racked wid pain

almost screams in mimicry:

> "Tote dat barge"
> "Lift dat bale!"

adds with resignation:

> Git a little drunk
> An' you'll land in jail.

then concludes in anguish:

> Ah gits weary an' sick of tryin'
> Ah'm tired of livin' and scared of dyin'

and triumph:

> But ol' man river,
> He jes' keeps rollin' along.

What makes him no ordinary character is created in this single lyric.

The element of coincidence in the book is not only silly but sloppy, for the action could have been motivated without resorting to nonsense. Nevertheless, the young showfolk, Frank and Ellie, just *happen* to want to rent a room in Chicago when Magnolia, to whose room they *happen* to be shown, just *happens* to have found Ravenal's farewell letter. As Magnolia now needs a job, they take her to audition for a nightclub manager who *happens* to have just been rehearsing Julie (unheard of since the early scenes on the show boat), and Julie *happens* to exit just in time not to be seen by Frank, Ellie, and Magnolia. But offstage *we* know that Julie, who is drunk, has heard Magnolia audition, realizes that Magnolia needs the job, and sends a

14

note to the manager saying that she, Julie, is quitting and he should hire Magnolia! Then Captain Andy, in Chicago for the World's Fair, *happens* into the nightclub in time for Magnolia's debut. And so on and on.

It has seemed worth spelling out the absurdity of the book of *Show Boat* only because it indicates in general the kinds of weaknesses to be found in the shows that followed a decade or two after. Except for *The Boys From Syracuse* and the monumental *Pal Joey,* the books of the Rodgers and Hart shows, which had great music and lyrics, are today virtually unrevivable. Except for *Porgy and Bess,* the Gershwin shows—*Girl Crazy, Oh, Kay!, Of Thee I Sing, Strike Up the Band,* and *Lady, Be Good* are also unrevivable in their original forms. The songs from *Babes in Arms, By Jupiter, On Your Toes, I Married an Angel, Jumbo, Higher and Higher,* and *A Connecticut Yankee* are again great and enduring, but not the shows for which they were written. Furthermore, as musical theater is by its nature a collaboration, I believe that a new author would be impotent to invent a plot and characters suitable for songs once conceived for other characters in other situations.

It is perhaps easy to underestimate the significance of this problem. But even a cursory glance at the list of works—entitled by the talents of their creators to endure for ages, if not forever—whose books make their life on the stage impossible, more than illustrates the great loss to the theater and to the world.

In any case, by 1940, when *Pal Joey* appeared, the notion that musical theater was like any other theater and had to meet its total standards had finally evolved out of decades of change and growth. From then on, in the best shows, drama and characters were to be believable; music, lyrics, and dancing were to become integrated and an inevitable part of the whole; performers would be required to act as well as sing; composers and lyricists would be free of the European traditions that had shaped their predecessors. The stage, by 1940, was set for the big period.

3

Revue

If the American musical grew out of European operetta, other forces were at work to help stamp its character and make it possible. One of the things necessary for the growth of the new musical theater was the liberation of its practitioners from the old romantic musical form. One of the primary instruments of this liberation was the revue.

The nature of the revue as a kind of catchall of musical numbers, sketches, and routines makes it difficult to characterize precisely. In one or another of its variations, it rose to enormous popularity during the first quarter of this century. Since the scores of most early revues were the product of many different writers, this kind of show provided a natural opportunity for new composers trying to break into the musical theater. Many composers worked as rehearsal pianists, and in such a position, entrée became easier. Producers were not hostile to new talent in a production because a song or two posed no threat to the whole project and could, if necessary, be replaced. If a song worked, its new composer was offered wider opportunities in the productions that followed. Also, since a revue had no unified musical style, a young songwriter was free to operate with little stylistic restriction.

The origins of revue are to be found in minstrel shows, pantomimes, variety shows, and extravaganzas of the previous century. Each of these contained particular distinguishing elements, yet all of them shared a looseness of structure that set them apart from operettas, which had plots and characters. Each of them was essentially a "program."

Although many people made notable contributions to one or another of them, revues were the full-time careers of a very few. Early teachers in the field were Harrigan and Hart, whose famous shows continued almost uninterruptedly for fourteen years. Harrigan wrote these shows (Irish-type vaudeville), including some of the music, acted and danced, produced and directed; Hart played opposite him and often in female roles. In E. J. Kahn's book *The Merry Partners,* an account of Harrigan and Hart, he relates an amusing story:

> Since Hart was often in need of ladies' apparel, he was apt to have special difficulties. Once, after he had boldly chased a frowzy woman into the heart of Five Points, and, on catching up with her, had offered her $25 for her raiment, he had a hard time convincing her it was only her clothes he wanted; she had never before heard of a man offering money just for *that*.

The Harrigan and Hart shows were the spiritual godfathers of the George M. Cohan productions, which began in 1901 and continued for twenty-seven years. Both dealt with Irish-American characters. However, the Harrigan shows emphasized the Irish part, and the comedy tended toward "low," whereas Cohan accentuated the American aspect (the U.S. flag was seldom less than star of the production), and Cohan as both writer and performer was more gentle. He made characters for himself to play who were—to his public—admirable, clean, upright, and patriotic. Beginning as author-composer-lyricist as well as star, director, and producer, he achieved his first success in book shows. When revues became most popular around 1915, he leapt on the bandwagon and wrote revues. His musical style was antithetical to that of operetta. Cohan was another American "first," and his contribution toward the future was large.

Meanwhile, in 1896, the great comedy team of Weber and Fields, who starred in and produced many of their own shows, came into prominence. They played low burlesque, Dutch-comedy characters with thick accents. Although their humor was broad, it was never vulgar. They played in their own very successful Music Hall for many years and employed stars such as Fay Templeton and Lillian Russell to share their billing. It was their avowed intention to keep their shows clean. Even with the predictable line of dancing girls, there was nothing about the costumes or comedy material to offend the family trade. For many years they themselves appeared in the same costumes, which became their trademark. Fields was tall, Weber, short and stout. Both wore flat derbies and both had short stubble beards. Fields wore checked trousers and a wide-lapel, plain-color jacket with velvet collar and cuffs, while Weber wore a loud checkered suit with velvet lapel and cuffs and a loud flowered waistcoat.

As early as 1894, a revue called *The Passing Show* appeared; but it was not until after 1900 that the term "revue" came more and more into currency. The style was then set for a group of larger shows that were to make show-business history: *The Ziegfeld Follies, George White's Scandals, The Passing Show, The Greenwich Village Follies,* and *The Earl Carroll Vanities.* The New York Hippodrome opened in 1905 and served as a great impetus to the production of spectacular extravaganzas, whose special breed was to flourish for nearly twenty-five years. The sheer size of the auditorium and stage, with its unique mechanical marvels, served to establish lavishness as a cardinal principle of this kind of show. At the Hippodrome, the Messrs. Shubert, Charles Dillingham, and others produced colossal spectacles replete with elephants, horses, fountains, swimming tanks, and—of course—girls. Florenz Ziegfeld, who had already begun his career as a producer, developed a show on similar lines, with the accent on girls; beginning in 1907, he presented twenty-two annual editions of his world-famous *Follies.* Lavish decors (frequently by Joseph Urban, who could be counted on to create a sensation), elaborate costumes, comedy sketches, clusters of stars, and, above all, pretty girls were the attractions of these shows. While there was frequently good new music in the *Follies*—by Berlin, Kern, Herbert, and Friml, for example—Ziegfeld brought in no new composers of any consequence. The above-named composers had already been well established through earlier productions.

The present Winter Garden Theater, opened in 1911 by the Messrs. Shubert, was initially a music hall featuring variety shows that could be watched by patrons who ate and drank during the performances. The format of these shows was in general the same as that of the late-19th-century extravaganzas: ballet or pantomime followed by vaudeville. Al Jolson, an alumnus of minstrel shows, was frequently starred. In a short time—but not before the Diaghilev Ballet Russe had been a part of the bill *—ballet disappeared from the Winter Garden program, for when ballet had proved to be unprofitable, the Shuberts shifted in the direction of Ziegfeld and mounted a revue series called *The Passing Show* (which had no connection with the 1894 production of the same title). This series was to continue through ten editions from 1913 to 1924. Though they had put together all the expected ingredients—stars, singers, dancers, girls, and new composers—*The Passing Show* never enjoyed the enormous popularity of *The Ziegfeld Follies*.

In 1919 there were stirrings in new directions. John Murray Anderson, already an established director, writer, dancer, and producer, began a new series of revues, *The Greenwich Village Follies,* which not only continued through eight editions, but also struck a new note in response to the sophisticated and irreverent spirit of the times. In Anderson's revues, girls occupied a position secondary to smart sketches by highly literate writers, scene and costume designs by such avant-garde artists as Reginald Marsh and James Reynolds, and a new serious dancer—Martha Graham.

George White, a dancer graduated from the Ziegfeld shows, produced the first of his *Scandals* in 1919, and his productions under this title ran to nine editions. Although the shows themselves were in many ways also copies of Ziegfeld's model, White

* The Diaghilev Ballet did not appear at the Winter Garden, but Gertrude Hoffman's *Saison des Ballets' Russes.*

introduced new theater music that was far more significant than any incorporated in previous revues. The composers included Gershwin, DeSylva, Brown and Henderson, and Sammy Fain.

Earl Carroll tried to outdo Ziegfeld when he initiated his *Vanities* (1923), a series which ran to nine productions. The accent was once more on girls. Carroll presented them in even more elaborate productions than had his mentor and exposed even more of their bodies. The music seldom was of real importance—though Carroll did use both Harold Arlen and Burton Lane (who were not his discoveries)—and the long string of stars he employed had already been established by Ziegfeld and others.

Only two years after the start of *The Greenwich Village Follies,* Irving Berlin presented the first of four editions of his *Music Box Revue.* Here also the girls were given second place, the humor and satire were considerably less crude than in the shows of his lavish predecessors, and, as in *The Greenwich Village Follies,* the music and style of production were less stereotyped.

Despite certain reservations expressed by the critics about revues in more than two decades, these shows had the support of an enthusiastic public. There were also frequent European importations, the most memorable of which were the Russian *Chauve-Souris* (1922) and the British *André Charlot Revue* (1924), which brought Beatrice Lillie, Gertrude Lawrence, and Jack Buchanan to Broadway. An edition two years later also boasted music by Noel Coward.

Among the performers who gained prominence in revues were: the Vernon Castles, W. C. Fields, Marilyn Miller, Jack Donahue, Clifton Webb, Elsie Janis, Raymond Hitchcock, Mae Murray, Marion Davies, Peggy Hopkins, Vivienne Segal, Ina Claire, Helen Morgan, Nita Naldi, Paulette Goddard, Norah Bayes, Eva Tanguay, Fannie Brice, Ray Dooley, Ruth Etting, Gilda Gray, Norma Terris, Irene Dunne, Harriet Hoctor, Gypsy Rose Lee, Fred and Adele Astaire, Bert Williams (Ziegfeld's enormously successful Negro star—a first), Leon Errol, Ed Wynn, Will Rogers, Eddie Cantor, Harry Richman, Van and

Schenck, Moran and Mack, Bert Wheeler, Paul Whiteman's Orchestra, John Philip Sousa with his band, Claire Luce, Morton Downey, James Barton, Mitzi Mayfair, Hal LeRoy, Jane Frohman, Willie and Eugene Howard, Gertrude Niesen, Bob Hope, Josephine Baker, Clark and McCullough, Jane Pickens, Al Jolson, Fred Allen, John Charles Thomas, Charles Ruggles, Phil Baker, Charlotte Greenwood, Ann Pennington, Texas Guinan, Frank Fay, Charles Winninger, Marie Dressler, Ted Lewis, Mary Lewis, Martha Graham, Leonard Sillman, Libby Holman, Ethel Merman, Frances Williams, Rudy Vallee, Ella Logan, Eleanor Powell, Bert Lahr, Grace Moore, Robert Benchley, Jimmy Savo, Milton Berle, Lillian Roth. The list is formidable and far from exhaustive.

In addition to Joseph Urban, Reginald Marsh, and James Reynolds, such theater designers as Adrian, Aline Bernstein, Watson Barratt, Norman Bel Geddes, and Cleon Throckmorton all served their apprenticeships in revue productions, as did the directors Hassard Short and Vincente Minnelli. Dancers who subsequently achieved prominence as choreographers, both in musical comedy and in the purer fields of concert dance, included Martha Graham, Fokine, Gertrude Hoffman, Chester Hale, Agnes De Mille, Anton Dolin, Tilly Losch, George Hale, José Limon, Charles Weidman, Doris Humphrey, Paul Draper, Helen Tamiris, Donald Saddler, Valerie Bettis, and Paul Haakon. Among American writers who contributed material for sketches were George S. Kaufman, Ring Lardner, and Moss Hart.

As impressive as is the list of young performers supported and nurtured by the revue, it played an even more significant part in providing a useful showcase for composers and lyricists. Because of the musical hodgepodge and absence of stylistic unity, it was possible for a new young composer to write in his own individual style.

When, for example, Richard Rodgers (with Lorenz Hart) at the age of twenty-three composed "Manhattan" for *The Garrick Gaieties* (1925) he was not breaking with tradition or writing an iconoclastic song. What he *was* doing, of course, was presenting his own fresh voice in an unusually good song for any period.

And how *different* is that song from "Indian Love Call" or *The Student Prince*'s "Serenade," both of which had appeared only one year earlier!

Also in revues the young composers had the invaluable experience of creating material for real productions, with the necessity of tailoring their songs for specific stars and judging audience reaction, but without the responsibility of composing an entire score. One example of the standard practice—and this will serve to illustrate the point—can be found in the list of musical material included in *The Ziegfeld Follies of 1921*:

4 songs by Gene Buck and Victor Herbert

1 song by Grant Clarke and James Hanley

1 song by Ballard MacDonald and James Hanley

1 song by Ballard MacDonald and Harry Carroll

2 songs by Gene Buck and Rudolf Friml

1 song by Channing Pollock and Dave Stamper

1 song by B. G. DeSylva and Jerome Kern

1 song by B. G. DeSylva and Rudolf Friml

2 songs by Gene Buck and Dave Stamper

2 songs by Grant Clarke and Jimmy Monaco

1 song by Channing Pollock and Maurice Yvain

1 song by Blanche Merrill and Leo Edwards

All of the principal composer-lyricist personnel in our contemporary musical theater came to their larger Broadway assignments via one or two song contributions in revue—all except Rudolf Friml, who had begun his American career in 1912 with the triumphant operetta, *The Firefly,* and Leonard Bernstein, whose Broadway credits started in 1944 with *On the Town.* Friml subsequently composed many successful operettas, but also made later revue contributions. Leonard Bernstein alone had no need of revue.

The list of the distinguished revue alumni includes Jerome

Kern, who contributed interpolated songs in 1905, at the age of twenty, and continued to do so until 1914, when he wrote his first full score. In 1907 Irving Berlin, at nineteen, made similar individual contributions and in 1914 also composed his first full score. In that same year, Sigmund Romberg, at twenty-seven, contributed to *The Winter Garden Extravaganza*. George Gershwin, who, like many of his confreres, entered the theater as a rehearsal pianist, provided *The Passing Show* of 1916 with his first stage songs; he was eighteen years old. Cole Porter at twenty-six had songs in *Hitchy-Koo of 1919,* which, although it was his second theater attempt, provided him with his first success. Richard Rodgers, after at least six amateur productions, at eighteen collaborated on a score with Romberg, and four years later wrote a slight show with Lorenz Hart and Herbert Fields. But his first successful score was with Hart for *Garrick Gaieties of 1925*—a revue score that contained "Romantic You and Sentimental Me" and "Manhattan" and focused the attention of a fascinated world on two new young men of exceptional promise.

The team of DeSylva, Brown, and Henderson succeeded Gershwin as composers of the *George White's Scandals* in 1925. Arthur Schwartz contributed single songs to shows from 1923 through 1925, but his first important collaboration with Howard Dietz was for *The Little Show* of 1929.

Both Harold Arlen and Vernon Duke were introduced to Broadway as composers in 1930. Arlen, also a rehearsal pianist, did some arrangements for the *George White's Scandals* and for one of Vincent Youmans's shows. His first song, "Get Happy," was written for the *9:15 Revue*. Following that, he contributed several songs to the shows at the Cotton Club, a Harlem night spot, among them "Between the Devil and the Deep Blue Sea" and "Stormy Weather." Vernon Duke, on the other hand, had started out as a serious composer and had done a considerable amount of work under the name of Vladimir Dukelsky. Like so many of his colleagues, Duke had worked as a pianist. His first contribution to the popular American theater was a song performed in *Garrick Gaieties of 1930*. Harburg, Lerner, Loewe, Bock, Harnick, Comden and Green, and many others began as cogs in the revue wheel.

But the lavish old shows were dead by 1930. As early as 1923, the *Ziegfeld Follies* had begun to slip in popularity. The great Ziegfeld tried harder than ever and spent even more money to keep his audience. The new editions were no longer annual affairs. Those of 1924 and 1925 were progressively less interesting. The 1927 show was a fiasco, and the next and last was in 1931. Ziegfeld died the following year in bankruptcy. *The Passing Show* had ended in 1924, the *Music Box Revues* in 1924, *The Greenwich Village Follies* in 1928, *Earl Carroll's Vanities* in 1931, and *George White's Scandals* in 1939.

By the time the newer composers were becoming established, the old revue which had launched them was dead. The public had wearied of ever-increasing lavishness, and the growing cost of this lavishness made the future for producers an impossibility. The formula of girls and scenery and costumes had become passé and no longer interested the public. The old revue passed totally out of existence.

Two factors clearly motivated the style of the new revue that the newest composers and writers became involved in. One of these was the need imposed by the new kind of audience to deal with literate ideas which would give a show some intelligent, audience-identifiable, and sustained interest. This need was also strongly reflected in the book musicals. Already in 1925 Ziegfeld himself must have sensed it, because for the first time he had begun to produce book musicals, although he failed to sense the possible application of the new style to his *Follies*. The element of ideas in the new revues took various definite and unified shapes. In *Pins and Needles* it was unionism, in *Call Me Mister*, the returning G.I., in *Inside U.S.A.*, some of the qualities and foibles of our country, etc.

The second factor—at least as important as the first—was money. These were Depression years, and even established giants in this area had failed and closed up shop.

Consequently, the newest creative people in musical theater worked in whatever theatrical enterprises were available to them. Since the established revue producers had begun noticeably to feel the financial pinch and were experiencing increasing difficulty in raising money, the most viable productions were

24

those on a small and simple scale; and the material itself for such productions had to be cast in new and revolutionary forms.

The new, sophisticated revues began—again, where today's equivalent often finds itself—off-Broadway. They were given in small theaters with small casts for small audiences, and they provided the entertainment world with an incomparable medium for satirizing and commenting on events and new cultural currents in the contemporary society. They declared their independence from the tradition of Broadway bigness by lampooning it, and expressed their familiarity with "high Culture"—still largely virgin terrain for Broadway audiences—by taking off on the serious contemporary drama of O'Neill, Dunsany, the Quintero Brothers, and Granville Barker—also seen only off-Broadway.

The first of eight seasons of *Grand Street Follies* appeared in 1922. In this, and in its successors, the chorus line made hilarious fun of their posh uptown sisters, but the music was subordinated to barbed and witty sketches and lyrics that were tailored to the smart few. Scenery and costumes were tasteful and simple, and the production was, of necessity, inexpensive, in a theater seating 296.

In 1925 Rodgers and Hart wrote the first *Garrick Gaieties* for the new Theater Guild. The real stars of this show, as it turned out, were its composer and lyricist, and in these revues, unlike the *Grand Street Follies,* the music was of paramount importance. The cast was small and talented, young and smart. (Libby Holman's first Broadway appearance was in the 1925 *Garrick Gaieties.*) The show had been scheduled for only two performances, but popular demand kept it running for 211.

Another sign of changing times was *Shuffle Along* (1921), an all-Negro revue, which was not only a success in its own right but helped to pave the way for a far better Negro revue in 1928, *Lew Leslie's Blackbirds.* Among other things *Lew Leslie's Blackbirds* was distinguished for having some extraordinary songs by Dorothy Fields and Jimmy McHugh, including "I Can't Give You Anything But Love," "Diga Diga Doo," "Doin' the New Low-Down," and "I Must Have That Man."

In 1929 Schwartz and Dietz enjoyed the first fruits of a long collaboration in a revue called *The Little Show*. This show took its inspiration from earlier intimate and sophisticated revues, but it was more opulent and had bigger stars—Libby Holman, Fred Allen, and Clifton Webb—scenery by the twenty-eight-year-old Jo Mielziner, and a sketch by George S. Kaufman. It was a smash hit, and other *Little Shows* followed.

In 1930 Schwartz and Dietz continued brilliantly with *Three's a Crowd*, in which they employed the same three stars who had graced the first *Little Show*. (It is interesting to note that *Three's a Crowd* was staged by Hassard Short, who had already come to fame as the guiding force for three editions of the *Music Box Revue*, and one of *The Greenwich Village Follies*.) The next year Schwartz and Dietz came up with their best revue, *The Band Wagon*, with the Astaires (Fred and Adele), Helen Broderick, Frank Morgan, and Tilly Losch. George S. Kaufman provided the sketches, with Hassard Short once again directing. Although in matters of taste and smartness *The Band Wagon* followed the new tradition established by the *Garrick Gaieties*, it was given a sumptuous production that Ziegfeld might have envied.

Vernon Duke wrote the songs for *Walk a Little Faster* (1932), which starred Beatrice Lillie and Clark and McCullough. The most memorable feature of the show was Duke's song, "April in Paris"; he would one day create *Cabin in the Sky* for Ethel Waters.

In 1933 Irving Berlin presented *As Thousands Cheer*. The cast, directed by the ubiquitous Hassard Short, included Marilyn Miller, Clifton Webb, Helen Broderick, and Ethel Waters.

One of the special novelties of this production was the inclusion of some serious avant-garde dancers: José Limon, Letitia Ide, and Charles Weidman's group. For *As Thousands Cheer*, Berlin created a score which included "Easter Parade," "Harlem on My Mind," "Heat Wave," and "Supper Time."

Leonard Sillman's *New Faces*—a revue series which ultimately ran to many editions—began in 1934. This revue served as a showcase for a considerable amount of new performing talent, which included Henry Fonda, Nancy Hamilton, Charles

Walters, Imogene Coca, Alan Handley, Gus Schirmer, Van Johnson, Alice Ghostley, Ronny Graham, Eartha Kitt, and Carol Lawrence.

In 1935 a grand extravaganza *a la* Ziegfeld was presented at the Hippodrome by Billy Rose. It was, appropriately, named *Jumbo*. Though really a revue, *Jumbo* had a book, by Hecht and MacArthur. Staged by John Murray Anderson, it boasted grandiose sets by Albert Johnson, costumes by Raoul Pène DuBois and James Reynolds, Paul Whiteman and his orchestra, and an enormous cast headed by Jimmy Durante. *Jumbo* never really came to life except in its marvelous score, written by the redoubtable Messrs. Rodgers and Hart. Their songs included "Over and Over Again," "The Most Beautiful Girl in the World," "My Romance," and "Little Girl Blue."

At the time of *Jumbo,* American society had been plunged for five years into the worst economic depression in its history. One might all too glibly go on at length chalking up the influences of the Depression (and of the Prohibition era that preceded it) on American art in general and on the musical theater in particular. Some of these influences are obvious; certainly, for instance, the ascendance of small and inexpensively produced musical shows during this period had more than a little to do with the shortage of money. Some results, however, are not as clear. If people were out of work and frightened—the most popular concept of the mood of those days—they were also strangely high-spirited. One has only to look at the plays, shows, films, and books of the Depression-New Deal era to see that this is so. The words are often sad or bitter, but the music somehow belies them.

The problem is further complicated by the fact that this was also the period in which both radio and talking movies came into their own. These undoubtedly had a strong effect on the musical theater. But to sort them out and discuss them properly would require at least another volume. Though the development of the American musical theater cannot be traced without some reference to the political, social, and cultural events against the background of which that development was taking place, it is not our purpose here to do more than note them.

27

The one revue of the '30's that contained the most explicit comment on its period was *Pins and Needles* by Harold Rome, written for the International Ladies' Garment Workers' Union. Produced in the same small theater in which Kern had given his Princess shows, with only a two-piano accompaniment, the simplest of scenery, and a cast of ILGWU members, the show ran for 1108 performances to a consistently enthusiastic audience and was subsequently taken on tour. The intention behind *Pins and Needles* was, quite naturally, to propagandize the trade-union movement. But Rome succeeded in making of it something so ebullient, witty, and engaging that without departing from its purpose it moved far beyond "public relations" and became a genuinely pungent, inspired, and serious-minded piece of hilarious entertainment. The show was roughly descended from the *Garrick Gaieties* and the *Grand Street Follies,* but its intensity and spirit made it unique.

Harold Rome's special talent for relevancy was once again to rise to the occasion when, after World War II, in collaboration with Arnold Auerbach, he wrote *Call Me Mister,* the unifying thread of which was the problems of the returning G.I. in readjusting to civilian life. Rome and Auerbach had just been separated from military service, and their intimacy with the subject produced brilliant results. Rome was able, as he had been with *Pins and Needles,* to be warm and funny without bypassing any of the sterner reality that lay beneath his theme. *Call Me Mister* was as alive as Irving Berlin's *Yip, Yip, Yaphank* and *This Is the Army.* However, Rome's show celebrated life in the aftermath of a ghastly war; Berlin's sounded a call to patriotism at any price.

It is, alas, necessary to mention Olsen and Johnson's *Hellzapoppin',* a would-be zany revue which descended upon the world in 1938 and ran for 1404 performances. Appealing to the lowest taste—and, to judge by its success, reaching its audience, *Hellzapoppin'* combined the least subtle elements of burlesque with the adolescent antics of a 1920's fraternity initiation.

Through the late '30's and '40's, various interesting small revues continued to make their appearance. Especially worthy

28

of mention are Morgan Lewis's and Nancy Hamilton's *One for the Money* (1939), featuring a new singer named Alfred Drake; Charles Gaynor's *Lend an Ear* (1948), featuring Carol Channing, particularly effective in a sketch called "The Gladiola Girl," with Gene Nelson, William Eythe, and Gower Champion; *Meet the People* (1940) by Jay Gorney, Edward Eliscu, and Henry Myers, with the then unknown Nanette Fabray; and *John Murray Anderson's Almanac* (1953), which introduced the songwriting team of Richard Adler and Jerry Ross, who would later do *The Pajama Game* and *Damn Yankees*. The cast included Hermione Gingold and Billy DeWolfe.

The 1950's were witness to the grandual disappearance of the revue from the Broadway stage. Probably the most important single factor involved—as in that of vaudeville before it—was its virtual engulfment by the three major mass media of entertainment—radio, movies, and finally television. These media followed the same old patterns set decades earlier. No single phase of live theater was as hard hit as revue.

As radio techniques developed in the 1920's, and millions of home sets were bought, much of what was offered on the stage could be had nightly in the home and without cost. Moreover, the radio drew people to it—for a time—simply by its novelty as a gadget, a modern wonder. In 1927 Al Jolson appeared in the first sound movie, *The Jazz Singer*. In it, and other sound films that followed, the new medium found its most congenial material in vaudeville programs featuring famous musical-comedy stars. For one thing, these early talking pictures tended to rely on a direct translation from stage to screen. And for another, movies now made stars accessible to the entire population. By 1932, the Palace Theater—the last variety stronghold—was compelled to cut its vaudeville bills in half and offer programs that included a feature motion picture, as well as some vaudeville; and in 1935, vaudeville disappeared completely from the Palace.

Then, in 1948, the theater's, and particularly revue's, most devastating competitor—television—invaded the entertainment world. As in the movies at the time of *The Jazz Singer*, the tech-

29

nique of the medium was still naked of invention. Its early fare, too, was to be variety shows, which were the easiest kind of programs to present and, again because of the novelty of television itself, were immensely popular. Beginning in 1948, Milton Berle had a weekly Tuesday evening show that affected the Tuesday evening economy so strongly that merchants closed their shops, theater business suffered new losses, and businessmen issued a concerted complaint.

Television variety shows, in a kind of posh contemporary Ziegfeld style, reached their height on all networks between 1956 and 1958. Ten years after the variety boom—there were in an average week, with schedules nearly around the clock on eight New York channels (1097 weekly hours), a total of twenty-two shows that could be classed as "variety." Most of these combined music, comedy, and dance but today they generally eschew elaborate production numbers. Once more the public taste had grown tired of the big spectacular, and the revue had grown small again.

The chancy, temporary part of the revue format—in whatever media it appears—is the comedy material that is an essential ingredient. As comedy songs and sketches are generally satirical, and train their wit on current political, social, and artistic events and celebrities, they go out of date almost as soon as they are written. Aristophanes' plays provide the classical example. Comedy, when it grows old enough to require footnotes, is no longer amusing. The comedy sketches written for the best of the stage revues by such master craftsmen as George S. Kaufman, Ring Lardner, and Moss Hart have all but vanished.

On the other hand, the best of the songs and song-lyrics remain. Good songs—even good comic ones—do not date. Among the best of our songs which were originally written for revues are:

"Shine On, Harvest Moon" (1908) Nora Bayes and Jack Norworth

"Rose of Washington Square" (1920) Hanley-MacDonald

"My Man" (1921) Yvain and Channing Pollock

"Who?" (1925) Kern and Harbach-Hammerstein II

"Manhattan" (1925)

"Mountain Greenery" (1926)

"Ten Cents a Dance" (1930)

"Over and Over Again" (1935)

"The Most Beautiful Girl in the World" (1935)

"My Romance" (1935)

"Little Girl Blue" (1935)

GEORGE AND IRA GERSHWIN

"Swanee" (1919)

"Somebody Loves Me" (1924)

DESYLVA, BROWN, AND HENDERSON

"Birth of the Blues" (1926)

"Black Bottom" (1926)

"Life Is Just a Bowl of Cherries" (1931)

"The Thrill Is Gone" (1931)

"That's Why Darkies Were Born" (1931)

IRVING BERLIN

"Oh How I Hate to Get Up in the Morning" (1918)

"A Pretty Girl Is Like a Melody" (1919)

"Soft Lights and Sweet Music" (1931)

"Let's Have Another Cup of Coffee" (1932)

"Easter Parade" (1933)

"Harlem on My Mind" (1933)

"Heat Wave" (1933)

HAROLD ARLEN–TED KOEHLER

"Get Happy" (1930)

"I Gotta Right to Sing the Blues" (1932)

"I Can't Give You Anything But Love" (1928)

"Doin' the New Low-Down" (1928)

"Diga Diga Doo" (1928)

COLE PORTER

"Let's Do It" (1928)

"You Do Something to Me" (1929)

"Love for Sale" (1930)

SCHWARTZ AND DIETZ

"Something to Remember You By" (1930)

"Right at the Start of It" (1930)

"Dancing in the Dark" (1931)

"New Sun in the Sky" (1931)

"I Love Louisa" (1931)

"Where Can He Be?" (1931)

"Miserable With You Again" (1931)

"If There Is Someone Lovelier Than You" (1934)

"In the Noonday Sun" (1934)

"I See Your Face Before Me" (1938)

"Moanin' Low" (1929) Rainger and Dietz

"Can't We Be Friends?" (1929) Swift and James

"Body and Soul" (1930) Green, Heyman, Sour, and Eyton

"April in Paris" (1932) Vernon Duke and E. Y. Harburg

"Franklin D. Roosevelt Jones" (1938) Harold Rome

"How High the Moon?" (1940) Lewis Hamilton

"It's a Big, Wide, Wonderful World" (1940) John Rox

"Boston Beguine" (1952) Harnick

"Guess Who I Saw Today?" (1952) Grand and Boyd

"Love Is a Simple Thing" (1952) Siegel and Carroll

Today, in New York, revue continues on a non-theatrical basis. Its theatrical survival is limited to the stage shows that complement the movies at Radio City Music Hall. On the other hand, the "girlie" aspect of revue—once celebrated by Ziegfeld, Earl Carroll, and George White—has been handed down to us only in such poverty-stricken form as the chorus line in nightclubs. Here are the semi-nude girls in their towering costumes: pale replicas of their sisters of the 1920's. The music now consists chiefly of quotations from the musical shows of Broadway—from the shows created by the alumni of old revue days.

Just as the lavish parent revue was forsaken by the small, unadorned offspring, today the girlie shows continue to perpetuate in poverty the older prototype, while the offspring, now livelier and less reliant on borrowing, has also continued. In smart nightclubs the fresh impulse results in such shows as Julius Monk's *Plaza 9* and *The Upstairs.* Here girls play no more a part than they did in the *Garrick Gaieties;* the success of the shows rests with the strength, wit, and originality of their sketches and songs; nothing is borrowed from anything. The general idea does stem from the *Garrick Gaieties* and, in topicality, from *Pins and Needles.* Just as in the early days, when the music consisted of a mélange of songs by many different new writers, in each of today's little revues, the material is once again provided by various composers. What they write finds and delights its own audience, which is necessarily small. The subject matter is "in" today and "out" tomorrow because it deals with yesterday's specific targets. The best of these shows achieve what they set out to do, but, it must be noted, they are strictly non-theatrical in size, character, and intent. What they *are* is nightclub.

Musical theater's debt to revue of all kinds is incalculable. The twenty-three-year-old Berlin who wrote "Alexander's Ragtime Band" gave us *Annie Get Your Gun.* George Gershwin, at twenty-one the author of a song for Al Jolson called "Swanee," gave us *Porgy and Bess.* Richard Rodgers, who at twenty-three gave the *Garrick Gaieties* "Manhattan," "Mountain Greenery," and "Romantic You and Sentimental Me," gave us, among other shows, *Oklahoma!, Carousel, South Pacific,* and *The King and I.*

33

It must also not go unmentioned that the developed revue in its most vulgar period broke with the operetta past. When Gershwin, Berlin, Rodgers, Porter, Arlen, Schwartz, and Rome made their almost unnoticed first entrances into the theater, they already were able to create—because of the antibook form and the latent eagerness for change—their very own musical images without regard for the recently celebrated conventions which were almost imperceptibly passing.

All those producers who took their chances in allowing young men to try their hands at a song or sketch were setting far more into motion than they knew. They were, in fact, unwittingly fathering the true American musical theater.

4

The Contemporary Musical

In order to analyze the character of the contemporary American musical theater—its ultimate and unique contribution to the history of musical entertainment—I have selected shows which seem to me to represent that theater in its most complete and mature state.

I have singled out these particular ones * because they are models of excellence in themselves (music, lyrics, and librettos) and they will best serve to illustrate a discussion of just what it is that gives the American musical its peculiar distinction. Despite many differences among them in subject matter, style, and invention, they are surprisingly similar in technical accomplishment and artistic form. Thus a discussion of these shows will, I believe, make it possible to distill certain working principles—not rules or formulas—imposed by the nature of the genre and of the world in which we live.

PAL JOEY (1940). Book by John O'Hara. Music by Richard Rodgers, lyrics by Lorenz Hart.

* In my opinion, *Cabaret* is a strong runner-up to the list of "best" shows.

35

OKLAHOMA! (1943). Book and lyrics by Oscar Hammerstein II, based on *Green Grow the Lilacs* by Lynn Riggs. Music by Richard Rodgers.

CAROUSEL (1945). Book and lyrics by Oscar Hammerstein II, based on *Liliom* by Ferenc Molnár. Music by Richard Rodgers.

ANNIE GET YOUR GUN (1946). Book by Herbert and Dorothy Fields, based on the life of Annie Oakley. Music and lyrics by Irving Berlin.

BRIGADOON (1947). Book and lyrics by Alan Jay Lerner, suggested by a German classic tale. Music by Frederick Loewe.

KISS ME, KATE (1948). Book by Bella and Samuel Spewack, based on *The Taming of the Shrew* by William Shakespeare. Music and lyrics by Cole Porter.

SOUTH PACIFIC (1949). Book by Oscar Hammerstein II and Joshua Logan, based on *Tales of the South Pacific* by James A. Michener. Music by Richard Rodgers, lyrics by Oscar Hammerstein II.

GUYS AND DOLLS (1950). Book by Jo Swerling and Abe Burrows, based on a story and characters by Damon Runyon. Music and lyrics by Frank Loesser.

THE KING AND I (1951). Book and lyrics by Oscar Hammerstein II, based on *Anna and the King of Siam* by Margaret Landon. Music by Richard Rodgers.

MY FAIR LADY (1956). Book and lyrics by Alan Jay Lerner, based on *Pygmalion* by George Bernard Shaw. Music by Frederick Loewe.

WEST SIDE STORY (1957). Book by Arthur Laurents, based on a conception of Jerome Robbins (*Romeo and Juliet* by William Shakespeare). Music by Leonard Bernstein, lyrics by Stephen Sondheim.

GYPSY (1959). Book by Arthur Laurents (suggested by the memoirs of Gypsy Rose Lee). Music by Jule Styne, lyrics by Stephen Sondheim.

FIDDLER ON THE ROOF (1964). Book by Joseph Stein, based on stories by Sholem Aleichem. Music by Jerry Bock, lyrics by Sheldon Harnick.

COMPANY (1970). Book by George Furth. Music and lyrics by Stephen Sondheim.

A LITTLE NIGHT MUSIC (1973). Book by Hugh Wheeler. Music and lyrics by Stephen Sondheim.

I. THE LIBRETTO

A. PLOTS AND CHARACTERS

To begin with, there is the question of librettos: In the issue of *Life* magazine for March 31, 1921, Robert Benchley published a review of a new musical comedy in which he said:

> The first act of *Love Birds* is just about what you would expect the first act of a musical comedy named *Love Birds* to be. . . . Something better may have come in the second act, but it was during the intermission that the big transfer scene was staged. By a peculiar coincidence the audience from *The Right Girl* were standing in excited groups in front of the Times Square Theater just as the inmates of the Apollo came out to get a breath of sea air right off the Forty-Second Street meadows. One thing led to another and your correspondent ambled a little too far to the left, with the result that when the doorman to the Times Square cried "Curtain!" we dashed impetuously in there. . . . There was really no way of telling that this was not the second act of the same show we had started out with. It might have been the second act of any musical show.

Apart from the opportunities they afforded men like Benchley to exercise *their* gift for humor, the books of early musical comedies were almost totally without virtue. Their main effect was to help drive intelligent theatergoers away from the musical theater. If this statement seems strong (it might be argued that what is primary to a musical show is the quality of the music), it must be remembered that musical theater is *theater*. In a form which seeks to integrate drama, music, and dance, the qualities of all its elements must hang together; and what they must hang upon are the characters and action they have been created around.

Until the 1930's, librettos for musical shows—with the qualified exception of Jerome Kern's *Show Boat*—not only were ineffectual and silly, but were expected to be. Alan Dale, critic for the New York *American,* expressed a rather widely held view when in his review of *Lady, Be Good* he wrote: "[the characters] have been jellied [sic] into some sort of a plot, which eluded me, as such plots invariably do, and I never worry. Let 'em go, I say.

Why worry with plots?" * The result of this view, which seemed to be shared by producers and audiences, was shows based on absurd books, containing songs that were mere interpolations, dances that were only divertissements, and comedy that was arbitrary, unreal, and considered unfunny even at the time.

During the '30's, perhaps as a consequence of America's new discovery that life was not a bowl of cherries, or perhaps just because audiences and creators tended to be more sophisticated and literate, a new sense of truth was brought to the musical-comedy libretto. These were the years of Gershwin's *Of Thee I Sing* (1931), Kern's *Music in the Air* (1932), Gershwin's *Porgy and Bess* (1935), and Rodgers and Hart's *The Boys From Syracuse* (1938).

By 1940, when *Pal Joey* opened, an effective book was becoming an essential part of musical-comedy production. A thoughtful public was beginning to return to the musical theater, where it could find dramatic satisfaction coupled with poetry and lyricism—the qualities that musical theater at its best provides.

A libretto, of course, is not a play. It must in the first place be highly compressed and able to make its important points succinctly. In printed editions, for example, *Liliom* runs to 132 pages, while the libretto of its musical version, *Carousel,* is only 88; *Green Grow the Lilacs* is 160 pages, and the musical, *Oklahoma!,* only 77. Song is elongated speech and therefore consumes more time in saying the same thing. In addition, there must be time for dancing and for reprises that may be essential. Also, music can instantly create an atmosphere, set a mood, or convey a spirit that would otherwise require a great many words to do. Sometimes a single musical number can do the work of an entire scene of a play.

Libretto-writing is an art in itself, and the success of our best shows is due first to the effectiveness of their books. The development of libretto-writing for the American theater neither paralleled nor depended on the development of contemporary

* Clive Barnes (*New York Times*) in 1968 wrote of *Hair* "Now the authors of the dowdy book . . . have done a brave thing. They have in effect done away with it."

38

drama; its growth took place within the musical-comedy form itself.

One of the most notable changes in the new musical books is in their conception of character. For a quarter of a century, two-dimensional Prince Charmings had ruled in a never-never land of happy endings—upright and infallible, pure and manly. In *Rose Marie,* the hero, Jim Kenyon, is a healthy, out-of-doors nitwit. D'Artagnan of *The Three Musketeers* is a stock romantic swashbuckler and gentleman. Despite his poverty, Francois Villon, the vagabond-poet of *The Vagabond King,* is a natural nobleman and savior of the French throne. Jimmy Winter of *Oh, Kay!* is gallant, though wealthy. In *Sweethearts,* Prince Franz's steadfast love for the daughter of a laundress is rewarded by the revelation that in reality (sic) she is a Crown Princess. The Red Shadow in *The Desert Song* is a fearless incognito Robin Hood. The hero of *The Student Prince* must turn his back on the girl he loves and marry a princess, sacrificing his own happiness for the sake of his kingdom, his sense of duty merely underscoring his all-round sterling qualities. The fact that Gilbert and Sullivan had as early as 1880 achieved an enormous success by poking fun at such characters—in *The Pirates of Penzance, or A Slave of Duty*—seemed in no way to affect their popularity.

Today, the principal male is often not a hero in the romantic sense. When *Pal Joey* opened in 1940, the odiousness of its leading character repelled critics and audiences alike, and the initial run was not long; by 1952, however, when the show was revived, the public had accommodated itself to the new anti-hero, and *Pal Joey* had a run commensurate with its quality. Joey is not an isolated example. *Carousel'*s Billy Bigelow is a libertine, a hustler, and a bum who makes no effort to support his wife until he learns of her pregnancy, whereupon he makes a desperate, stupid, and disastrous attempt to meet his oncoming financial responsibility: cornered in an abortive robbery, he commits suicide. Sky Masterson in *Guys and Dolls* is a professional gambler whose theatrical ancestry can be traced to Gaylord Ravenal in *Show Boat* and MacHeath in the old *Beggar's Opera.* The sadistic Siamese King with whom Anna Leonowens must contend is hardly a heroic model, nor is the self-centered Professor Higgins, nor the swindling Music Man.

There has been a further break with the tradition of leading men; they not only do not have to be of sterling character, but they no longer have to be young. Emile De Becque, the King of Siam, Professor Higgins, Captain von Trapp, Tony (*The Most Happy Fella*), Mr. President, Robert Baker (*Wonderful Town*), Hubert Cram (*Do Re Mi*), Phil (*Milk and Honey*), Fiorello, and Uncle Sid (*Take Me Along*) are middle-aged. What is more important, in middle age they are still romantically attractive. In most of the shows in which these characters appear there are also young lovers; but in no case is the audience's loyalty to the more seasoned hero diminished.

The heroines have also taken on a lifelike dimension. They are—in the best of our shows—motivated human beings. Vera Simpson in *Pal Joey* has no scruples; she wants her kind of pleasure and can afford to buy it and get rid of it at will. The seemingly frail Julie in *Carousel* is actually a determined and strong young woman. She understands that Billy Bigelow will never be a conventional husband and is aware of his temper, laziness, and vanity; nonetheless she wants, and quietly sets about to get, him. The worlds of Annie Oakley (*Annie Get Your Gun*), Nellie Forbush (*South Pacific*), Fiona MacLaren (*Brigadoon*), Eliza Doolittle (*My Fair Lady*), Anna Leonowens (*The King and I*), Sarah Brown (*Guys and Dolls*), and Maria (*West Side Story*) are concretely defined and plausible ones, and the problems they confront, like those of the heroes, are universal.

Perhaps the most important reason that the librettos of the best musicals work is their use of prototypes. In selecting (maybe an instinctual choice) characters who are ordinary, everyday, and recognizable, the method of particularization is at work. In other words, a large, simple point of view is set in motion and expressed by means of two people who are representative of many. These two are well known to everyone, and so audiences clearly identify with them. What is universal is expressed through just two. The necessary limitations and simplicity of librettos (as compared with "idea" plays) are then employed fully. Man, in many different guises and situations in many different shows, becomes important. We, belonging to the same human race, understand, feel, laugh at, and celebrate him because he is ourselves. All of us participate in his drama—that is, when the man is truly representative of some phase of us and is pinpointed sufficiently for us to recognize and then react.

The earlier cardboard characters sang lovely songs for a quarter of a century and, through music and stardust, successfully beguiled the more naive audiences of their day into imagining that they were experiencing dramatic satisfaction. A girl like Nellie Forbush, on the other hand, has a background, social roots, prejudices, in short, a recognizable heart and mind. She is in conflict with Emile De Becque, but also with herself. What happens to her grows naturally out of her own behavior, because, like all living human beings, she has been endowed with the ability to act.

In earlier times romance and comedy were two disparate elements, each represented by its own "couple" or "team." On the other hand, the ladies and gentlemen in contemporary musicals—because they are allowed to be people—are involved in both the humor and the romance of the show. Everyone in *My Fair Lady* has his or her comic moments. Anna and her King, Joey and Vera, Nellie, and Annie Oakley are at once romantic, "serious," and funny. And so are Tevye in *Fiddler on the Roof* and Rose in *Gypsy*.

Still another significant character innovation has gradually taken place. The best of the operettas had—at the very least—some melodramatic qualities. These qualities, like everything else in operetta and in most of our early musical comedies, originated in grand opera. Melodrama almost invariably presupposes the presence of at least one hissable villain. It has happened in our time, so gradually as to have been almost imperceptible, that the villain has vanished! In the musicals we are currently concerned with, there is truthfully not one. The conniving pair in *Pal Joey* are funny; Jud in *Oklahoma!* is pathetically psychotic, even if he does pose a threat to the heroine; the rejected suitor in *Brigadoon* is an object of pity; Jigger in *Carousel* is as amusing as he is villainously ineffectual. The pogrom in *Fiddler on the Roof* does not strike us as an act of villainous men as much as a concomitant of life in czarist Russia. In the other shows on the present list, there is no suggestion of a villain. In our times, he has been hissed into oblivion.

All of this is new, not so much as a result of new kinds of

plots, but because of the discovery that it is possible to present human beings even in musical shows—and, furthermore, that the greater reality produces a more powerful and more immediate impact upon an audience than all the false moustaches, glittering costumes, and powdered wigs put together.

On the other hand, in the new Stephen Sondheim-Hugh Wheeler *A Little Night Music,* we are again concerned with fairy tales. Act I shows a variety of mismating (seldom complained about), and the end of Act II has everyone paired off just as we wish them to be. Reality is tossed to the winds; logic, the precise machinery, is needed to affect these changes. But it matters not a whit. We *believe* in fairy tales and accept the "happily ever after" syndrome without one doubt. We do it because we are led to want it that way and we want it because we recognize underneath the lovely dressings of the people the natures and hearts of human beings we know. The style of the music and the graceful humor of the lyrics prevail upon us to swim with the current. And, in the end, the people are abbreviations. They are not two-dimensional, but they are never allowed to go deeper than the style and wit of the show find essential. We fly on a cloud made of whipped cream and rejoice and celebrate: what, we have no need to discover, or is it perhaps in the end a more blissfully romantic life than we will ever know?

B. PRINCIPLES AND SUBPLOTS

Characters, no matter how real, can only grow and evolve through the processes of the plot in which they function. They do not exist outside and alone.

The fifteen shows on the preceding list employ a wide variety of periods, settings, characters, styles, and points of view, but are nevertheless similar in dramatic structure. These similarities are peculiar *only* to librettos of musical shows, which differ essentially in structure from plays and opera librettos. I think it is important to illustrate these differences; and they operate at no place more vividly than in the shows' openings.

Take, for example, a most distinguished play from the contemporary American theater, *A Streetcar Named Desire* by Tennessee Williams. The play opens in a general atmosphere of the New Orleans French Quarter. The hero and his pal enter the scene in front of the building in which he lives. He bellows to his wife, who comes out onto a landing. Playfully, he throws her a package of meat and says he is going bowling. The wife says she will join him, and a moment later follows. After the exit of these three, the show's heroine, older sister of the wife, enters uncertainly in search of this very address. A neighbor assures her that this *is* the place and lets her into the sister's flat. The heroine is disappointed in the poor and untidy place revealed to her. There is a discussion in which we learn that the heroine is from Mississippi, that her family had formerly lived in a mansion on a plantation, that she taught school, and that at this moment she wants to be left alone.

In *A Streetcar Named Desire,* though all three important characters are introduced early in the show, what we learn about them is simple and brief. We are *not* certain—nor does it matter here—which of the women the heroine is. We observe a kind of "ladylike" quality about the older sister (in contrast to the younger one), but there is no hint of how she is to develop—a slow, painful evolution—and we see no serious conflict among them.

The librettos of musical shows—on the other hand—operate from a set of dramatic principles which are essential to their effectiveness. In the opening scenes of each of these shows, the author introduces, as such, his two principal characters, indicates directly or implicitly some conflict of position or personality that separates them, and sets up a *need* in the audience to see a genuine resolution of their differences.

These three basic principles may seem obvious; they are simple, but they are, for a musical libretto, essential. Occasionally an author has deviated from these principles and has succeeded, but if he has succeeded, it is because a workable substitute has replaced what would normally be—according to principle—essential. To anyone, like me, who has reason to read large numbers of new scripts or to see all of each year's new crop of plays and musicals, it is—alas—apparent that the three principles are not nearly obvious enough. In any case, let us examine just these as they are applied in the shows under discussion here.

In Scene 1 of *Pal Joey*, Joey is auditioning. He is immodest, brassy, and ignorant, but likeable because in his brashness he is transparently naive. When, in Scene 2, he tries to pick up an innocent girl, he sings:

> I could write a preface on how we met
> So the world would never forget
> And the simple secret of the plot
> Is just to tell them that I love you a lot.

His intentions are clearly far from honorable—but not evil; and their lyrical expression makes Joey rather attractive.

Then, in Scene 3, Mrs. Prentiss Simpson—Vera—enters. She is all of the things Joey *says* he is, and he is no match for her. She has *really* been around; he only thinks he has. She has status, education, and money; he, none. This disparity becomes truly complex when we realize that both of them are enormously proud. In Joey's case, pride protects him from admitting that he is nothing, knows nothing, and has nothing. He fancies that success and wealth are, for him, only just around the next corner. Vera's pride, on the other hand, rears itself in defense of real things: her approaching middle age, her money, and her social position. Vera tacitly offers Joey potential financial security: a place to live, clothes, money to spend, a car, and an opportunity to perform—untalented as he is—in his own club. For Joey, this is what he has always aspired to. For Vera, an affair with Joey is the most desirable amusement available at the moment. She knows it will be expensive, but she can afford it; she recognizes Joey's tastelessness, but smiles at it. She is aware that at her age this involvement is foolish. She has the advantage of knowing that when she becomes bored—and from past experience she knows she *will*—she can buy herself out as easily as she bought herself in.

If the sexes of these two characters were reversed—if Joey were a young girl and Vera, a middle-aged man—such a situation would by now hardly interest us. Unless there is something extraordinary about them, young girls hustling rich middle-aged

44

men present a pretty tired and conventional spectacle. Turning the tables in this way makes the drama between Vera and Joey new and interesting. Moreover, Joey, ungallant as he is, in taking on such an unequal match for himself, comes to have a certain Don Quixote-ish quality. Vera, indulging herself in a scandalous pleasure—and escaping retribution—must become an object of envy to most adult audiences. The contest between them is one whose outcome may be keenly awaited by the audience without its necessarily caring who is winner.

Vera and Joey meet for the first time, Act I, Scene 3, in a honky-tonk nightclub:

VERA: Oh, you're going to be difficult. Secretive.
JOEY: Sure. If I gave it to you all at once you wouldn't come back.
VERA: You're about the freshest person I think I've ever met. What makes you think I care enough to come back?
JOEY: Lady, you can level with me. You'll be back.
VERA (to one of the gents): Shall we go? I don't like this place.
JOEY: Wait a minute. I'm liable to get the bounceroo if you walk out like this.
VERA: You worry about that. (She exits.)

Joey has met his superior and she has challenged him. Vera, well aware of her prominence in Chicago, knows that Joey can easily get in touch with her—and will. She has only to wait. It is clear, however, that their match has not been made in heaven.

In the opening scene of *Oklahoma!*, there is the following exchange between Laurey, the heroine, and Curly, the hero:

CURLY: I've a good mind not to ask you to the Box Social.
LAUREY: If you did ast me, I wouldn't go with you.

It is obvious that Curly and Laurey love each other and belong together. Only Laurey refuses to allow Curly to take her for granted. On this ordinary, girlish refusal rests the entire dramatic conflict in *Oklahoma!* For in accepting Jud Fry's invitation—again from the girlish impulse to teach Curly a lesson—Laurey puts herself in the way of those dangers that create a life-size problem.

The first scene of *Carousel* constitutes a pantomime played against the music of a waltz suite. The stage directions read: ". . . now Billy (the barker on the carousel) starts his spiel and the entire stageful turn toward him and the carousel. . . . Everyone on the stage starts to sway unconsciously with the rhythm of Billy's words (unheard by the audience)—all but Julie. Julie just stands, looking at him over the heads of the others, her gaze steady, her body motionless. Billy becomes conscious of her. . . . She takes his mind off his work. . . . The heads turned up at him now follow his eyes and turn slowly toward Julie. . . . (It must be understood that Billy's attitude to Julie throughout this scene is one of only casual and laconic interest. He can get all the girls he wants. . . .) . . . Once he has got her on the carousel, he dismisses her from his mind. . . ."

In Scene 2, when the characters are allowed to speak and sing, we learn that Julie has never had a fellow. She is opposite in every way to the insatiable Billy, who is almost frighteningly and reluctantly drawn to her. Julie, the frail one, is strong; Billy, the powerful, is weak. They are impossibly mismated and inevitably drawn together. How, then, will it end?

In *Annie Get Your Gun,* Scene 1, Annie Oakley, an ignorant, awkward country girl, outshoots the renowned marksman Frank Butler, to whom she is attracted. The exhibition of her skill as a marksman is offhand; for her, it is nothing. But Butler, who has worked hard to achieve a national reputation based on the same skill, is a man, and his ego is wounded; he suddenly becomes a defenseless boy. Annie, who adores him, wants only to be in his good graces. Without intending it, these two simple and attractive people, who like each other—and whom the audience likes equally—are now in competition. Through the drama that follows, we feel that they must be brought together. It is they themselves who prevent what they both want from happening.

In *Brigadoon,* a contemporary American traveler on a walking tour through Scotland falls in love with a girl whom he meets in a town that comes alive only one day in each century. She may not leave. For him to remain would mean his having to share in a life which is lived only one day in every hundred years.

We learn at the outset that the boy is unhappily engaged to a girl in America. A moment later and before she meets the American, we hear the Scottish girl telling her friends who worry that she is not married:

> Waitin' for my dearie
> An' happy am I—
> To hold my heart till he comes strollin' by.*

It is clear that *this* boy and *this* girl are destined for each other, but their situation looks hopeless: the boy will be long dead before she lives her next single day.

In *Kiss Me, Kate* the two stars of a touring company of *The Taming of the Shrew,* who were once married to each other, play their offstage roles onstage. The male star is also the director of the play, and as the show opens, he and his leading lady are obviously at war. Although he is paying court to the ingenue and the female star has a wealthy fiance, it is clear that the two stars are still very much attracted to each other. The audience recognizes the petty provocations they hurl at one another as a game—which indeed it is in *The Taming of the Shrew*—and wants the players to resolve their antagonism and get back together again.

In *South Pacific,* set during World War II, Navy Ensign Nellie Forbush from Little Rock, Arkansas, falls in love with a French plantation owner who lives on the Pacific island where she is stationed. Everything is happy until the Arkansas girl learns that Emile De Becque is the father of two Eurasian children by his first wife, now dead.

Although Nellie and Emile are in love and ideally suited to each other, Nellie's bigotry—the automatic workings of her

---

* © 1947—Alan Jay Lerner & Frederick Loewe. World Rights Assigned to Chappell & Co. Inc. World Rights Assigned to and Controlled by Sam Fox Publishing Company, Inc.

background—takes possession of her. Because we like her and want her to be with Emile, we wish her to become as understanding as we have already come to feel she could be.

The hero of *Guys and Dolls*, Sky Masterson, is a gambler; the girl he becomes involved with, Sarah, is a prudish mission worker. Each of them feels the utmost disdain for what the other represents. We know that Sarah has an important lesson to learn about life, that her sense of its possibilities is narrow, pinched, and unreal. For the audience, the lovers-to-be are like pictures out of focus; it will be part of the dramatic purpose of the show to correct the focus.

Guys and Dolls departs in one significant way from the plot form of all the other shows: while Sky Masterson is clearly the leading man, his romantic partner is not really the leading lady but a secondary character. The leading lady is Miss Adelaide, who has for fourteen years been the fiancee of Nathan Detroit. Thus the resolutions of two romantic conflicts share equal prominence in the working out of the story. I do not know of another show in which this has been the case. And because of it, *Guys and Dolls* has one or another of its leading characters playing in every scene. In effect, each principal's opposite partner is just short of being *the other principal,* but, in fact, is not.

Guys and Dolls is also unique in that it is a satiric fable, and thus its characters are more symbolic than real.

The theatrical principles outlined above apply in exactly the same way to the rest of the shows under discussion. *My Fair Lady*'s Professor Higgins is an arrogant, self-centered, well-to-do phonetician. His Eliza Doolittle is a poor, dirty, cockney flower girl with an atrocious accent. This is a Cinderella tale, and we want the finally-to-be-lovely Eliza to charm all of London for both their sakes.

In *West Side Story*, Tony and Maria are hopelessly in love, but they have been committed by birth to violently irreconcilable factions. In this only truly tragic one of these shows the lovers are the predestined victims of society.

The fact that, when they meet, the two lovers (as in *Romeo and Juliet,* on which the show is based) are clearly intoxicated with each other, also presents a treatment of hero-heroine relationship which makes *West Side Story* different from all other musicals in this study. Whereas in all of the others, there is a schism *between* the two at the outset, in this one show, they are hopelessly in love. The threat to their happiness is apparent at the beginning, but it is the opposing societies to which each belongs that create the conflict.

In *The King and I,* the arrogant King of Siam has sent for a Welsh schoolmistress, Anna, to educate his numerous children and wives. It is the King himself, however, who needs Anna's help—although he doesn't admit it and seldom accepts it without protest. Anna, a widow with a young son, has needs of her own. The audience's strongest wish is to see both of them helped, and each of them in this situation is the only one who has the power to help the other.

In *Fiddler on the Roof,* there is an exception (proving the rule) to the practice of introducing the two principal romantic characters at the outset. For Tevye, the husband and father is the human hero, while his antagonist is the generation gap with which he is at war. The romantic element is divided like Gaul into three parts: three of Tevye's daughters together with their chosen amours.

There is still another original combination of characters in *A Little Night Music,* in which the two principal couples and two singles are so unhappily intertwined that re-grouping becomes mandatory. Here we are presented literally with six individuals whose relationships must become more satisfactorily arranged—for them as well as for us. We *will* it and it happens. That is all we need. We do not care or need to care about the messy if all-important details that realistically must be taken into account as the result of so drastic a rearrangement.

Rose, the heroine of *Gypsy,* is an ambition-ridden mother of two daughters. She sacrifices her own chance of a comfortable married life in an effort to achieve success on the stage for her oldest daughter who runs away from her. Undaunted, Rose turns her unalterable intentions toward creation of the same career for the younger daughter. In the process—near the end of

49

the show—she almost loses this second one—now successful—because of her attempt at continued supervision. We are horrified by Rose's inhuman steam-roller tactics but sympathize with her failure to comprehend her daughter's need for freedom. We are happy at the end when they become reunited. The mother-daughter reconciliation is substituted here for the more usual boy-girl reunion.

In all the rest of these best librettos the two principal characters are defined, their apartness is clearly stated early in the exposition, the story line is in every case simple and a direct outgrowth of the "who" of the characters, and there is not a single situation or character that is not readily identifiable with, and understandable to, the average theatergoer. Laurey and Curly are the girl and boy next door. Joey is the boy hanging around the corner poolroom. If we don't actually know Vera Simpson, she is nevertheless a familiar type: the wealthy society lady we read about who always has a new young man. Julie Jordan might be one's cousin, and Billy Bigelow, the ne'er-do-well whom she inevitably marries. And so on. They are all intimately connected in some way with all of our lives: real, hoped for, or read about.

In librettos (as in plays, for that matter), situations, like characters, must be particularized if they are to be effective. The camera must be in focus, pinpointing the characters and their specific problems. A newspaper headline reporting the death of three thousand people in a Chilean earthquake indeed may cause readers to cluck their tongues in some kind of transient astonishment; but—on the other hand—this same story may become deeply moving when narrowed down to a single family, or to two people, whose personal anguish can be recorded. The general situation is nondramatic, the specific compels the audience to identify with the particular human beings involved.

This point of view is not limited to serious or tragic situations: it applies also to comedy. It is impossible for a crowd or army or nation to evoke laughter. One or two people may create a precise situation which can be humorous. Ten people falling down a staircase could constitute a catastrophe, whereas a single man involved in the same action may be laughable. I suppose this is why jokes begin: "An Irishman walking down a street encounters a Jew," etc.

No situation—comic or tragic—can achieve any theatrical effect without particularization. The same principle applies also to lyrics which, at their best, are personal and achieve their effect when employing clear, precise images.

> The corn is as high as an elephant's eye
> —HAMMERSTEIN

> You want to talk of Keats or Milton;
> She only wants to talk of love
> —LERNER

> Artificial roses 'round the door,
> They are never out of bloom
> —HART

> The most beautiful sound I ever heard: Maria
> —SONDHEIM

> For I've imagined ev'ry bit of him,
> From his strong moral fiber to the wisdom in his head,
> To the homey aroma of his pipe
> —LOESSER

> The girl that I marry will have to be
> As soft and as pink as a nursery
> —BERLIN

In these and all other fine lyrics, the images are fresh and precise.

Generalizations achieve no effect and are the hallmark of amateurs.

C. SUBPLOT

In the best of our shows the central plot does not tell the whole story. Each of them has at least one subsidiary drama, a subplot whose conflict is resolved side by side, or in connection with resolution of the main story. Conversely, one of the things that unsuccessful musicals—of which there have been so many in recent seasons—have in common is their dependence on a single story.

In musicals, simplicity of plot is a prerequisite. The "filling out" is accomplished by the other material that is unique to the genre: songs and dances. However, the story as such—interrupted, embellished, and delayed—cannot fulfill the total requirements of a satisfying show. I believe that this dictates the necessity for a true, working subplot.

The need for a subplot was established in operetta at its high point. Almost invariably, there were subplots in the works of the Viennese composers, in Gilbert and Sullivan, and in Offenbach. This subplot idea did *not* descend from grand opera—the source of almost all the rest of operetta traditions—where it has never been used and was never missed. (*Never* is a large word; in *Don Giovanni,* for example, there is the semblance of a subplot in the Zerlina-Masetto characters, but it is never fully developed.)

Die Fledermaus—Viennese operetta at its peak—has such plot complexities, involving all of its characters in such an almost inexplicable mishmash, that a subplot is unthinkable. In *The Merry Widow,* however, the principals—Sonia and Prince Danilo—carry on a light coquettish affair while the subplot characters—Natalie and Camille—are involved in a more serious and romantic one.

This latter example of secondary-plot characters is unusual because a tradition seems to have evolved which dictated that the leading couple be "romantic" and the secondary pair "comedic." In the climax period of American operetta—circa 1924—this method was invariable: *The Vagabond King, Rose Marie, Desert Song,* and the others. Furthermore, the comedians (strange to say) occupied a larger portion of the operetta as a whole than the two leading characters! In *The Vagabond King,* for example, the three comics, Guy Tabarie, Oliver le Dain, and Margot, have infinitely more to do (and sometimes more to sing) than Francois Villon and Katherine de Vancelles, the hero and heroine. And in the operettas of this period, the subplot characters carried all of the comedy while the pristine leads were never allowed to stoop to anything (and I mean it) so low.

52

The necessity for a subplot possibly stems from the nature of the musical-comedy form. Musical shows inherently preclude the kind of complexity or depth of psychological or intellectual exploration that—in ordinary drama—can sustain a single conflict for two-and-a-half hours. Try, for example, to imagine *Oklahoma!* with only the Laurey-Curly-Jud triangle. The events themselves are too quickly told; something more had to be added to this simple tale of a nice girl and boy temporarily pulled apart by a psychotic farmhand. Or, imagine *Guys and Dolls* told only as the romance between Sky Masterson and Sarah, or, on the other hand, only as the struggle between Miss Adelaide and Nathan Detroit.

Typically, the subplot functions as a counterpoint to the main plot, with a life and line of its own. At the same time, while they are involved in a subsidiary conflict of their own, the secondary characters invariably play an integral part in the general story line. Take *South Pacific*. Emile De Becque and Nellie Forbush are the principal characters and are in love with each other. Bloody Mary, a native woman, and Luther Billis, a serviceman, are both involved in a comical con game at the expense of Billis's fellow sailors. Bloody Mary also has a young daughter, Liat, who falls in love with Lieutenant Cable. When Nellie breaks with De Becque because of his Eurasian children, he volunteers to go with Lieutenant Cable on a dangerous mission for the U.S. forces. De Becque returns afterward to an enlightened Nellie; meanwhile, Cable has been killed, and the sticky problem of an "impossible" marriage with Liat is settled. All these are vital elements in *South Pacific*.

Subplot characters (as pointed out previously) traditionally provided most of the comedy material. In *Pal Joey,* the secondary characters, Gladys and Ludwig, function both as villains and as comic foils. In *Carousel,* Carrie and Mr. Snow provide comedy, as does Jigger, the evil one. In *Oklahoma!* a comic triangle counterpoints the one formed by the principals and Jud. In *Brigadoon,* there are two sets of subplot characters: the comedic Meg and Jeff, and the young, romantic Jean and Charlie Dalrymple, who have Harry Beaton, the threat to Brigadoon's very existence, to contend with. There are also three sets of characters in *Kiss Me, Kate,* the principals, the gangsters, and Lois with her wealthy Harrison.

It seems important that librettists be aware of the subplot as an essential complement to the non-complex, sometimes shallow (especially shallow without music), and non-intellectual characters who are indigenous and probably inescapably necessary to musical shows of all kinds. (I am not derogating musicals!) Mimi, Carmen, Tosca, Nellie Forbush, Bess, and Rosabella are simply not on the same intellectually developed plane—nor, for intelligibility and in the available time, could they have been—with Blanche Dubois, Albee's Martha, Wilder's Dolly Levi, or Willy Loman.

It is consciousness of principles that is of first importance, because if in a particular instance and for sound reasons the librettist wishes to dispense with the subplot, doing so is not an impossibility. Doing so, however, without awareness and without a fully workable substitute, or a basic change of form that makes the use of a subplot unnecessary, may leave the libretto unworkable. Without a "workable substitute," what would remain would be too insubstantial.

The Kurt Weill-Moss Hart *Lady in the Dark* has a unique form. The heroine is pitted against four male characters, none of whom is clearly defined as the hero until the very end. The heroine—with the aid of a psychoanalyst—is searching for an understanding of her confused life. In the whole work, there are three seperate fantastic little operettas—complete musical sequences. In these, all of the characters of the realistic play appear in differing roles. The first sequence is an enlargement of glamor, the second relives high school days, and the third has a circus background. Besides these three musical sequences, there is only one single song and a final reprise of it. But because there are four male protagonists and each appears constantly in a different role, there is more than enough to sustain the audience's interest.

In *Fiddler on the Roof,* a single character—Tevye—battles with his traditions. There is no subplot but there is an overhanging and increasing threat of a pogrom carrying along the thread of suspense, as well as a continuing war between

Tevye and his traditions through each of his daughters' marriages. The emotions (intermingled with humor) mount to the very end when Tevye, with what remains of his family, is forced to move away: the wandering Jew, now emboldened by the very same traditions which have cost him three daughters and his home. Interest, concern, identification, and deep feeling are all present. These are accomplished because of a rich texture, without the need or aid of a subplot.

Company is a mosaic of tiny plots—five couples presented in cameos. All relate to a single principal character who in turn has encounters with three single girls. The whole is a merry-go-round revolving about a center pole.

In *A Little Night Music,* although we are made to care more about one man and one woman, all of the characters—all clearly identified—are closely related, so that whatever happens to one will affect the rest. They are all tightly knitted together. The movement of a single character in any direction will radically alter each of the others. We watch, want, wait, anticipate, and rejoice at the reshuffling which should replace misery with satisfaction.

Any principle can be discarded under certain circumstances, only it is essential that basic principles be known to creative people so that—consciously and deliberately—they can be employed helpfully, or replaced when they are clearly not needed.

D. SOURCES AND TRANSLATIONS

In the contemporary musical theater, practically most books are based on novels, stories, plays, biographies, and films. The practice of adapting literary or dramatic material for musical treatment is, of course, time-honored: one has only to mention *La Traviata* and *Otello, Faust, The Merry Wives of Windsor, Salome,* and *Wozzeck.* There are a number of partisans of "originality" who have voiced their opposition to this translation between media, but their arguments have so far led nowhere, since not a single musical based on an original idea (*Lady in the Dark* is best classified as a "play with music" and *Hair* had no book) has succeeded. This is not meant to imply that I am opposed to new book ideas. To the contrary, I know that they ought to exist. The fact is that—as yet—they do not.

In an article in the *New York Times Magazine* (September 11, 1966), Arthur Laurents, the playwright, wrote:

> Many people object to musicals on the ground that they are merely the reworking of old and familiar material. The trouble, rather, is that the material is not reworked: it is merely edited and songs are dropped in. . . .

I am in complete agreement with Mr. Laurents and I know that the paucity of thoroughly original librettos, is due to a general lack of understanding of the requirements of musical theater as opposed to those of non-musical plays. The dramatic form of the musical is necessarily a different one, and one of its aspects—the skeletal quality which allows music and lyrics to assume functional roles—is not generally known by many of even our best writers.

Alan Jay Lerner, in his preface to *Brigadoon*, suggested that the use of already tested material for libretto purposes was a good idea and concluded:

> I can tell you the book is all-essential. It is the fountain from which all waters spring. So start off on the right foot and select a story that is all prepared for you. The translation of that story to musical form is quite complex enough. Within that frame you will find more than adequate challenge to your originality and enough on which to experiment.

Whatever might account for it, the fact is that "original" books for musical shows have not been as workable as adaptations of existing material.

A few figures will illustrate the point. In the decade from 1920 to 1930, there were produced on Broadway 423 musicals, including many revues and some revivals. Of these, some dozen shows were based on known books or plays, including Dumas's *The Three Musketeers* (Friml), Edna Ferber's *Show Boat* (Kern), and *The Prisoner of Zenda* by Anthony Hope (Romberg).

Between 1930 and 1940 (the Depression years), there were only 179 musicals (a drop-off of nearly 50%), including revues, and there were an increasing number of revivals. About half a dozen of these shows were based on books and plays, including DuBose Heyward's *Porgy and Bess* (Gershwin), Pedro del Alarćon's *El Corregidor y la Molinera* (*Revenge With Music* by Schwartz and Dietz), and Shakespeare's *The Comedy of Errors* (*The Boys From Syracuse* by Abbott and Rodgers and Hart).

Between 1940 and 1950, 162 musicals were produced, and about twenty were based on known books and plays, the proportion of adaptations enlarging considerably. These included:

John Cecil Holm's *Three Men on a Horse* (*Banjo Eyes* by Vernon Duke and John La Touche)

Brandon Thomas's *Charley's Aunt* (*Where's Charley?* by Frank Loesser)

Russell Medcraft and Norma Mitchell's *The Cradle Snatchers* (*Let's Face It* by Cole Porter)

John O'Hara's *Pal Joey* (by Richard Rodgers and Lorenz Hart)

Julian Thompson's *The Warrior's Husband* (*By Jupiter* by Rodgers and Hart)

Lynn Riggs's *Green Grow the Lilacs* (*Oklahoma!* by Rodgers and Hammerstein)

Ferenc Molnár's *Liliom* (*Carousel* by Rodgers and Hammerstein)

Elmer Rice's *Street Scene* (by Kurt Weill and Langston Hughes)

Alan Paton's *Cry, the Beloved Country* (*Lost in the Stars* by Kurt Weill and Maxwell Anderson)

Anita Loos's *Gentlemen Prefer Blondes* (by Jule Styne and Leo Robin)

James Michener's *Tales of the South Pacific* (*South Pacific* by Rodgers and Hammerstein and Joshua Logan)

In earlier days, one man, Harry B. Smith, a bookwriter, collaborated with a variety of composers and lyricists, including De Koven, Herbert, Kern, Lehár, Oskar Straus, etc., in creating

57

more than three hundred "original" librettos. Where are they now? More recently, many distinguished playwrights have become involved in the musical theater, either as authors, or adaptors, or both. These have included S. N. Behrman, Maxwell Anderson, Robert Sherwood, Moss Hart, George S. Kaufman, Arthur Kober, Paul Osborn, Lillian Hellman, and many more.

Let us examine the production records of shows by the leading composers for nearly three-quarters of a century and see what they tell us on the question of librettos.

HAROLD ARLEN, one of the most gifted of our composers, did seven shows between 1931 and 1961. The most thoroughly workable one was *Bloomer Girl* (1944) with eight unforgettable songs and an entertaining book by Sig Herzig and Fred Saidy based on a play by Dan and Lilith James.

IRVING BERLIN, since 1914, has had twenty-one shows on Broadway. *Annie Get Your Gun* (1946) has a great score with a workable book by Herbert and Dorothy Fields and will probably be around forever. There are countless marvelous songs in other shows, and there is the charming *Call Me Madam*. But *Miss Liberty*, in spite of the otherwise eminent Robert Sherwood, has a poor book that nothing could save then or now.

JERRY BOCK has produced eight shows and several songs for revues between 1955 and 1970. All but the first show, *Mr. Wonderful* (1956), written with Larry Holofcever, were written with Sheldon Harnick. These included *Fiorello!* (1959), *Tenderloin* (1960), *She Loves Me* (1963), *Fiddler on the Roof* (1964), *Generation* (1965), *The Apple Tree* (1966), and *The Rothschilds* (1970).

VERNON DUKE began in 1932 and by 1944 had been represented by seven shows, most of them revues.

RUDOLF FRIML had produced thirty-four shows on Broadway from 1912 to 1934. *Rose Marie* and, far less frequently, *The Vagabond King* are still revived. (*Rose Marie*—a romantic melodrama—somehow still works despite its unthinkable comedy material.)

GEORGE GERSHWIN, from 1919 until 1935, had twenty-five shows produced. Here a few curious facts emerge. Gershwin had written ten not very outstanding shows before 1924, when he wrote *Lady, Be*

Good. (Was it coincidence that the preceding ten were done without the lyrics of his brother, Ira, with whom—afterward—he always collaborated?) Of the twenty-five shows that Gershwin wrote, only one really survives as it was written: *Porgy and Bess* (1935). This survival, in my opinion, is due to more than the unique quality of the score; it is because the book stands up in any time or place. Despite the richness of the *Girl Crazy* score (1930) and the celebrated first Pulitzer Prize-winning musical, *Of Thee I Sing* (1931), neither can be revived because of their out-of-date books.

VICTOR HERBERT, from 1894 to 1924, had thirty-three shows produced. Out of them about fourteen songs are still often sung. The books make all of the shows impossible for today's audience although *Naughty Marietta, The Red Mill,* and *Mademoiselle Modiste* are occasionally revived by amateurs.

JOHN KANDER, beginning on Broadway in 1961, has had six shows produced: *The Family Affair* (1961), with William Goldman, *Morning Sun* (1963), music and lyrics and with lyricist Fred Ebb, *Cabaret* (1966), *Zorba* (1968), *The Happy Time* (1968), and *70, Girls, 70* (1971).

JEROME KERN, from 1910 to 1939, had twenty-five shows produced. Of these, *Show Boat* (based on Edna Ferber's novel adapted by Oscar Hammerstein II) has one of the best scores, by far the best book to that date, and is a "standard" everywhere. Though many of the songs of *Roberta, Music in the Air,* and others are still frequently performed, the shows are seldom revived.

BURTON LANE first appeared in 1940 and had three produced shows to his credit by 1947, among them the distinguished *Finian's Rainbow.* The songs (lyrics by E. Y. Harburg) in this show are fine, and its book was, for its time, prophetic. *Finian's Rainbow* will probably endure.

FRANK LOESSER, in 1948, came along with *Where's Charley?* (based on Brandon Thomas's *Charley's Aunt*), and of the six book shows he wrote subsequently, four have been enormously important. *Guys and Dolls* (1950) based on Damon Runyon's Broadway folk tales, brought the first new characters into the theater since *Pal Joey* (1940)—and perhaps the most original ones since John Gay's *The Beggar's Opera* in 1728; then there was the opera, *The Most Happy Fella* (1956)—about which we will have more to say later—based on Sidney Howard's play *They Knew What They Wanted,* and finally, *How*

59

to Succeed in Business Without Really Trying, based on the book of the same name by Shepherd Mead, adapted by Abe Burrows, Jack Weinstock and Willie Gilbert. All four shows are important in the repertory of our musical theater.

FREDERICK LOEWE, first represented in 1938, had seven shows produced by 1961. Two of these were *Brigadoon* (1947) (written by Alan Jay Lerner, based on a German short story), which contains eleven outstanding songs, and *My Fair Lady* (1956) (based on George Bernard Shaw's *Pygmalion*), which broke all previous theater records. Both shows contain every book element needed to keep them alive indefinitely.

COLE PORTER, from 1916 to 1950, had twenty-two shows produced. Some of the American theater's best songs are in his folio, but despite a recent off-Broadway revival of a revised *Anything Goes*—with its tutti-frutti score—the only Porter show with a reasonable book (by Sam and Bella Spewack out of Shakespeare) is *Kiss Me, Kate.* It took Porter thirty-two years of successful songwriting, including three theater hits, to arrive at his best work.

RODGERS AND HART had twenty-four shows produced between 1925 and 1942. The list of songs with which these men enriched the American theater is as astonishing as the number of successful shows they created. Yet out of the lot (in my opinion), only two books will last: *The Boys From Syracuse* (1938) and *Pal Joey* (1940)—the first adapted by George Abbott, the latter by John O'Hara.

RODGERS AND HAMMERSTEIN's first collaboration, *Oklahoma!,* made 1943 an important year in the American musical theater. From that date until Hammerstein's untimely death in 1964, these men created nine shows, four of which are permanent monuments of the American theater. (All four—*Oklahoma!, Carousel, South Pacific,* and *The King and I*—were adaptations, two from plays, one from a short story, and one from a biography.) Their scores contained no fewer than thirty of Rodgers and Hammerstein's best songs. Their five other shows—two of which had original librettos—were less successful in the artistic sense, but one of them (*The Sound of Music*) was a box-office triumph.

SIGMUND ROMBERG had produced fifty-six shows from 1914 to 1948. *The Desert Song* and *The Student Prince,* with archaic books, are still revived because of the opulent scores: *New Moon,* less often.

HAROLD ROME made a sensational success at his musical-theater debut in 1937 with his revue, *Pins and Needles,* produced at the Labor Stage by the International Ladies' Garment Workers. Between that time and 1962, he had produced three other revues and six book shows. Of the four book shows that came to Broadway, *Wish You Were Here* was adapted from Arthur Kober's play, *Having Wonderful Time, Fanny* was based on Marcel Pagnol's motion-picture trilogy, *Destry Rides Again,* on a story by Max Brand, and *I Can Get It for You Wholesale,* on the novel by Jerome Weidman.

ARTHUR SCHWARTZ had fourteen shows (most of them revues) produced between 1929 and 1952. He wrote a number of memorable songs; but the best of the book shows, and Schwartz's best score after *The Band Wagon,* a revue, was *A Tree Grows in Brooklyn* in 1951. Again—good as this was—the indifferent quality of its adaptation from the novel prevented the show from becoming one of Broadway's best.

STEPHEN SONDHEIM has been active first as a lyricist, then as a composer-lyricist. He has produced nine shows since 1957. There were *West Side Story* (1957), with music by Leonard Bernstein, *Gypsy* (1959), with music by Jule Styne, *A Funny Thing Happened on the Way to the Forum* (1962), music and lyrics, *Anyone Can Whistle* (1964), music and lyrics, *Do I Hear a Waltz?* (1965), with music by Richard Rodgers, *Company* (1970), music and lyrics, *Follies* (1971), music and lyrics, *A Little Night Music* (1972), music and lyrics, and *The Frogs* (1974), music and lyrics.

JULE STYNE began in 1947 and had been represented by six shows by 1964. *Funny Girl* and *Gypsy,* both biographical, were the biggest box-office successes of the six. Styne's 1949 show, *Gentlemen Prefer Blondes,* boasted only a moderately workable book. *Bells Are Ringing,* and especially *Gypsy,* are excellent shows with Styne's usual exceptional scores.

KURT WEILL composed his first show in America in 1938 and died prematurely after his ninth in 1949. Individual songs from his American shows, such as "September Song" and "Speak Low," are unforgettable, and *Lady in the Dark,* based on an original libretto by Moss Hart, will come back again and again.

VINCENT YOUMANS had twelve shows produced from 1921 to 1932. His was one of the freshest and most original talents the theater had ever known; yet in spite of the fact that his shows contained by now classic songs like "Tea for Two," "Hallelujah," "Great Day," "Without a Song," and many others, the books to the Youmans scores are so particularly wedded to their own day that the fruits of this talent can only be handed on piecemeal. (The recent successful revival of *No, No, Nanette* [1971] had a new book by Burt Shevelove.)

To date, we have the evidence of history that adaptations have provided a sounder basis on which to build a musical show than original ideas. To be sure, there have been some highly successful original books: Mike Stewart's for *Bye Bye Birdie,* E. Y. Harburg's and Fred Saidy's for *Finian's Rainbow,* Betty Comden and Adolph Green's for *Bells Are Ringing,* and Don Appell's for *Milk and Honey* are prime examples.

There are, however, shows without really workable books that are nevertheless successful as vehicles for stars. Such shows exist only for their currency value, though, and their existence at all or for any length of time cannot be calculated with any degree of certainty.

It might *appear* that the adapter's task of reworking already tested material into a libretto is a relatively easy and straightforward one. After all, he is given a plot, setting, characters, and a kind of overall dramatic conception upon which to work. While it is true that good adaptations are far more numerous than good original books, nevertheless the adapter's job is an extremely complex one, fraught with difficulties and dangers of all kinds. In adapting, he must reorganize the material to meet the special requirements of his genre. He must shape the plot so that it can include song and dance and distill the essence of his characters, who, in the musical form, reveal themselves in new and different ways—and more succinctly; he may have to create some additional characters or delete others who make insufficient contribution to his new form, inject appropriate comedy material where there is none, and divide his story so as to provide a single workable act ending for the mid-performance break.

Particularly if he is a playwright, he will need to employ a form which may seem alien to him. His play—now to become libretto—*must* be incomplete without music and lyrics: he may have to surrender, for example, a written scene to a musical one that may accomplish the same purpose more effectively. He will have to tighten his own material to allow time and space for the musical materials, which can not *repeat* what has already been said in dialogue. He must simplify, be more succinct than would otherwise be his custom, eliminate complex intellectual ideas, which, to the audience, can only be confusing in a musical (because of the natural difficulties of comprehending such ideas within music, and because of the shortened space he has in which to expose them) and be willing to surrender to musical and lyrical purposes the peak emotional moments which can be more effectively expressed by these means.

Some comparisons between source material and corresponding librettos will, I think, demonstrate some of the principles of successful adaptation.

The conversion of *Green Grow the Lilacs* into *Oklahoma!* provides an excellent case in point. This adaptation was in most respects a simple affair, which is to say that the order of the play was adhered to in the musical. (This is not always possible.) The play was in six scenes, and the musical is in two acts or six scenes (three in each act). The scenes, however, do not always parallel one another.

In addition, Hammerstein created a new character of major interest, Will Parker, whom Riggs had given only one offhand mention—in his Scene 3 in the smokehouse:

CURLY: You know Will Parker?
JEETER: Never heard of him.
CURLY: Ole man Parker's boy up here by Claremore? He can shore spin a rope.*

Early in Scene 1, Hammerstein introduces Will Parker, who has just returned from winning the steer-roping contest in Kansas City. He is full of enthusiasm for his first glimpse of "modern," big-city life, and he has won a prize of $50—the amount Ado Annie's father has insisted he must have to be allowed to marry Ado Annie.

Will becomes an opposite number to Ado Annie and adds to

* Copyright 1930, 1931 by Lynn Riggs. Copyright 1957 (In Renewal) by Howard E. Reinheimer, Executor. Copyright 1958 (In Renewal) by Howard E. Reinheimer, Executor.

the fun of Ado Annie's relationship to the Peddler. In fact, Will's existence helps to give the character of Ado Annie a new dimension. In the original play, the author describes her: "She is an unattractive, stupid-looking farm girl, with taffy-colored hair pulled back from a freckled face. Her dress is of red gingham, and unbecoming." In the musical, she becomes something far more interesting—in fact beguiling, and a full "comic."

The secondary triangle—Will, Ado Annie, and the Peddler—supply indispensable comedy for *Oklahoma!,* but their shenanigans also form a perfect example of a complete subplot. Their story line is complete in itself and can be told separately, although its function is contrapuntal to the main plot—Laurey, Curly and Jud, also a triangle.

The idea of having Curly sing a song at the very opening comes from the original, and the lyrics of "The Surrey with the Fringe on Top" are largely indicated in the Riggs play. "Pore Jud Is Dead" is, in essence, to be found in the original smokehouse scene, and in that same scene Curly talks about "the purtiest mornin'," which gives a hint of the song that became the musical's opening.

The Rodgers and Hammerstein changes in the proportions of several scenes are of great import; and the addition of Will, with its chain-effect on everything around him, adds the comedic color so wanting (at least for a musical) in the original.

In his introduction to the play, Riggs wrote: "Two people in a room, agreeing or not agreeing, are to me truly dramatic. The edges of their being can never be in accord; psychically, as well as physically, they are assailed by an opposing radiation." And later on: ". . . I thought of the first three scenes as The Characters, the last three scenes as The Play."

Rodgers and Hammerstein seem to have tried as much as possible to work within Riggs's conception—particularly in the ballet at the end of Act I, which explores Laurey's psyche through her dream and provides some of the motivation for her subsequent behavior. (It is interesting to note that while the original play ended its run without making back its investment, *Oklahoma!* earned profits of historic proportions.)

The following is a chart comparing the progress of the play with that of the musical libretto:

PLAY	MUSICAL
Scene 1 The (Laurey) Williams farmhouse. (This is a living room interior.)	*Act I, Scene 1* The front of Laurey's farmhouse. (This is out of doors.)
Scene 2 The same, showing Laurey's bedroom. (The material in this scene is included in the musical's first scene.)	
Scene 3 The same, showing the smokehouse.	*Scene 2* The smokehouse.
	Scene 3 A grove on Laurey's farm. (This scene is an invention of the adapter. It leads into Laurey's dream ballet, which ends in Jud's awakening her and taking her to the social.)
INTERMISSION	INTERMISSION
	Act II, Scene 1 The Skidmore Ranch. (This is a new scene in which Will Parker is duped into getting back enough money from the all-too-willing Peddler to be able to marry Ado Annie. Also (and more importantly) there is an auction of picnic baskets, and Jud almost outbids Curly, who has had to sell horse and gun in order to win. Bad feeling between them is expressed.)
Scene 4 The porch of Old Man Peck's house. (The party is in full swing. Laurey has her confrontation with Jeeter, discharges him, and decides to marry Curly.)	*Scene 2* Skidmore's kitchen porch. (Jud dances on with Laurey. She has the confrontation scene with him and discharges him. She is eager to marry Curly.)

65

Scene 5 The hay-field back of William's house, a month later.

Scene 6 The living room of the Williams house three nights later. (Ado Annie and Aunt Eller discuss Curly's trial scheduled for next day. Laurey is worried. Curly enters, having broken out of jail. He is pursued by a crowd of men who mean to return him to jail. Aunt Eller talks them into letting Curly spend the night with his bride.)

Scene 3 Back of Laurey's house. (The setting is the same in both. The wedding of Laurey and Curly is over, and their friends give them a "shivaree"—a customary folk celebration—which is a prankish annoyance to the couple. Here, as in the play, Jud enters, starts an argument and, in a fight with Curly, falls on his own knife. In the musical Aunt Eller amusingly arranges Curly's trial on the spot, and the show ends with the happy couple leaving on their honeymoon.)

To recapitulate, in Act I of the musical, the material follows closely the first half of the play but divides itself differently and concludes with a ballet. Act II, Scene 1 of the musical is an invention, and the events of Scene 2 happen in Scene 1 of the play. Act II, Scene 3 of the musical contains the fight, the trial and the happy ending, whereas in the play the fight and the arrest of Curly occur in Scene 5, and the reuniting of Curly and Laurey is in Scene 6—with the trial not as yet having happened but a strong feeling that everything will come out happily.

I would like to mention briefly several other of these conversions to libretto.

South Pacific, based on the stories by James Michener, has a well-integrated plot line. Logan and Hammerstein took three of the nineteen tales: "Our Heroine," the story of Ensign Nellie Forbush and Emile De Becque; "Fo' Dolla," the story of Lieutenant Cable, Liat, and Bloody Mary; and "A Boar's Tooth," which describes Luther Billis. Some of the other tales have contributed extra color, background, or nuances, but the above three supply the principal ingredients. Although the characters in all three tales are in the same location or nearby in the book they are never brought together. The Forbush-De Becque story as told in the musical *South Pacific* is elongated by De Becque's agreeing to go on a dangerous military mission after Nellie's break with him.

The suspense created by De Becque's mission and by the prolongation of the separation between the lovers is a major contribution of the librettists; in the original story, the break and reconciliation occur during the same night. The musical treatment is theatrical, as it needs to be.

Further, the libretto's use of Luther Billis as part of this particular tale (in which he fits admirably), making him Bloody Mary's complement, is brilliant. By being paired with Luther, Bloody Mary becomes more developed, and in addition to her original qualities she also becomes a major comedienne.

The dovetailing of these elements with the poignant story of Liat and Lieutenant Cable completes a model three-couple plot. In addition, there is the marvelous contrast between mature and very young love. And finally, in the libretto it is Lieutenant Cable who accompanies Emile on the dangerous mission. The knowledge of Cable's death is in itself deeply moving, but it also serves to conclude the Liat-Cable plot satisfactorily without Cable's having to refuse to marry her (on racial-social grounds) as he does in the original *Tales*.

Margaret Landon's novel (based on fact), *Anna and the King of Siam*, was the basis of *The King and I*. Each chapter of the novel contains a harrowing episode, complete in itself, and linked to other episodes through the personalities of the King, who is responsible for creating most of the issues, and Anna, who tries to resolve them.

Hammerstein's treatment alters the King's physical presence by making him attractive, not, as according to Miss Landon, "of medium height and excessively thin." The subplot involving Tuptim comes from one of dozens of horrifying tales in the novel and occurs more than three-quarters of the way through it; the man involved with her is a priest who neither has any amorous relationship with Tuptim nor has he ever been previously aware of her. The libretto has altered this story to make the King's two luckless victims lovers even prior to Tuptim's "arranged" marriage to the King, and their subplot extends throughout the musical.

Hammerstein's achievement here is in his selecting, simplifying, and bringing into focus a few of a multitude of characters and situations and in his ability to create one direct, effective main plot line. Almost none of the details of the original is left unchanged, and yet there is in *The King and I* an essentially truthful distillation of the book's intention. Everything has been telescoped so as to become more viable. The death of the King at the end—a radical alteration of the book—presents a far more effective (and conclusive!) piece of dramaturgy. Humor, entirely absent from the novel, is wholly original with Rodgers and Hammerstein and appropriate to their show. It is especially felicitous in the songs such as "A Puzzlement," "Shall We Dance?" and "Shall I Tell You What I Think of You?"

In *Carousel,* the most striking single element in the transformation of Molnár's *Liliom* is the alteration of time and place. *Liliom* is set in Budapest about 1919, and *Carousel,* on the New England coast between 1873 and 1888. Naturally, such a change had a profound influence on the color and style of the musical. The action in the musical has a fluency which the original does not have, and the comic characters of Carrie and Mr. Snow soar high above their dour literary alter egos, Marie and Wolf Beifeld. In *Liliom,* after plunging a knife into himself, the title character spends a long scene dying, during which everything that is capsulized in *Carousel* (and *after* Liliom goes to heaven) is argued or spelled out. The play's heavenly scene is much longer, further spelled out, and drab. The dialogue between the heavenly magistrate and the characters in his court sounds like an object lesson for prospective Eagle Scouts. In *Carousel* Billy dies without seven pages of dialogue; he simply says, "Julie!"—following which he exits, then is seen in heaven arguing with charming heavenly people, who instantly communicate the passage of time by telling him that his daughter is fifteen years old.

In the conversion of *Pygmalion* to *My Fair Lady*, neither the characters (except for Doolittle) nor the plot (except for the ending) was significantly altered, but the proscenium was opened up to show us what we had never seen before: Eliza's native habitat, Ascot, the outside of Higgins's house, the Embassy ball, the Covent Garden flower market, and other parts of Higgins's house besides the study. Almost all of the song ideas are generated by the text of the play.

If we are ever to have excellent original librettos, it will be necessary for playwrights to study the techniques that musical theater peculiarly requires of its librettists. The same is true of songwriters. Regardless of their talents or achievements, men who write songs will not be able to compose a proper musical score without a considerable knowledge of theater.

Since the largest share of the responsibility for a show's success rests on the librettist—and since today's exorbitant production costs seriously diminish the beginner's opportunities for learning through doing, it is essential that potential librettists learn everything possible from the growing list of musical-show models—as well as from the formidable catalogue of failures.

E. TIME AND DRAMATIC SEQUENCE

In the plays of Shakespeare, the action is almost always continuous. On those few occasions when time has lapsed between scenes or acts, its passage is made clear in the dialogue that follows; and generally the lapse has been so well prepared in the previous scene that the audience knows at once what the interval is. Writing in this way is of course most dramatic, since the audience is propelled ahead at the end of every scene and the action is seldom interrupted.

In operas, time-lapses are usually great. The action is not, as a rule, continuous. *Madame Butterfly*, in three acts, typically makes no overt reference to the passage of time. But Butterfly marries Pinkerton at the end of Act I; in Act II, she already has a baby of unspecified age, and she is hopeful of Pinkerton's return; in Act III he does arrive—accompanied by his American wife. Thus considerable time has passed, at least between the first two acts.

In modern plays, although there are many which carry the action continuously (despite the traditional two intermissions), there are many others with wide time spans between acts and/or scenes.

In *A Streetcar Named Desire,* the three acts are set in "spring, summer, and early fall."

In *Born Yesterday,* two months pass between Acts I and II, and Act III takes place the night after Act II.

In the biographical *Abe Lincoln in Illinois,* thirty-four years go by during the three acts.

In *The Fourposter,* thirty-five years pass.

In *Desire Under the Elms,* two months elapse between Acts I and II, and Act III is "late spring of the following year."

In today's best musicals, however, as in the plays of Shakespeare, the action is continuous, or nearly so. In *West Side Story,* the scenes follow precipitously. Everything takes place within a period of about two days. In *My Fair Lady,* there is a time-lapse in Act I in order for us to see Eliza's progress. All of the rest moves rapidly headlong. *South Pacific, Oklahoma!, Brigadoon, Kiss Me, Kate,* and *Guys and Dolls* are nearly continuous. In *The King and I,* there is a time-lapse after Scene 1 to show that Anna has not been received by the King immediately. And later, weeks have passed to show that Anna has not seen the King. In *Carousel,* Act II, between Scenes 3 and 4, there is a lapse of fifteen years which is announced as a surprise in the preceding scene in heaven:

STARKEEPER: . . . fer one thing you might do yer little daughter some good.
BILLY: A daughter! It's a girl—my baby!
STARKEEPER: Ain't a baby any more. She's fifteen years old.
BILLY: How could that be? I just come from there.
STARKEEPER: You got to get used to a new way of tellin' time, Billy. A year on earth is just a minute up here. . . .

In *Pal Joey,* time is nearly continuous, and in *Annie Get Your Gun,* the second act opens as Annie, after her break with Frank Butler, is returning from a triumphant tour of Europe.

This time continuity gives a feeling of immediacy which, in turn, helps to propel the action and give the audience a sense of going forward. This is not a new method. It was already old in Shakespeare's day, and it has always, for instance, helped to accentuate the suspense in melodrama.

The fact is that while it is quite unnecessary to opera librettos and to many plays—the continuity of time is one of the hallmarks of contemporary musical theater, where it is helpful.

F. SCENE AND ACT ENDINGS

Operettas had traditionally been divided into four or five acts. The twenty-minute intermission following each act's curtain allowed time for changing the cumbersome scenery. Although these shows frequently began as early as seven in the evening and lasted until midnight, the actual playing time was often less than three hours. The strain this put on the librettist was enormous, for one of the trickiest problems is persuading the audience to return for the next act.

In the two-act version of *Rose Marie* (1924) (the original was in three acts), in the finale of Act I, the heroine reprises the "Indian Love Call" (across a mountain) as a signal to her beloved, Jim, that she is not going to go away with him so that Jim will himself then go away at once. She wishes to prevent his arrest on a murder charge (of which he is not guilty). It is self-sacrificing of her. The audience hopes that somehow they will be together again.

During the first quarter of this century, as stage machinery improved and conventions changed, shows were boiled down to a standard three acts. This still obligated the librettist to *try* to bring the restless natives back twice. After the 1930's, nearly all musicals were done in two acts. Though this system generally entailed as many as twelve to twenty speedy scene shifts, the librettist has only *one* major "break" to cope with. Still more recently, several major musicals were given in a single act.

In *Annie Get Your Gun* at the end of the act the hero goes away, leaving an angry note for Annie. In *Oklahoma!* the heroine, after a nightmare in which Jud nearly kills Curly, is awakened by Jud to go to the social with him. Frightened by her dream, she acquiesces.

In *Brigadoon* at the height of the dance celebrating the marriage of Jean MacLaren to Charlie Dalrymple, Harry Beaton, the bride's disappointed suitor, savagely interrupts the revelry. He is bitter and exclaims to the astonished crowd, "I'm leavin' Brigadoon. 'Tis the end of all of us! The miracle's over!" The miracle he refers to has just been explained: "One day in every one hundred years the town of Brigadoon comes to life, but if anyone living in it ever leaves, the town will be dead forever." The angry Harry has rushed out, threatening to leave. Can he be stopped?

My Fair Lady breaks at the Embassy Ball when Professor Karpathy, a phonetics expert and former pupil of Professor Higgins who has bragged that he can detect any imposter, succeeds, against Higgins's wish, in dancing with Eliza. As the curtain descends we are anxious to know if Karpathy will discover Eliza's true background.

The first act of *A Little Night Music* ends after Couple A has received an invitation to a weekend in the country, and Couple B, who is at odds with A, has decided to turn up at the same place, uninvited. There is certainly going to be a scrambled mess, which we will delight in watching.

Although the act break must persuade the audience to return for the second half of the show, each of the many scenes in each act must complete itself and, at the same time, point ahead to the future by suggesting where the characters are going, what they hope to accomplish, and over what hurdles they must leap. In a sense, this is the same technique that was employed with great success several decades ago in magazine and movie serials and that today persuades millions to return daily to their favorite comic strips.

This dual function of completion and promise is well illustrated in the scene endings of *Guys and Dolls, Carousel,* and *West Side Story.*

GUYS AND DOLLS

ACT I

Scene 1 Masterson accepts a bet from his friend, Nathan Detroit, that he can take Sister Sarah to Havana.

Scene 2 Masterson and Sister Sarah part in anger after their first meeting.

Scene 3 Where will Nathan's crap game be held?

Scene 4 Nathan, in order to go to the crap game, leaves his unhappy "fiancee," Adelaide.

Scene 5 Two gamblers are philosophizing about the interference of women in the lives of men (the title song).

Scene 6 Masterson learns that Sister Sarah's mission is to be closed unless there are people at their midnight prayer meeting and offers to provide "sinners" if Sister Sarah will go to dinner with him in Havana.

Scene 7 Men are gathering on a street in preparation for the crap game, the place for which is still uncertain. A detective questions them and is told they are giving a bachelor dinner to celebrate the impending wedding of Nathan and Adelaide. Adelaide appears and is excited. Nathan is shocked to learn that Sister Sarah has gone to Havana with Sky!

Scene 8 Sky and Sarah are in Havana. Sarah is getting drunk—not realizing that there is rum in her milk.

Scene 9 Although the now happy Sarah wants to remain in Havana, Masterson insists on taking her back home.

Scene 10 Sky and Sarah, back from Havana, are saying good-night in front of the mission. They declare their love. On hearing a police siren, gamblers rush out of the mission, where they have had a game, the other mission personnel having just returned from an all-night canvassing of "sinners." Sarah feels that Sky took her away for this purpose. She breaks with him.

ACT II

Scene 1 Nathan again stands up Adelaide.

Scene 2 (on the street) Arvide—the head of the mission—tries to reason with Sarah. He knows she is in love. Sky appears and makes it clear that he will furnish the "sinners" at the prayer meeting: *his* part of the bargain.

Scene 3 The game ends with Sky rolling the dice once for $1,000 for each man against promises to attend prayer meeting if they lose. The scene ends on the dice roll; the outcome is unknown.

73

Scene 4   Nathan meets Adelaide, who is preparing for their wedding that evening, and tells her he is going to a prayer meeting, which she believes is his biggest lie.

Scene 5   The prayer meeting. Sky having won, delivers all the gamblers and leaves. The commander is impressed: "Isn't it wonderful that even evil can be used for good!" Sarah feels she's been a fool.

Scene 6   Adelaide and Sarah meet. Both have identical problems, and both have made the same error: they should have married first and *then* reformed their men. They want to do something about it now.

Scene 7   Both couples are united.

CAROUSEL

ACT I

Prelude   In pantomime, we see Julie and Billy's attraction to one another.

Scene 1   Julie and Billy meet. Julie knows all about Billy's unstable character but sets out quietly to win him. At the end of the scene, Billy is unable to resist.

Scene 2   Billy, now married to Julie, learns he is to become a father and for the first time recognizes some responsibility. Because he must have money to support his child, he agrees to join his evil friend Jigger in a holdup. The two men join Julie and the villagers, who are leaving for a clambake. Billy, unwillingly, is armed with a knife; the men plan to slip away from the party.

ACT II

Scene 1   Julie, suspecting some unsavory plan, begs Billy not to go with Jigger. He goes.

Scene 2   The holdup is a fiasco. Jigger escapes. Billy is caught and stabs himself. The returning clambake party enters, Julie runs to Billy as he dies. Two heavenly friends "resurrect" Billy and escort him to heaven.

Scene 3   The heavenly friends are understanding, but they want Billy to return to earth to do some good before admitting him to heaven. He thinks he has just died, but discovers that Julie now has a fifteen-year-old daughter. The Starkeeper makes Billy return to earth to look at her.

Scene 4   Billy's daughter, Louise, is snubbed because of her dead father's disreputability. He is persuaded to visit earth, where, if he wishes, he can be invisible.

Scene 5   Billy, visible, tries to make Louise accept a star he "stole" from heaven. When, because she is afraid of him, she refuses, he hits her. As Julie comes out of the house, Billy disappears. Louise tells Julie the stranger "Hit me—hard— . . . but it didn't hurt." Julie feels that somehow this was Billy. Although again he has failed to do good, Billy wants one more chance; he is told he can attend Louise's graduation.

Scene 6   At the Graduation exercises, the Starkeeper, now the village doctor, tells the graduates: "You can't lean on the success of your parents. That's their success." (Directing his words to Louise) "And don't be held back by their failures! Makes no difference what they did or didn't do. You just stand on your own two feet." Billy, who is invisible, asks Louise to believe the doctor. The graduates sing "You'll Never Walk Alone." During the singing Billy goes to Julie and whispers, "I loved you, Julie. Know that I loved you!" She appears to understand. Billy is led back by the heavenly friends, having redeemed himself.

WEST SIDE STORY

ACT I

Scene 1   The Jets ("Americans") want to rumble with the Sharks (Puerto Ricans). They feel that their former member, Tony, can be counted on to participate. Riff says he will get Tony to challenge the Sharks.

Scene 2   Tony refuses to rumble but agrees to meet his buddies at a dance that evening. He is mysteriously happy in anticipation of something he cannot comprehend.

Scene 3   In a bridal shop where they both work, Maria and Anita (the girl-friend of Maria's brother, Bernardo, the head of the Sharks) are preparing to go to the dance. Maria, like Tony, is filled with anticipation.

Scene 4 At the dance, the social director instructs everyone—the members of the rival gangs and their girls—to form two concentric circles; when the music stops, the boys and girls are to dance with whoever is opposite them. The object is to mingle the dissident factions. Tony and Maria meet and are instantly in love. Bernardo confronts Tony. The Sharks and Jets agree to meet in half an hour at Doc's drugstore to set the time and place for the rumble.

Scene 5 Maria on her fire escape; Tony standing below. They declare their love, and it is agreed Tony will come at sundown next day to the bridal shop to see Maria.

Scene 6 The rival gangs meet at the drugstore for a "council of war." Tony is contemptuous of them for using deadly weapons; why not fight with fists, if they must fight? They agree that only the best man of each gang will fight. Tony is convinced it will be a fair fight.

Scene 7 Tony at the bridal shop. Maria wants Tony to stop the rumble. Tony and Maria go through a marriage ritual without benefit of clergy.

Scene 8 The neighborhood—a song scene about "Tonight." To the spotlighted rival gang members "tonight" means their approaching fight. To Maria and Tony it means being together.

Scene 9 The rival gangs meet under the highway. Riff and Bernardo start fighting; Tony enters and tries to stop them. Bernardo offers to fight Tony, who declines. A general melee ensues, during which Bernardo and Riff produce knives. Tony tries to part them. Bernardo kills Riff, whose knife Tony takes. He kills Bernardo. A police whistle is heard. Everyone runs, but not before Tony, staring at Bernardo's body, cries "Maria!"

ACT II

Scene 1 A few minutes later. Just as Maria tells her girl friends there will be no rumble, Chino bursts in and reveals that Tony has killed Bernardo. Maria—alone at prayers—is interrupted by the arrival of Tony. She is savage at first, but soon understands. He plans to give himself up to the police.

Scene 2 The Jets are confronted by police officer Krupke, from whom they escape. They are concerned about Tony's whereabouts, fearful that the Sharks will find him and kill him. They go in search.

76

Scene 3 Tony and Maria are still together in her bedroom. Anita knocks at the door. Tony leaves via the fire escape to go to the drugstore, where he will hide. Anita, entering, knows that Tony has just left. She is savage because Bernardo is dead and Maria, his sister, is having an affair with his murderer. Maria convinces her of her love, and Anita's hatred softens. As a police officer enters to interrogate Maria, Anita leaves for the drugstore to tell Tony to wait there until Maria can come.

Scene 4 Tony's gang is at the drugstore to prevent the Puerto Ricans from killing Tony, who is hiding in the basement. Anita enters to deliver Maria's message. The boys taunt her. She is so abused that she blurts out "Tell him [Tony] that Chino found out and—and shot her [Maria]!

Scene 5 Doc tells Tony Maria is dead. Tony runs out yelling, "Chino? Chino? Come and get me, too, Chino."

Scene 6 Immediately after Tony enters the street yelling for Chino, Maria enters. As they run toward each other, Chino shoots Tony.

All scenes of the best musical shows have strong finishes of their own—periods—but each also projects the audience toward what will happen next. For maximum effect, each scene should be essential to the plot line.

What I have come to feel is a fair test of the strength of a scene's closing is whether the audience knows that the scene has ended *before* there is a blackout or curtain. Its completion must be clearly felt as a result of what it has had to say. As for the all-important second part—the pointing ahead—the scene should leave the spectator with the simple question "Now, what will happen next?"

II. ELEMENTS OF THE MUSICAL SHOW

A. THE MUSICAL OPENING

Prior to the 1940's, there was scarcely a musical show that did not open with an ensemble song-and-dance. These, moreover, seldom had very much relation to what followed. Their chief functions were to settle the audience, assure everyone at once that there would be beautiful girls, and identify the ensemble itself.

In *The Red Mill* (1906) the girls lead off:

> By the side of the mill with its sails
>   hanging still and the bridge so quaint,
> We've been posing for hours with our baskets of
>   flow'rs as they paint, paint, paint.*

and later the boys, all of whom are painters, respond with:

> Girls, as you know we are wed alone to art and
>   it breaks our heart but we have to
>   devote all our own to art.*

In *No, No, Nanette* (1925):

ACT I The home of James Smith, New York, all of the choristers sing:

	How do you do?
	How do you do?
	Go and tell your mistress we're here.
PAULINE (*the cook*):	I shall let you know just as soon as I can go.
CHORUS:	Take our names to Miss Nanette.
PAULINE (*spoken*):	Flappers!
CHORUS:	Flappers are we,
	Flappers are we,
	Flippant and fly and free,
	Never too slow,
	All on the go,
	Petting parties with the smarties,
	Moonlight dances,
	Oh, what chances,
	Keeping our beaux
	Upon their toes.
	Dizzy with dangerous glee.
	Puritans knock us
	Because the way we're clad.
	Preachers all mock us
	Because we're not bad,
	Just flippant young flappers are we! †

* Lyrics by Henry Blossom.
† Copyright 1925 by Harms, Inc. Used by Permission. Lyrics by Mandel, Harbach, and Caesar.

The years from 1906 to 1925 had brought about no changes in musical openings. Although the best contemporary musical shows fulfill certain dramatic obligations by introducing characters and definitions of place, the musical forms in which today's openings are cast vary widely. That openings do differ so much is one of the marks of the theater's maturity. Like everything else in the best contemporary musicals, the opening number has become functional.

At the start of *Pal Joey*, the title character is auditioning for a nightclub job. He sings "A Great Big Town," which is a kind of "throwaway"—a song not intended to be a feature of the main score. The tone is set: Joey is immediately established as corny, naive, and untalented, and the audience is introduced to his needs and limitations.

Oklahoma! has the most original beginning of any show. The curtain rises on the front of Laurey's farmhouse. The backdrop represents a cornfield. It is morning. The orchestral introduction is bucolic. Offstage the unaccompanied voice of Curly is heard: "Oh, what a beautiful mornin' . . ." and as he enters, the orchestra sneaks in to support him. (*Green Grow the Lilacs* opens in a similar way.) Time, place, and period are established. We meet Curly as the guileless, romantic young cowhand that he is.

The opening of *Carousel* is again distinctly different. The entire first scene—"An Amusement Park on the New England Coast"—is performed in pantomime against an orchestral suite of waltzes. The audience observes the two principals, Billy and Julie. We see that they have never met, but that some vague mutual attraction exists. We also meet Mrs. Mullin, the owner of the carousel, Julie's friend Carrie, and the girls' boss, Mr. Bascombe—all of whom reveal themselves in dumb show against the background of the music.

Annie Get Your Gun opens with light underscoring to set the scene of a summer hotel on the outskirts of Cincinnati, late in the 19th century. This music is followed by a march which brings on members of the Buffalo Bill Show troupe and, following a single announcement of the tent show, there is an opening song, "Colonel Buffalo Bill," which advertises the evening's performance. It is a solid, serviceable opening for what can be described as plain American musical comedy at its best.

Brigadoon opens in the atmosphere of a storybook. In the dark, an offstage chorus quietly sings:

> Once in the Highlands, the Highlands of Scotland
> Deep in the night on a murky brae;
> There in the Highlands, the Highlands of Scotland,
> Two weary hunters lost their way.
> And this is what happened,
> The strange thing that happened
> To two weary hunters who lost their way.*

A mystic theme is heard in the dark. The lights fade on, and two lost American hunters play a comedy scene.

The audience knows that there is an indefinable strangeness in the air, but against this, a scene of contemporary comedy is played. The show which follows will combine these two disparate elements, an indefinable mystical atmosphere and contemporary realism.

Kiss Me, Kate begins with a dialogue scene: actors on a bare stage having finished rehearsal of a play. There is a sense of antagonism, of haste, of half-understood undercurrents. There is underscoring using "Another Op'nin', Another Show," which finally erupts into the song itself. The dialogue has established the principal characters and then what amounts to the "opening chorus" is performed by a minor principal and the ensemble: in a sense, the exact reverse of the old formula.

In *South Pacific* the curtain rises on the garden of Emile De Becque's plantation home, where two Eurasian children sing a simple happy French song, "Dites-moi." The song ends, and a servant playfully chases them into the house just as Emile and Nellie enter. It is Nellie's first visit to the house; she is thrilled with the beauty of everything, and Emile basks in her happiness.

Guys and Dolls has a long choreographic opening. Set on Times Square, it introduces Runyonesque characters: Cops,

Dolls, Guides, Tourists, a Pug, Bobby-Soxers, a Celebrity, a Photographer, etc. They exit, leaving three gamblers onstage. The dance music melts into the "Fugue for Tinhorns"—a trio about horse racing and betting. At the conclusion, the Mission Band enters, playing a hymn. These mission workers are the opposite number to the gamblers, and among them is Sister Sarah, one of the two heroines.

The overture of *My Fair Lady* melts into the opening music. We see the outside of the Royal Opera House, Covent Garden. The opera has just ended. It is raining. The well-dressed crowd emerges in search of taxis. A young man (Freddy) collides with a flower girl (Eliza), inadvertently knocking her flower basket out of her hands. She complains in full, rich cockney. She encounters another taxi seeker, Colonel Pickering, who gives her some change. A bystander calls Eliza's attention to a man standing behind a pillar writing down everything she says. Eliza thinks he's a detective and wails her innocence. There is a hubbub. Colonel Pickering defends her. The man, of course, is Professor Higgins, who is making phonetic notes of her speech. He sings "Why can't the English teach their children how to speak?" Higgins and Pickering meet, discovering that they are both speech specialists and know one another by reputation. Higgins has boasted that he could pass Eliza off as a "duchess at an ambassador's garden party" in six months. He goes off with Pickering, and Eliza hears him give his address.

The King and I opens on the deck of a small ship in the 1860's. (There is musical underscoring.) The captain is talking to a child when the child's mother, Anna Leonowens, enters. They are in sight of their destination, Bangkok. There is excitement and apprehension. The child and the captain express their fear, which the mother (while sharing the feeling) tries to calm by singing:

> Whenever I feel afraid
> I hold my head erect
> And whistle a happy tune,
> So no one will suspect
> I'm afraid.*

* Lyrics by Oscar Hammerstein II.

81

The music and lyrics have charm and humor in the face of apprehension. In the song Anna meets the situation with courage and at the same time obliquely gives the audience an accurate view of her character. This is a dainty beginning which prepares for, while giving no actual hint of, the arduous and painful problems which lie ahead.

The opening of *West Side Story:* "half-danced, half-mimed . . . is primarily a condensation of the growing rivalry between two teen-age gangs—Puerto Ricans and . . . what is called Americans." Seeing and hearing a kinetic, finger-snapping, fragmentary dialogue and music—that accompany the mime-dance and in an extraordinary way communicate tension and evil—we become immediately aware of the dark, hopeless social web that hovers menacingly in the very air. It will destroy. No one will be safe.

A Little Night Music has an original opening. Five individual characters—two men and three women—attired in evening clothes enter separately and sing (they are the "chorus") a ro-mantic "overture" about remembrance. On finishing the vocal quintet, they begin to waltz. The curtain rises "revealing in dim light, the main characters doing a strangely surreal waltz of their own, in which partners change partners and recouple with others."

Gypsy begins with rehearsal of a kiddie show. "The kids are in horrible, homemade costumes; the mothers wear clothes of the very early twenties"; Jocko (the M.C.) is ordering everyone to shut up. He calls out light cues to the front light men. A kid begins an accordion solo and is cut short. "Baby June and Company" are next. Jocko instructs the conductor to play half of their material. As June and Louise begin to sing, an instructive female voice is heard from the rear of the theater. Rose, the heroine of *Gypsy* (who had shouted) rushes down the aisle and onto the stage. The show has begun.

To recapitulate: each of these openings defines the style in which its particular show will be cast. Each introduces impor-tant characters and, in a manner, describes them. These methods are functional and constitute a notable departure and advance from the slight, almost unconnected stereotyped openings which characterized shows of an earlier period. The mere introduction of important characters in this manner shatters one age-old convention: the principals, formerly, were never exposed before a good deal of setup revealing their characters, problems, attractiveness, peculiarities, and in one of many ways, a preparatory "Here he (she) comes now!" In the best shows of our time, functional things are given first and primary consideration.

B. THE PLACE OF THE LYRIC

Once during the rehearsal of a show when two characters began to sing a song, Abe Burrows said to me, "Now begins unreality!"

Literally, of course, this is true. Sky Masterson (*Guys and Dolls*), an archetypical Broadway gambler, sings:

> My time of day is the dark-time
> A couple of deals before dawn
> When the street belongs to the cop
> And the janitor with the mop
> And the grocery clerks are all gone.
> When the smell of the rainwashed pavement
> Comes up clean and fresh and cold
> And the street lamp light fills the gutter with gold
> That's my time of day.
> And you're the only doll I've ever wanted to share it with me.*

These lines are lyrical, imaginative, introspective, and poetic. Because they are sung, they rise above literal mundane considerations, and we therefore feel no incongruity between their unexpected lyricism and Masterson's ordinary lingo. We are seeing *inside* him.

Unreality of this kind is an important central part of musical-theater convention. We accept it, as we accept any genuine working convention, unquestioningly.

A character (male) on the stage is talking to a girl. A man in the pit in front of the stage begins to wave his arms. A sound of

* MY TIME OF DAY by Frank Loesser © 1950 Frank Loesser, All Rights Reserved. Used by Permission.

musical instruments begins to permeate the atmosphere. The "daylight" of the stage quickly fades, and the boy and girl are standing on a street focused in two spotlights. The boy sings a verse and a chorus. (The girl does not interrupt.) Then the orchestra changes key. The girl (who until now was a stranger to the boy) sings the same verse the boy sang, but with changed lyrics, followed by a chorus identical to his. Furthermore, the chorus lyrics sung first by a "heel" and reprised by an innocent girl contain the lines:

> And the simple secret of the plot
> Is just to tell them that I love you a lot; *

These sentiments seem rather natural and real: we are not even conscious of how precipitously the two have come to a declaration of love. This is the scene in front of the pet shop in *Pal Joey*.

It is, as Burrows said, "unreality." But being sung, it reaches us on a different plane because music is able to create a special super-real world; and the artificially constructed and lighted scene emphasizes the idea that what is seen is not intended to be merely lifelike. If the theatrical illusion thus created is successful, it will indeed seem larger than life. And by now, this mechanism is totally accepted as convention.

In *Oklahoma!* the psychotic Jud—now alone—lays himself bare:

> But when there's a moon in my winder
> And it slants down a beam 'crost my bed . . .
> And a dream starts a-dancin' in my head. . . .
> And the girl that I want
> Ain't' afraid of my arms . . . .
> And her long, yeller hair
> Falls across my face,
> Jist like the rain in a storm! †

The unrealism of this passage brings us to a higher truth. Jud is no longer only a sniveling, frightening, hideous, threatening

* Lyrics by Lorenz Hart.
† Lyrics by Oscar Hammerstein II.

misfit, but a pathetic human being. We recognize his dream, and we pity him even as we fear him.

With Joey and Linda, music (and lyrics) gives a sympathetic tenderness to an artful "pickup." Sky Masterson's revelation gives us an insight into a guy who had seemed responsive only to the material world. In Jud—by himself—we are shown the emotional torment that drives this fellow creature to being repellent.

How else but in song could the bully Billy Bigelow reveal so much of himself as he does in the "Soliloquy"—something he could never be capable of doing in *reality* to anyone? In this number, and for the only time in the whole of *Carousel*, he is able to express tenderness, boyish enthusiasm, and, for a moment, something bordering on maturity when he recognizes his responsibility as a prospective father:

> I got to make certain that she
> Won't be dragged up in slums
> With a lot o' bums
> Like me!
> She's got to be sheltered
> And fed, and dressed
> In the best that money can buy! *

Even these few examples should indicate the wide range of emotion and character revelation that the musical lyric is capable of expressing. Each of them is closely related in function to the classical soliloquy; but if spoken soliloquies were employed today in the American theater, they would embarrass the audience, to whom they would appear stilted, self-conscious, and artificial. The musical soliloquy, long famous in grand opera (Iago, Rhadames, Figaro, Boris Godunov, Marguerite, Hans Sachs, Wotan, and hundreds of others), is one of the few ancient devices which has been continuously employed in operetta and in all other kinds of musical theater. Victor Herbert took advantage of it in *Mademoiselle Modiste* (1905); Leonard Bernstein used it most effectively in both *Candide* (1956) and *West Side Story* (1957). Soliloquy is most important, especially in

* Lyrics by Oscar Hammerstein II.

85

contemporary musical theater, because by means of it, a character—whether comic or serious—can comprehend through a single "song" what might otherwise require an entire prose scene.

A song or ballad in general terms might mean a love song, a narrative, a soliloquy, or a character ballad. In it, composer and lyricist share an almost limitless opportunity to create the most expressive kind of composition. To be sure, at this point in history both of them must face a problem created by many centuries of precedent. The lyricist, while retaining the verbal simplicity essential to all good songs and making the lyric appear to be generated by the character who is to sing it, must also be able to create freshness through an un-stereotyped idea. The composer on his side must be able to combine melodic and harmonic warmth with rhythmic simplicity and a feeling of emotional and musical inevitability.

In many of the best revues of the '30's there were important lessons to be learned about ballads. Four or five times during these revues—as I recall vividly—a pretty soprano or handsome baritone was given the impossible chore of stepping in front of a velour drop to sing a ballad immediately after some boff comedy sketch. The singers, I remember, were always attractive and always sang well, but they were invariably so boring that at the mere sight of them, the audience grew restless. People talked, others went to the lavatories; nearly everyone rustled through the program to be assured that something—anything—*else* was going to follow!

In other words, in a show, for even a good ballad to succeed fully, it has to be properly set up. In a revue, of course, there was no setting up at all. How or why was one to care about some singer in a tuxedo trying suddenly and out of nowhere to tell you that his heart was breaking or that he had found the girl of his dreams? You couldn't have cared less.

In a good musical book show the ballad—and all the other songs—grows out of a situation which is already engaging the attention, interest, and emotion of the audience. It then becomes a high point in a fully comprehensible scene, and the listener, understanding the problems, must care.

86

Of course, an exceptional ballad can work perfectly well outside the theater as either a piece of instrumental music or as a vehicle for a singer. The point is that *in* the theater it must be important: it must "hold the stage." It is essential that the lyrics be a logical extension of the scene in which the ballad is sung, that they expand the character whose expression they are, that both words and music seem to be essential when they occur, and above all, in the marvelous words of E. E. Cummings:

> I would suggest that certain ideas gestures rhymes, like Gillette Razor Blades having been used and reused to the mystical moment of dullness emphatically are Not To Be Resharpened.

If a ballad's lyric has freshness and the music is meaningful, the love song or love scene can soar. "Tonight" in *West Side Story*, the "Bench Scene" in *Carousel*, containing "If I Loved You," the simple "Come to Me, Bend to Me" in *Brigadoon*, the title song in *Fanny*, will serve to illustrate what I mean. Even in the old shows, when everything else might fail—when the comedy songs were unfunny, the openings ricky-ticky, and the charm songs merely coy—the love ballads usually worked. In the old shows, they worked because of extraordinary tunes. They work even today: "One Alone" from *The Desert Song*, "Indian Love Call" from *Rose Marie*, "Serenade" from *The Student Prince*, "Kiss Me Again" from *Mademoiselle Modiste*, "Oh Promise Me" from *Robin Hood*, are still very much alive. But in today's more developed and more literate musical theater, the ballads must have—besides good tunes—lyrics which make a new point. They must begin with a fresh idea and progress with it to a satisfying and meaningful conclusion.

The most difficult task for the lyricist is the creation of good comedy songs—a problem that we shall discuss in a later section.

An offshoot of comedy songs is the charm song. This term—charm song—which I believe I have made up, designates a song that embodies generally delicate, optimistic, and rhythmic music, and lyrics of light though not necessarily comedic subject matter. The lyrics and music are usually of equal importance. "To My Wife" in *Fanny*, when fat old Panisse toasts his young wife on their fifth wedding anniversary and thanks her for the joy she has given him, achieves just the right lightness, sweetness, and sentimentality. One of the most perfect examples of the use of the lyrical charm song is "The Surrey with the Fringe on Top" in *Oklahoma!* Compare it with its original prose equivalent. In Scene 1 of *Green Grow the Lilacs* the following exchange takes place:

CURLY: A bran' new surrey with fringe on the top four inches long— and yeller! And two white horses a-rarin' and faunchin' to go! You'd shore ride like a queen settin' up in *that* carriage! Feel like you had a gold crown set on yer head, 'th diamonds in it as big as goose eggs.

LAUREY: Look out, you'll be astin' me in a minute!

CURLY: I ain't astin' you I'm *tellin'* you. And this yere rig has got four fine side-curtains, case of rain. And isinglass winders to look out of! And a red and green lamp set on the dashboard, winkin' like a lightnin' bug!

LAUREY: Whur'd you git sich a rig at? (*with explosive laughter*) Anh, I bet he's went and h'ard it over to Claremore, thinkin' I'd go with him!

CURLY: 'S all you know about it—

LAUREY (*jeering*): Went and h'ard it! Spent all his money h'arin' a rig, and now ain't got nobody to ride in it.

CURLY: Have, too! Did *not* h'ar it. Made the whole thing up outa my head—

LAUREY: What! Made it up?

CURLY: Dashboard and all!

LAUREY (*flying at him*): Oh! Git outa the house, you! Aunt Eller, make him git hisself outa here 'fore I take a stove arn to him! Tellin' me lies!

CURLY (*dodging her*): Makin' up a few—Look out, now! Makin' up a few purties ain't agin no law 'at I know of. Don't you wish they *was* sich a rig though? Nen you could go to the party and do a hoe-down till mornin' if you was a mind to. Nen drive home 'th the sun a-peekin' at you over the ridge, purty and fine.*

Hammerstein's lyric uses the identical idea and many of the images. The song has a setup verse, chorus, second verse, sec-

* Copyright 1930, 1931 by Lynn Riggs. Copyright 1957 (In Renewal) by Howard E. Reinheimer, Executor. Copyright 1958 (In Renewal) by Howard E. Reinheimer, Executor.

ond chorus, third verse (with development) under dialogue, and third chorus. The lyrics have been organized to tell a continuous tale. With Rodgers's music, the whole is unremittingly charming.

"June Is Bustin' Out All Over" in *Carousel* tells wittily of the coming of summer in terms of the flora and fauna of the region.

Almost at the very opening of *The King and I* Anna sings "I Whistle a Happy Tune," which not only beguiles the audience but tells them indirectly and enchantingly that Anna Loenowens *is* frightened. The listener chuckles half out of amusement and half out of anxiety.

Brigadoon is full of charm songs which differ considerably from one another. "Waitin' for My Dearie" is a kind of oblique love song about someone the character has not yet met. This is followed by "I'll Go Home with Bonnie Jean," also an oblique love song and delivered by the young lover who is to be married that day. In it, he is renouncing all other love. This in turn is followed by "The Heather on the Hill," a duet between the two principal characters and also an oblique love song, for love is hinted at, though not expressed. All three of these songs are charming, they move, they have musical lilt, they flirt, they are witty, they are about love and are not love songs.

Charm songs occupy a peculiar place in the musical program of contemporary shows. Their music has a stronger profile than that of the comedy song and helps to lead the lyric with its rhythmic lilt. It lends an air of cheerful pleasantness to the scene, in contrast to the more serious tone of the ballad or the jocularity of the comedy song. It infuses a sense of brightness and well-being without being obligated to the "payoff" of a joke. It is an easier kind of song for the lyricist to come by than a successful comedy song and permits the composer a more graceful musical opportunity.

C. MUSICAL SCENE

In most of the earlier shows, there were long musical scenes in which the words shifted back and forth between dialogue and lyric (sung) verse. This practice was handed down from grand opera by way of operetta. Such musical scenes usually occurred at moments of high dramatic tension and appeared particularly as part of the finale of Act I. But as musical comedy grew farther away from operetta, this practice fell more and more out of use. Recently, musical scenes have been revived; abandoning them had been a loss to the musical theater. Their "revival," however, has generally taken a form which gives them certain new dimensions.

A contemporary example—one which adheres very closely to the tradition—is found in *West Side Story* in the passage where Maria, the heroine, is savagely confronted by her friend Anita in "A Boy Like That." Anita's lover, Bernardo (who was also Maria's brother), has been killed by Maria's beloved Tony. We know that the murder was provoked and unintentional. This musical scene commences fiercely; Anita, grieving, is savage, but Maria overcomes her savagery. Together, at the conclusion, they sing:

> When love comes so strong,
> There is no right or wrong,
> Your love is your life! *

In the same show the "marriage" scene—a combination of speech and song ("One Hand, One Heart")—is tender, sometimes humorous, and always moving. The music-lyric treatment ending in:

> Make of our lives one life,
> Day after day, one life.
> Now it begins, now we start
> One hand, one heart—
> Even death won't part us now.*

is nearly unbearable because of its simplicity and impossibility. The poetic-musical treatment suffuses a kind of magic without which the scene could not exist. It is interesting to note that in *Romeo and Juliet,* which provided the plan and idea for *West Side Story*, the marriage ritual is indicated—it is about to take place as the scene ends—but Shakespeare omitted the ceremony itself, which could only have been a reproduction and therefore dull. The authors of *West Side Story*, however, taking advantage of the musical possibilities, created a scene in which a simple ritual is performed by the two lovers alone. Only through the employment of music could this have been accomplished. Again, this is an example of musical theater potential which is here exploited in its own peculiarly unique way.

In two other shows, *The King and I* and *My Fair Lady*, the musical scene achieved something new in the theater. It was employed for charm and amusement; originally, musical scenes had usually been only dramatic—even melodramatic. In *The King and I*, the "Song of the King" (a scene between Anna and the King) extends into another long musical section, "Shall We Dance?" The scene begins with an enchanting discussion of male and female, contrasting Eastern and Western points of view, and travels quite naturally to the King's outrage at seeing Western people dance together with the man's arm around the woman's waist. This becomes "Shall We Dance?" in which Anna explains Western decorum and finally begins to teach the King to dance in Western fashion. It is amusing in itself, but it also serves to touch on, with just the slightest passing reference, an amorous undercurrent between the two characters. This is cut off dramatically with the entrance of the Prime Minister. "Shall I Tell You What I Think of You?" belongs in the same category.

In *My Fair Lady*, in "Why Can't the English" (teach their children how to speak?), the author manages all at once to establish Higgins's philosophy of phonetics, his hostility toward sloppy speech, his potential relation to Colonel Pickering (the speech enthusiast) and to Eliza, with her dreadful cockney accent. A single line in Shaw's play has been developed into an important, witty and functional musical scene.

The same is true of "I'm an Ordinary Man" and "Just You Wait, 'enry 'iggins"—this last being a display of Eliza's feelings that Lerner and Loewe added to Shaw. "The Rain in Spain" and "You Did It" come straight out of the original *Pygmalion* and, like "Why Can't the English?," they transform the material of the play into musical scenes of charm and enchantment.

Lyrics may function in still another way. To illustrate: two pieces belonging to what I like to call the "hopeless-hope" category are "Somewhere" in *West Side Story* and "You'll Never Walk Alone" in *Carousel*. This kind of expression is not new. At the end of *Porgy and Bess* it reaches a great height when Porgy sings "Oh Lord, I'm on My Way." In *West Side Story* a voice is heard singing quietly and concludes:

> There's a place for us,
> A time and place for us.
> Hold my hand and we're halfway there.
> Hold my hand and I'll take you there
> Somehow,
> Someday,
> Somewhere! *

In this "place" happy couples would be moving "in a world of space, and air and sun." For the people in *West Side Story*—for all of them, but especially for the lovers, Tony and Maria—such happiness is a total impossibility. And there is in its way nothing more moving than the expression of hope in the face of what we know to be inevitable catastrophe.

We are similarly moved in *Carousel* when we see Billy lying dead, the bereaved Julie being held up firmly by her Aunt Nettie, who sings:

> Walk on
> Through the wind,
> Walk on
> Through the rain,
> Though your dreams be tossed and blown. †

One of the most original musical scenes occurs in *Fiddler on the Roof* when Tevye, who is afraid of telling his wife that he has consented to their daughter's marriage to the poor tailor instead of a wealthy butcher, fabricates a yarn about the threatening ghost of the butcher's dead wife. The scene—a comic night-

* Copyright 1957 by Bernstein & Sondheim. Lyrics by Stephen Sondheim.
† Lyrics by Oscar Hammerstein II.

mare—unfolds in song, dialogue, pantomime, and dance. Nothing quite like it has been created elsewhere.

The average theatergoer today refers to musical shows generally as musical comedies—and with reason. Comedy, of course, from well before Shakespeare and through the centuries that followed, has always been an indispensable element in theater—finding its essential place even in such tragedies as *Macbeth* and *Hamlet*. Musical theater in particular has from the beginning leaned most heavily, after romance, on comedy. There is a not uncommonly held view among many people that comedy is included in musical shows in order to attract a larger audience—in other words, to make shows more "commercial." Such a notion is absurd. Comedy is to musical theater—to all theater—as red is to the spectrum of colors: primary in itself and necessary for the existence of purple and orange and a whole range of shades. The comic view of reality provides an enriching comment on the serious or straightforward; sometimes, like a mirror, it reflects ourselves, and we laugh at our own foibles. Without comedy, most drama would be off-balance.

In earlier musical-theater works, comedy consisted of extraneous jokes introduced out of nowhere and without relationship to characters or plot. Often it consisted of topical comment that all too soon became meaningless. Frequently, it was left to the discretion—or indiscretion—of the performer, who would improvise whatever he felt at any performance.

The point of view in regard to comedy that existed in our musicals from the start was reexpressed as late as 1963 in the "Author's Note" (Burt Shevelove) to the published version of *A Funny Thing Happened on the Way to the Forum*.

This is a scenario for vaudevillians. There are many details omitted from the script. They are part of any comedian's bag of tricks. The double take, the mad walk, the sighs, the smirks, the stammerings. All these and more are intended to be supplied by the actor and, hopefully, the reader.

93

According to a recent poll, *The Student Prince* * (1924) and *The Desert Song* (1926) are today the American public's two most beloved musical heirlooms. The enduring popularity of these shows can be attributed primarily to their scores, timeless in their loveliness, and to nostalgia. They are performed year after year throughout America. There have been two film versions of each. Their songs are newly arranged and recorded every year. Their comedy scenes, however, not only do not work today, but, judging by the reviews of their premieres, they were never considered funny. Audiences expected comedy scenes in musicals to be poor and simply shrugged them off as an inevitable part of the fairy-tale romance and the opulent music.

In *The Desert Song,* for example, the comic character, Benjamin, while riding in the Moroccan Desert, is captured by the Riffs:

SID: Speak.
BENJAMIN: Certainly. Mr. Chairman, Ladies and Gentlemen.

Same Scene:

SID: What are you doing in Morocco?
BENJAMIN: Nothing. Make me an offer?

Later:

HASSI (*sharpening his knife and pointing it*): When I see a spy I want blood.
BENJAMIN: Don't look at me, I'm anemic. . . .

In another scene:

SUSAN: Got any news?
BENJAMIN: One about the size of a tea-tray.
SUSAN: I said news.
BENJAMIN: I thought you said bruise. . . .

* It is interesting to note that the principal dancer in *Desert Song* is a secondary, though important character and that her dances are quite well integrated into the plot. Also, in both *Desert Song* and *The Student Prince* the finales of the shows are most unusually *not* (for their period) ensemble numbers, but vocal duets!

The same Benjamin has a comedy song called "It":

> There was a time when sex
> Seemed something quite complex.
> Mr. Freud then employed words we never heard of.
> He kept us on the string—we kept on wondering,
> But the seed of sin now at last has been
> Found by Elinor Glyn.
> In one word she defines the indefinable thing.

1ST CHORUS

> She calls it "It,"
> Just simple "It."
> That is the word
> They're using now . . .
> For that improper fraction of vague attraction
> That gets the action somehow! *

The Desert Song has not been singled out here because it is one of the old "classics" most vulnerable to exposure. On the contrary, this show is one of the most durable. Its comedy material, however—and the same is true of all earlier shows—was not acceptable then and is especially not today.

In most of the early shows, comedy material was of a general nature: jokes about just anything, or puns. In *Of Thee I Sing* (1931) most of the comedy comes out of contemporary political situations. In its own time it worked well enough to win the Pulitzer Prize. Today it is meaningless, and the show, because it is built on comedy that has long ago perished, cannot be revived. It is significant that—and this is surely an important indication of modern-day artistry—the songs, *including* the lyrics, are not dated. The lyrics are universal and therefore enduring. Only the "comic" dialogue is dated, and *Of Thee I Sing,* once funny *because* of it, is now impossible to revive because of it.

A glance at more recent shows will demonstrate clearly that the comedic point of view has changed considerably. Today it does not consist of jokes, gags, or hotly current allusions strung loosely together, for these are what go quickly out of style. The humor of contemporary comedy grows naturally out of the char-

---

* Lyrics by Oscar Hammerstein II.

95

acters and the situations they are placed in. Since the majority of enduring comedy songs have lyrics that reveal the character's personal problems, difficulties, and plaints, they are almost invariably autobiographical. Sometimes the comedy song is a soliloquy and sometimes a kind of "confession" to another character. The comic lyric, through its revelation of character and its employment of witty, fresh rhyme schemes and rhythmic predictability—the kind of predictability that prepares the audience for the precise moment of the "payoff"—achieves what prose dialogue cannot. The music in the comedy song, however, tends to be more discreet than in the ballad: it usually has a less well defined profile and is more complementary than assertive. ("Bewitched, Bothered and Bewildered" is a strong exception.)

There is another departure from earlier comedy material—one that has sharpened with the passage of time. For example, in *Rose Marie,* whenever Lady Jane and Hard Boiled Herman play a scene together, or either is pitted against another character, a kind of neon sign lights up to announce "COMEDY!" Each of the comedy teams, Herman and Lady Jane in *Rose Marie,* Benjamin and Susan in *The Desert Song,* etc., wear instantly recognizable labels—"Comedian" and "Comedienne"—and their connection with the plot (if any) is artificial and fabricated. The performances of these people were exaggerated to the point of stylization: they were performers in an out-of-the-blue vaudeville sketch interpolated between the legitimate parts of a play. Their costumes often suited this exaggeration: outrageous colors, enormously large shoes, disproportionate designs, and so on. Sometimes their makeup suggested the circus or the *commedia dell'arte.* Until the mid-1930's, this was the pattern. The appearance of the comedy team interrupted the show until its exit from the stage.

In recent musicals, comedy scenes of this sort have disappeared. Comedy teams have disappeared, leaving the romantic principals with the comedy responsibilities. Today they can handle it without damaging their once-sacred two-dimensional romantic characters.

That this process has been one of evolution can be seen somewhat more clearly by a chronological listing of examples:

96

In *Pal Joey* (1940) Joey and Vera, the two principals, carry more of the comedic weight than three minor comedy characters. Gladys (the hoofer) and Ludlow Lowell (the blackmail artist) have vital connections with the plot and are essentially comedic. Melba (the reporter) has only one scene which is humorous. But nothing in *Pal Joey* is funnier than Joey's scene in front of a pet shop window trying to "make" the innocent Linda:

> LINDA: Oh, tell me something about him. I never had a dog myself. Wouldn't you like to talk about him?
> JOEY: Well, you understand, this was an Airedale I used to have. Oh, he wasn't much. We had champion dogs in those days. That was when the family still had money.
> LINDA: Your family?
> JOEY: Sure. Mother breeded dogs for a hobby.
> LINDA: Huh?
> JOEY: Well, sort of a hobby, the way Daddy played polo!
> LINDA: Oh.
> JOEY: Well, one day I came home from the Academy. I was going to an academy then, about ten miles from the estate. I didn't learn much there, except how to play polo and of course riding to hounds. So this particular day I have reference to, I was returning to our estate. They opened the gate for us and about a mile up the road I saw Skippy coming. He was up near the main house, about a mile or so, and I instructed the chauffeur, I said—Chadwick—be careful of old Skippy, and he said—yes. But with Skippy you couldn't tell, because his eyesight was so bad. Well—do you want to hear the rest of it?
> LINDA: Did you run over him?
> JOEY: It wasn't the chauffeur's fault, really. Not actually. But Daddy discharged him anyway. Mother erected a monument over his grave.

And a minute later:

> The estate fell into other hands when Daddy lost his fortune. That was when I resigned from the Princeton College. Hy-yuh, Skippy, boy.

Among the autobiographical comedy songs not addressed to another character—soliloquies, if you like—is Vera's "Bewitched, Bothered and Bewildered." It is a simple confession of her own foolishness in wanting Joey. It is honest, forthright, self-critical, and sophisticated.

> I'll sing to him—
> Each spring to him
> And worship the trousers that cling to him.
> Bewitched, bothered and bewildered am I.

What other form could an expression of this kind take? If it were prose dialogue, it would be vulgar. But in its sparse (even dainty and elegant) lyrical style, sung and delivered self-critically, it is piquant and amusing.

In *Oklahoma!* (1943), three comics, Ado Annie, Will Parker, and Ali Hakim, the peddler, function in the show as separately from the rest, as their counterparts in *Rose Marie* and *The Desert Song*. But their scenes are timeless and durable because the situations in which they are so comically caught relate to ordinary recognizable human behavior. There is, for example, the scene between Ado Annie and the Peddler:

> ADO ANNIE: . . . what you meant when you said that about drivin' with me to the end of the world.
> PEDDLER (*cagily*): Well, I didn't mean really to the end of the world.
> ADO ANNIE: Then how fur did you want to go?
> PEDDLER: Oh, about as far as—say—Claremore—to the hotel.
> ADO ANNIE: Whut's at the hotel?
> PEDDLER (*ready for the kill*): In front of the hotel is a veranda—inside is a lobby—upstairs—upstairs might be Paradise.

Ado Annie's song "I Cain't Say No!" is another "confession" comedy song, but unlike Vera Simpson's soliloquy, this one is a reply to Laurey's:

> Well, you jist can't go around kissin' every man that asts you! Didn't anybody ever tell you that?

Ado Annie: "Yeow, they *told* me. . . ." Then she proceeds to explain her weakness:

> . . . Other girls are coy and hard to catch
> But other girls ain't havin' any fun!
> Ev'ry time I lose a wrestlin' match
> I have a funny feelin' that I won!

The song is an important exposition of Ado Annie's problem, it sets up her character clearly, and it could not have been done so fully in any other way.

In *Carousel* (1945), the dark-souled Jigger is trying to seduce the fun-loving betrothed Carrie Pipperidge:

JIGGER: Every girl ought to know how to defend herself against beasts like that. (*Proceeding slyly up to his point*) Now, there are certain grips in wrestlin' I could teach you—tricks that'll land a masher flat on his face in two minutes.

CARRIE: But I ain't strong enough—

JIGGER: It don't take strength—it's all in balance—a twist of the wrist and a dig with the elbow. . . . Suppose a feller grabs you like this. (*Puts both arms around her waist*) Now you put yer two hands on my neck. (*She does*) Now pull me toward you. (*She does*) That's it. Now pull my head down. Good! Now put yer left arm all the way around my neck. Now squeeze—hard! Tighter! (*Slides his right hand down her back and pats her bustle*) Good Girl.

CARRIE (*Holding him tight*): Does it hurt?

JIGGER (*Having the time of his life*): You got me helpless! . . .

CARRIE: Mr. Craig— (*She stops, because something terrible has happened. Snow has entered. Jigger sees him and stops, still holding Carrie over his shoulders, fireman style. After a terrifying pause, Carrie speaks:*) Hello, Enoch. (*No answer*) This is the way firemen carry people.

SNOW (*Grimly*): Where's the fire?

In *Annie Get Your Gun* (1946) Annie herself is the principal source of humor. Her naive explanation of her and her family's way of life—"Doin' What Comes Natur'lly"—works in exactly the same way as Ado Annie's song.

> Folks are dumb where I come from
> They ain't had any learnin';
> Still they're happy as can be
> Doin' what comes natur'lly.*

* Copyright 1946 Irving Berlin. Reprinted by permission of Irving Berlin Music Corporation.

This one also is developed at length and runs through an entire catalogue of family practices—"doin' what comes natur'lly." As a straight, prosy piece of information, coming as it does early in the show, it would have been an unmitigated bore.

To me, the general humor in *Annie Get Your Gun* stands as a model of timelessness. A revival of the show—twenty years later—proves its workability.

One of the great examples of the long-joke lyric—as opposed to a short-joke lyric as in "Bewitched"—is Meg Brockie's lament in *Brigadoon*, "The Love of My Life." The song begins as an autobiographical narrative to Jeff, the whimsical, if exhausted, American traveler; Jeff, however, falls asleep at once, and the song becomes a soliloquy. In it Meg relates the sagas of four separate pursuits of love: a flower-picker, Christopher McGill, then a friend of McGill's:

> —how was I to know
> That of all the lowland laddies there was never one so low!

Then comes a poet who:

> writes about the things he cannot do,

And finally a soldier:

> But when I was drowsin' I snored to my dismay,
> An' he thought it was a bugle an' got up and marched away.

After each of these failures, Meg reports to her father, who always encourages her to make another try:

> Daughter there must be one.
> Someone who's true or too old to run. . . .*

In effect, Meg is telling us that every man runs away from her and that her father wants to be rid of her. She does not *say* these things, but we comprehend them clearly. For her, this is a sad story; for the audience, her misfortunes are funny.

South Pacific (1949) owes a good deal of its laughter to Ensign Nellie Forbush, a fact that, by the contrast it presents, serves to deepen and enrich her emotional scenes.

In *Guys and Dolls* (1950) the two principal comics are as clearly labeled as the comic team of *Rose Marie,* but in this case, they carry an important plot of their own, are closely related to the other characters, and are genuinely and timelessly funny.

One of the best autobiographical comedy songs of any character is the hypochrondriacal "Adelaide's Lament," which, in part, says:

> In other words, just from waiting around
> For that plain little band of gold
> A person . . . can develop a cold.
> You can spray her wherever you figure the strept-o-cocci lurk,
> You can give her a shot for whatever she's got but it just won't work.
> If she's tired of getting the fish-eye from the hotel clerk,
> A person . . . can develop a cold.*

Adelaide's entire character comes alive in this song. The lyrics tell you not only how she speaks but even the nuance of her inflection. Before the song is finished, you know the entire history of Adelaide's romance, and the more tragic she makes it out to be, the funnier it becomes.

The total comedy of *My Fair Lady* (1956) is preserved as it was in the original. There is not a single character uninvolved in the outrageous humor of every scene, and all of the comedy songs are generated out of Shaw's perception of the personal dilemmas and problems of human beings. Nothing is funnier than the first line of one of Professor Higgins's songs—the man who is bigoted, selfish, and oblivious to the needs of everyone else—when he sings simply and naively "I'm an ordinary man."

In *The King and I,* the tyrannical King sings a soliloquy called "A Puzzlement." He is incapable of admitting personal imperfection to anybody. He expresses self-doubt only to himself when he is alone. A clipped, precise lyric, coupled with the rhythmic bounce of the music, makes his confession sincere, believable, and amusing, and at the same time suggests our own concept of Oriental (translated) speech:

> Shall I join with other nations in alliance?
> If allies are weak am I not best alone?
> If allies are strong with power to protect me,
> Might they not protect me out of all I own? . . .
> And it puzzle me to learn
> That though a man may be in doubt of what he know,
> Very quickly will he fight,
> He'll fight to prove that what he does not know is so.*

In this the audience perceives ordinary humanity, always publicly masked behind pomp. Which, then, is the "real" King, the tyrant or the man in "A Puzzlement"? While he is undoubtedly a mixture of the two, he is far more the latter: in "A Puzzlement," being off guard, he has no responsibility to keep up appearances or prove anything. He becomes sympathetic to us, and funny; and we see unmasked, for the first time in the show, the man who is King.

In these examples of comedy scenes and lyrics, it should be evident that, aside from humor, they also furnish character revelations which are essential to a fuller comprehension of the people themselves. In this way, the contemporary use of comedy makes it an integral and important function to the show.

The usual practice of having comedy songs delivered by a single character helps to focus more sharply on the "setup" and the "payoff." This is to say, the subject matter is limited usually to a single idea ("setup") which becomes developed in a series of variations, each of which explodes in its own farcical conclusion ("payoff"). Humor—to be effective—must be concrete; it cannot be general or vague, either in its concept or its performance. It is nearly impossible for a joke to change hands in the

* Lyrics by Oscar Hammerstein II.

telling without suffering a loss of effect through the dissipation of attention. Occasionally, a successful comedy piece *seems* to change hands, but closer scrutiny usually reveals that it does not.

For example, near the end of *Guys and Dolls* the two contrasting leading women find themselves suffering the same misery: each has dismissed her man. In the ensuing song (a duet), "Marry the Man Today," the setup (a verse) is divided into two conversational parts. The chorus is bandied back and forth between them, and they sing together now and then. Actually, since the two situations are identical, the two characters become one. They are not arguing but concurring, and the "point" lines are assigned (for absolute clarity) to only one voice.

"Gee, Officer Krupke" in *West Side Story* involves six boys. This marvelous charade could only be done as a musical scene because it is a series of comic autobiographical verse-vignettes in the manner of children's games. Although six boys (with identical problems, experiences, and points of view) are involved, each section of the song is delivered as a solo; each is sufficiently long (seven lyric lines) to prevent the attention from becoming dissipated or choppy; and both the setup and the payoff are completed before the singer changes. The solo section each time is followed by an ensemble (unison) refrain. Example: after Diesel (as a judge) orders Action to go to a psychiatrist:

(ACTION, TO A-RAB)

My father is a bastard,
My ma's an S.O.B.
My grandpa's always plastered,
My grandma pushes tea.
My sister wears a mustache,
My brother wears a dress.
Goodness gracious, that's why I'm a mess!

(A-RAB, AS PSYCHIATRIST)

Yes!
Officer Krupke, you're really a slob.
This boy don't need a doctor, just a good honest job.

103

Society's played him a terrible trick,
And sociologically he's sick!

(ACTION)

I am sick!

(ALL)

We are sick, we are sick,
We are sick sick sick,
Like we're sociologically sick! *

Whether the autobiographical character of today's best comedy songs is merely coincidental or has deeper geneses it is impossible to say, but I would guess' that there are at least two good reasons for the success of this method. First, since the performer is telling the audience about himself, what he is conveying is something human enough for the listener to identify himself with. Therefore, his song takes on the one quality that imparts universality. And second, since the song's effect is to be comedic, it must follow that the character is complaining, for audience-performer relationships work by opposites. Just so, the author-composer-lyricist, in supplying the material for the performer, must *provide* substance that can generate the desired reaction. A complaining song presented in proper comic terms, and on a level with which the audience can identify, evokes in people the amusement of seeing themselves (or others whom they recognize instantly) and being entertained by the spectacle of their own foibles.

Any writer who would dare to create a song of personal complaint meant to rouse sympathy would be guilty of a fundamental artistic miscalculation. Such a song could only express self-pity—a tiresome bore—and would drive the audience out of the theater.

In the contemporary solo comedy songs referred to above one basic quality of character is held in common: Ado Annie, Adelaide, Annie Oakley, Meg Brockie, Carrie Pipperidge, and even Joey, communicate their innocence above all. They are the eter-

* Copyright 1957 by Bernstein & Sondheim. Lyrics by Stephen Sondheim.

104

nally bewildered victims of their own weaknesses. Perhaps this is a basic requirement of the comedic character and of the quality of his material.

E. THE MUSICAL PROGRAM

One of the things that any composer of a successful book show must consider carefully is his musical program. No less than the organizer of a concert or a vaudeville program, he is involved in the problem of avoiding monotony and must—perhaps even more than the arranger of a straight musical program— find the means to present his audience with sharp and interesting contrasts. Such contrasts will depend on the *kinds* of songs that follow one another, their moods, their subject matter, and the characters who sing them.

To begin with, the show itself will contain contrast between scenes—which may involve a change of scenery, or merely a shift in the characters on stage, or in the quality or subject matter of their dialogue. These larger contrasts will, of course, result in differences in the qualities of the songs themselves.

Though the above seems almost too obvious to mention—and has of course been the practice in good musical production for a long time—the business of proper programming seems to have occurred *only* to the composers of the best shows. The library of less successful musical shows contains failure after failure in which the composer—by neglecting to concern himself with program balance—succeeds only in adding ennui to boredom. Those of us who have occasion to "read" musicals have seen large numbers of them in which ballad follows ballad in an endless parade; in addition, this shortcoming is often further intensified by the total absence of workable comedy songs. This is the case more often than not (particularly among shows that go unproduced).

To analyze the question of the musical program, it is necessary first to give a few definitions:

1. *Song*   The musical setting of a lyric. It may consist of a verse and chorus. The verse is free in form, usually establishes or sets up a subject, and is melodically secondary to the chorus—which introduces and develops the main theme. In

musical-theater and popular-song practice, the 32-bar chorus (or variants of its component parts and lengths) is the commonest form. Broken down into its components, it usually consists of four 8-bar sections:

AABA. The "A" part contains the main theme. "B" (called a "release") generally contrasts with the "A" parts in tonality and usually provides rhythmic and melodic differences.

This form has deep classical roots in the old dance forms (which also contained the germs of sonata form). It is, broadly speaking, the basic form of all Western music. An example of the precise use of this 32-bar song form is "There But for You Go I" in *Brigadoon*.

The variations on this form are of course so numerous and so extraordinarily different from one another that a list would fill volumes. However, I should like to illustrate a few variant examples in *Oklahoma!*:

"I Cain't Say No!" (the refrain) AABBA plus 16-bar extended ending plus a "trio" with its own AABA and a return to the primary AABA.

"Many a New Day" A(12 bars), B(8 bars), A(8 bars).

"People Will Say We're in Love" A(16 bars), A(16 bars), B(8 bars same motif inverted), A(8 bars).

"Out of My Dreams" ABACA.

"Oklahoma!" ABABCA.

2. *Ballad* Most often a love song, but it can also be a narrative, soliloquy, or character song.

"There But for You Go I" (*Brigadoon*) has the character of a ballad. "People Will Say We're in Love" (*Oklahoma!*) is a rhythmic ballad, as is "Tonight" (*West Side Story*). "Come to Me, Bend to Me" (*Brigadoon*) is a love ballad. "Lonely Room" (*Oklahoma!*) is a character ballad or soliloquy. "Mister Snow" and "When the Children Are Asleep" (*Carousel*) are narrative ballads, which also belong to the charm song category.

3. *Rhythm Song* One primarily carried along on, or propelled by, a musical beat which is most usually a regular one.

Its character may include ballad, dance, comedy song or charm song (the latter two differentiated by the quality and content of the lyrics). "I'm an Indian Too" (*Annie Get Your Gun*) is a rhythm song, as are "Luck Be a Lady" (*Guys and Dolls*) and "I'm Gonna Wash That Man Right Out of My Hair" (*South Pacific*). An example of the rhythm ballad is "Tonight" (*West Side Story*). "Happy Hunting Horn" (*Pal Joey*) is a dance song. "My Mother's Weddin' Day" (*Brigadoon*) is a rhythm-comedy song, and "I Whistle a Happy Tune" (*The King and I*) is a rhythm-charm song.

4. *Comedy Song* Divided into two main and quite opposite forms—each of which has many variants. These forms might be generally classified as the "short joke" and the "long joke."

"Bewitched, Bothered and Bewildered" in *Pal Joey* is in the "short-joke" category:

> Sweet again,
> Petite again,
> And on my proverbial seat again.
> Bewitched, bothered and bewildered am I. . . .
> Though at first we said "No, sir,"
> Now we're two little dears.
> You might say we are closer
> Than Roebuck is to Sears. . . .*

In each of the first two sections of the song and in each of the subsequent (and different) refrains, there is a separate "joke" (4 bars each plus 4 bars of the recurrent "Bewitched, bothered and bewildered am I" refrain). Then in the "release," or middle section (8 bars), there is a third joke. The final 8 bars of each chorus has still another 4-bar joke plus the 4-bar title refrain. Thus there are, in all, four separate punch lines, each with its own necessary setup, in each chorus. The sequence of the jokes is determined here by their comparative strength. Each is stronger than its predecessor, and the use of the reiterated refrain (three times in each chorus) is also functional: the refrain occurs during the laughs, all the while assuring the audience that it is missing nothing.

* Lyrics by Lorenz Hart.

In the same "short" category is "Doin' What Comes Natur'lly" from *Annie Get Your Gun*. Here, however, there is a joke every eight bars and a four-sectional form to each chorus (ABCA). There are four jokes to every chorus; and in each chorus, the images, subjects, and punch lines are basically unconnected with those of the preceding or following ones.

The best, fullest, and clearest example of the "long-joke" category is "The Love of My Life" in *Brigadoon*. Here, after a verse (16 bars) which sets up the overall situation, there are four choruses (34 bars each—containing an interior 2-bar extension) each of which is followed by a 16-bar conclusion. The entire number proceeds uninterruptedly from start to finish, and the big jokes come at the end of each 34-bar chorus. Each chorus tells the story of a different attempt by the singer to find a "love of my life," and each conclusion tells what "Pa" said when she went home and recounted her failure. Although this song is extremely long, it is fast-moving and successful. The development is so clear, the setups so excellent, and the jokes so funny that it never seems to lag in performance. And although there are four separate tales, the relation of each to the other, and the wonderful cumulative buildup of all, works so superbly that the song's uncommon length is not in the least a hindrance.

5. *Charm Song* One usually combining music and lyrics in equal importance. The subject matter of the lyrics is light, and there is no attempt to make a comedy point. The musical setting is generally delicate, optimistic, and rhythmic, and may have, more than the music of comedy songs, a life independent of its lyrics.

Examples of charm songs are:

"I Whistle a Happy Tune" (*The King and I*).

"Dites-moi" and "A Cockeyed Optimist" (*South Pacific*).

"Waitin' for My Dearie" and "The Heather on the Hill" (*Brigadoon*).

"The Surrey with the Fringe on Top" (*Oklahoma!*).

6. *Musical Scene* A theatrical sequence—dramatic, comedic, lyrical, narrative, or a combination of several of these—set

to music, for one or any number of characters. It may include a song and may be held together formally by its literary structure, guided by a feeling of musical balance. It may include speech, recitative, song, and incidental music (underscoring).

The scene which contains "A Boy Like That" and "I Have a Love" (*West Side Story*) is a dramatic musical scene. It also contains a song. "Song of the King" and "Shall We Dance?" (*The King and I*) together comprise a musical scene which has comedy, a charm song, and a dance. "Wouldn't It Be Loverly?" and "Just You Wait" (*My Fair Lady*) are charm musical scenes. "Why Can't the English?" from the same show is a comedic musical scene. "Soliloquy" (*Carousel*) is a musical scene containing lyrical, dramatic, and comedic elements. "Down on MacConnachy Square" (*Brigadoon*) combines a number of ingredients. Nearly all of these musical scenes contain some spoken dialogue.

"Finale, Act I" (*Desert Song*) and "Finale, Act I" (*Rose Marie*) both of which contain dramatic and lyrical elements, are direct ancestors of the above musical scenes.

F. LAYOUT

In a discussion of musical programs, it is necessary to say a word about musical "layouts." "Layout" refers to the manner of verse and chorus juxtaposition plus the number of times— wholly or in part—and the ways a song is presented in any one sequence. Layouts can vary considerably; moreover, their final shapes are usually determined by the way things work on both sides of the footlights.

Hearing a song sung through just once is usually an unsatisfying experience because insufficient time has been allowed for the song to create a definite impression. It is too fleeting, too unimpressive, too difficult to catch hold of and remember. On the other hand, if a song is indiscriminately repeated, it can, of course, easily become dull and boring. Thus the shape of its layout has to be carefully thought out, and the possibilities are virtually limitless. The final choice must rest on a number of considerations:

1) The tempo.

2) The mood of the scene in which it appears.

3) The song's position in relation to the whole show.

4) The inherent value of the song itself.

5) The relative importance of the character who delivers it.

Each of these considerations will, of course, have its own effect on all the others:

1. *Tempo* The slower a song is, the less likely it is to bear extensive repeating. This follows from the simple physical fact that a slow song will occupy more time than a faster one. Much repetition would therefore tend to make it tedious. "You'll Never Walk Alone" (*Carousel*) and "More I Cannot Wish You" (*Guys and Dolls*) are slow and are sung through only once. ("You'll Never Walk Alone" is reprised at the end of the show in a choral version.) In addition, they are both sung by secondary characters.

2. *Mood* The song's particular layout has to be governed to a large extent by its relationship to the scene in which it occurs and by the degree to which it is integrated into the scene. This factor is also affected by the functional quality of the lyrics. In *Oklahoma!* the lyrics of "The Surrey with the Fringe on Top" are narrative. They describe the surrey in detail, the effect it has on animals and nature along the road to the box social where Curly wants to take Laurey, and the joy of the lazy ride home after the party is over. There are no lyric repeats. The surrounding scene is light and gay. The words are charming and inventive. The tune has a hypnotic quality and moves smoothly over a jogging rhythm. The layout consists of three verses (the third used as musical underscoring of dialogue) and three choruses! It holds.

"Something's Coming" (*West Side Story*) concludes the second scene of the show. The hero, Tony, sings it and the song points ahead to the magical, intangible unknown (Maria) which the boy only senses. The song is charged with energy and magic. It is swift: a rocket aimed at another world. Musically it consists of two elements: a clipped, fast musical motif alternating with a lazy, lyrical, floating one. The fast motif section recurs almost six times, the lyrical one, twice. The song begins as a reply to a question in the dialogue:

> RIFF: Who knows? Maybe what you're waitin' for'll be twitchin' at the dance! (*He runs off*)
> TONY: Who knows? (*Then he sings:*) Could be! . . .*

Incidentally, this is an example of a rhythm song based on a beat set in a changing time scheme.

"Wunderbar" (*Kiss Me, Kate*) occurs during a scene of badinage between the two principal characters. They are charmingly caustic to each other and trying to remember the waltz in a flop show they once played in together. This layout is unusual. The last 16 bars of the waltz are introduced instrumentally under dialogue. The two principals then *sing* the same final 16 bars as a duet which leads into the verse. This is followed by an entire chorus, then the *release* and the final 16 (as duet) again. That is:

Last 16 bars of chorus twice (instrumental, duet).

Verse.

Chorus.

Release (instrumental).

Final 16.

There is a rationale behind this treatment. Both characters are trying (in dialogue) to recall the old waltz. The man says, ". . . something about a bar." Two lines later they both recall:

> Wunderbar, wunderbar!
> There's our fav'rite star above.
> What a bright shining star!
> Like our love, it's wunderbar! †

Then the verse sets up the song, which follows in its entirety.

3. What is meant by "the song's position in relation to the whole show" is whether it is close to beginning or end or intermission. This might have a great influence on the length of a song. Again, the quality of the particular song would play a great part in the decision. *Oklahoma!* opens with "Oh, What a Beautiful Mornin'." At the very outset of the show, there is a verse (16 bars) followed by a chorus which is only 16 bars long, or half the length of the average chorus; the verse and chorus are of equal length. The entire layout consists of three verses and three choruses with a small extension (4 bars) at the very end. This much repetition of a song at the very opening of a show would usually be excessive, but "Oh, What a Beautiful Mornin' " is only half the length of a usual song.

No other show that comes readily to mind has had the temerity to open with a solo song in this way. In *Guys and Dolls,* the trio "Fugue for Tinhorns" that follows a pantomime sequence at the very opening is not repeated at all. The first vocal number in *Annie Get Your Gun* is "Colonel Buffalo Bill," which is repeated once at the time and heard four times subsequently as change music. "Dites-moi" in *South Pacific* is reprised only at the end of the show. The first song in *The King and I,* "I Whistle a Happy Tune," consists of one chorus, a coda, and an encore.

In today's musical theater there is something that in the trade goes by the name of "11 o'clock spot" or "11 o'clock number." This is usually a piece of comic or dramatic special musical material created specifically to be a showpiece for the star near the end of the evening. Its avowed purpose is to give the show a late-evening "lift" and to provide the star with fresh, last-minute brilliance. Apart from star consideration, writers frequently try to find a late lift for the show. The introduction of an important new tune just before the end of the show is not usually done because the proper layout of a song—that is, offering it in sufficient repetition for adequate impression on the ear and the mind—is not feasible so late in the audience's experience. Therefore the choices of good 11 o'clock material are fairly lim-

ited. Sometimes something new does grow out of the show itself, and then 11 o'clock lights up for everyone.

In *Oklahoma!* the title song explodes out of the situation
in the beginning of the final scene. The verse sets up the idea
and, by employing seven principals in small solo bits, evokes a
community feeling. The first chorus (mostly sung as a solo by
Curly) is quick as light. The second chorus includes a busy
choral arrangement, then a transition that could belong to a
cheering squad at a football game, the release and the last section (altogether, verse and 2½ choruses). Then the last 1½
choruses again as an encore. The show itself ends with two par-
tial reprises of earlier songs.

West Side Story puts its one comic song, "Gee, Officer
Krupke," in this late spot between the heartbreaking lyrical bal-
let "Somewhere" and the savage musical scene that begins "A
Boy Like That." From this latter scene to the bitter end, it is all
fire. The comedy song here occupies the same position as the
Musicians' Scene in *Romeo and Juliet* and the Gravediggers'
Scene in *Hamlet*.

In this same spot, *Carousel* has Agnes De Mille's ballet,
which reveals to the disembodied Billy the painful humiliation
his daughter is forced to suffer on his account. It furnishes the
audience with an integrated ballet which constitutes the principal dancing in the show. Similarly, *The King and I* has Jerome
Robbins's enchanting ballet, "The Small House of Uncle
Thomas."

At a slightly earlier spot in the second act of *South Pacific*
there is the raucous show-within-a-show, "Honey Bun." From
there on, there is drama on top of drama, speed, and suspense—
and then the concluding reprise of the delicate "Dites-moi."

Late in the second act, *Guys and Dolls* has a minor character
(backed by chorus) sing the rousing, bouncy, spiritual-like "Sit
Down, You're Rockin' the Boat." And in roughly the same spot,
Annie Get Your Gun exposes a fast new comedy duet for the
two principal characters, "Anything You Can Do," consisting of
3 choruses and an extension.

The examples I have cited have not been created for star-exposure. A notable 11 o'clock number which grows directly out of the show but is a powerful star vehicle is "Rose's Turn" from *Gypsy*.

From these examples it would seem obvious that contemporary practice favors little repetition of opening musical material (*Oklahoma!* is a notable exception)—which is often unimportant musically—but that usually a little past midway in Act II, there is something new and, hopefully, astonishing. Near the close of the show, by-then-familiar songs are often reprised. Two notable exceptions to this kind of practiced formula—the non-introduction of new songs very near the end of a show—are to be found in two of Sondheim's scores. The final song in *Company* is "Being Alive," and quite close to the end of *A Little Night Music,* a moving ballad, "Send in the Clowns," is heard for the first time. In both of these instances, the new songs work well in their unorthodox positions.

It seems to me that the usual practices in musical programming grow out of psychological considerations. At the beginning of a show, the audience is seldom completely settled in and quiet; therefore at this point, the best songs would tend to get lost. (The single exception to this proposition is "Oh, What a Beautiful Mornin'," which is reprised four times in the show and heard also in the ballet.) Then again, because late in the second act the audience may be getting sleepy or restless, the use of "fireworks"—something new where newness is least expected—has the effect of creating new life. The use of reprises not only promotes familiarity with—perhaps also nostalgia for—previously heard songs, but adds the pleasure associated with recognition of the familiar.

4. It is probably futile to attempt to discuss the "inherent value of the song itself." Nearly every composer is certain that nearly every song he writes is the best one ever written. Experienced composers have learned better. Most inexperienced composers will attempt to repeat every song ad nauseam. Only audience response (or lack of it) will possibly dislodge them from their lofty perch.

5. The relative importance of the character who sings the song will affect the extent of the layout. Sometimes this effect

may be opposite to what is expected. In *Pal Joey,* for instance, "Zip," a comedy song, is sung by Melba in her only scene in the show. For a single song to work under these conditions (and "Zip" does) it must be given adequate dimensions. "Zip" has a long verse and 3 choruses. Hattie, a minor character in *Kiss Me, Kate,* leads the ensemble in "Another Op'nin', Another Show" early in Act I. It consists of two refrains (no verse)—one solo and one with ensemble. After a dance, Hattie reprises it from the release (solo) and continues to the end with the ensemble. In *My Fair Lady,* Freddie, the young man, has only one solo. This, "On the Street Where You Live" (Act I), consists of a verse, a long chorus (64 bars, or twice the ordinary length), 16 bars played under dialogue, plus 16 bars sung. In Act II, there is a reprise of nearly all of the song which ends instrumentally under dialogue.

Lady Thiang in *The King and I* has only one song, "Something Wonderful." It has a verse and only one chorus, but the theme is so composed that its main motif occurs in the one chorus seven times. The motif is used for a scene-change immediately afterward, and the song is mostly reprised in the next scene and is followed by a "postlude" (based on the song) which concludes the scene. Near the end of Act II, the entire chorus is played as underscoring to a scene. Neither the song nor the single-song character with whom it is closely associated is lost.

Arvide, who sings "More I Cannot Wish You" in *Guys and Dolls,* and Jud, who sings "Lonely Room" in *Oklahoma!,* each have only the one solo song, and that song is sung only once. Both songs are extremely effective and each in its own way amplifies the actor's character and functions for the show, but each song is sung once only.

The foregoing should illustrate the fact that good programming does not follow a set of fixed rules, but rather, seems to grow from the need to suit material to the particular requirements of the particular show.

Having defined the musical components, presented illustrations from well-tested sources, and discussed some of their respective rationales, it might be well to chart programs of several shows. In this way, the creation of interior contrasts and similarities will become instantly apparent. (The layouts of individual numbers are not indicated, nor is the scene-change music listed.)

The letters appearing after numbers identify the singing characters: M—hero; F—heroine; MC—male comic; FC—female comic; V—villain; Mch—male chorus; Fch—female chorus; ChaC—character comedian; Mix ch—mixed chorus; SM—secondary male.

OKLAHOMA!

1. Ballad (rhythmic) (M).

2. Short Reprise of #1 (F).

3. Charm Ballad (rhythmic) (M, F, Ch and FC).

4. Comedy Song (MC and Mch) and Dance.

5. Reprise of #3 (M).

6. Comedy Song (FC).

7. Encore of #6.

8. Reprise section of #6 (MC and FC) into Short Reprise of #1 (Mix ch and M).

9. Rhythmic Ballad (Soft shoe) (F and Fch) and Dance with Fch ending.

10. Comedy Scene (ChaC and Mch).

11. Rhythmic Ballad (M and F) into underscoring, reprise, and underscoring.

12. Comedy Scene (M and V).

13. Dramatic Ballad (V).

14. Underscoring, into Waltz Ballad (F and Fch), into Dream Ballet.

ACT II

15. Country Song and Dance (Solos [all] and Mix ch).

16. Comedy Song (MC and FC) and Dance.

17. Reprise of #9 (M and F).

18. Fast March (Solos [all] and M and Mix ch).

19. Encore of #18.

20. Finale (#1—Mix ch) and (#9—Mix ch).

GUYS AND DOLLS

1. Pantomime (brisk music) into:

2. Rhythm Song (Trio—secondary characters).

3. Hymn (F and secondary characters).

4. Musical Scene (Fox Trot) (MC and secondary characters and Mch).

5. Reprise #3 (F and secondary characters).

6. Ballad (F and M).

7. Short reprise of #6 (F).

8. Show Song and Dance (FC and Fch).

9. Comedy Song (FC).

10. Recitative and Fox Trot Song (two secondary characters).

11. Production Dance with Occasional Rhythmic Dialogue (M and F and dancers).

12. Rhythmic Charm Song (F).

13. Ballad Introduction (M), into Rhythmic Ballad (M and F).

14. Agitated Musical underscoring.

ACT II

15. Show Song and Dance (FC and Fch) Comedy.

16. Short Reprise of #9 (FC).

17. Charm Song (secondary character).

18. Dance (male ensemble).

19. Rhythmic Song (M and Mch).

20. Comedy Duet (MC and FC).

21. Fast Spiritual (SM and Mix ch).

22. Reprise #3 (Mix ch).

23. Slow Short Duet (parts of #9 with parts #13) (F and FC).

24. Comedy Duet (F and FC).

25. Pantomime based on many themes.

26. Short Reprise (instrumental) #3.

27. Finale, Reprise Chorus #10 (all).

MY FAIR LADY

1. Background Music (Bustle) under pantomime.

2. Comedic Musical Scene (M and F and SM).

3. Charm Song and Dance (F and Mch).

4. Rhythmic Comedy Song (MC and two minor males).

5. Comedic Musical Scene (M).

6. Reprise of #4 (MC and Mix ch).

7. Comedic Charm Scene (F).

8. Comedic Musical Scene (M and F and SM and Mix ch).

9. Charm Song and Dance (F and M and SM).

10. Gay Ballad (F and Sec. Fs).

11. Charm Song and Dance (Mix ch).

12. Coda to preceding #.

13. Ballad and Scene (SM and Sec. Char. F).

14. Underscoring #10.

15. Procession and Waltz, introducing Ball Scene.

16. Procession and Waltz proper.

ACT II

17. Charm Can Can and Soft Shoe (Musical Scene).

18. Reprise #7 (F) into (M and SM and Sec. Ch. and Mix ch).

19. Reprise #13 (SM and F) into:

118

20. Dramatic Musical Scene (F and SM).

21. Charm Song and Dance and Scene (Reprise #3) (F and Mch).

22. Charm Song and Dance (MS and Mix ch).

23. Comedic Musical Scene (M and SM).

24. Charm Scene and Ballad (F and M).

25. Charm Dramatic Soliloquy and End (M).

These three quite different shows: *Oklahoma!* set in rural, early 20th-century America, *Guys and Dolls,* among contemporary New York underworld characters, and *My Fair Lady,* in London the ordinary and the elegant, 1912, are models in our theater; and all were enthusiastically received. Each is different from the others in style, period, content, and feeling. Yet from the point of view of musical sequence, they have basic features in common—with one another and, in fact, with all shows that work.

Above all, there is liberal contrast within the musical sequence. *Especially do ballads not follow ballads.* Interspersed among the slower and more serious pieces is a generous sprinkling of charm and comedy material. (*My Fair Lady* has more charm songs and comedy songs than any other show.) Ensemble choruses alternate frequently with solos, which are themselves distributed among a variety of different characters. Dancing appears at intervals, according to opportunities determined by the libretto and the character of the show.

Although nearly every musical number is separated from the next by a dialogue scene, there is nevertheless a kind of "hangover" memory that makes musical contrast essential for a proper theatrical ebb and flow. It is my belief that the contrasts revealed by the above skeletal outlines of musical sequence are not accidental. They are the result of planning which involves self-criticism on the composers' part. In the theater especially, fortunate accidents are rare.

One final point about the musical program: most first acts have a duration of from about one-and-a-half to one-and-three-quarters hours. Second acts generally run from about forty to fifty-five minutes. This rather large disparity in length between the two acts, by itself, contributes only a little to the kind of variation in program we have been discussing, but in contemporary practice, the strongest material is usually assigned to Act I. Let us examine simply the numbers of musical pieces in Act I and II of four scores.

OKLAHOMA!

ACT I	ACT II
10 songs	3 songs
2 reprises	4 reprises
2 major dances	1 major dance

GUYS AND DOLLS

ACT I	ACT II
9 songs	6 songs
2 major dances	2 reprises
	2 dances

ANNIE GET YOUR GUN

ACT I	ACT II
11 songs	5 songs
2 reprises	4 reprises
3 dances	2 dances

BRIGADOON

ACT I	ACT II
9 songs	3 songs
6 dances	5 reprises (partial)
	3 dances

What actually happens in these four—as well as the others of the best contemporary shows—is that the first act must capture and hold the audience's interest—entertaining as it progresses, and involving the mind and emotions to the point of personal identification. If the audience is "captured" within the first-act situation development, and if it is moved to care about the characters and how they will ultimately resolve their difficulties, the author's biggest and most serious problems have gone a long way toward resolution. The composer, then, must be concerned with the needs of the musical program, which should be full, rounded, and diverse. The musical problems of the second act are less demanding than those of the first, and the composer has available to him, provided he uses it with taste, a most potent aid in the form of the reprise. For the creative people involved in the making of a musical, it is in Act I that the best foot must be put forward.

It should be noted that in the "programs" of three of the shows listed above there is liberal use of song reprises. In *Oklahoma!* there are seven; in *Guys and Dolls,* six; and in *My Fair Lady,* three. This use of reprise or encore has always been quite usual. In addition, the songs are used as scene connections, in overtures, entr'actes, out music, etc.

More recently, scene designers in collaboration with directors and authors have brought the form of musical theater into a new phase—one which has affected reprise. The clearest example of this is in *A Little Night Music,* designed by the extraordinary Boris Aronson, staged by Harold Prince, with libretto by Hugh Wheeler. Although the show is in two acts, there are no "crossovers" (usually attributed to George Abbott), but a completely fluid production. The basic set does not change except that a slider containing a chaise longue is shoved on stage (on a green lawn), and with a concentration of light on the couch, the audience believes quite easily that this is—suggested by the lady's presence—a lady's bedchamber. This and similar treatments can be totally acceptable and credible.

This technique of abbreviating sets eliminates the crossover with its water-treading and loss of time. It also, incidentally, has had an effect on the music.

The closing of the traveler curtains to permit scene change and/or the accompanying crossover in front of it in order to continue some kind of action, most often required music. This consisted generally of a reprise of a recently heard song. With the crossover in ill repute today, the reprise has fallen more and more into disuse. Fewer musical repetitions result in a diminishing of the audiences' erstwhile dinned-in familiarity with the songs. In consequence, a general public feeling is expressed that composers today don't create memorable tunes. In many cases, the idea is erroneous and the tunes simply have not had the repetitious exposure which audiences have grown accustomed to experiencing.

In *A Little Night Music,* just before the end of Act I, a single song, "A Weekend in the Country," is repeated seven times, back-to-back as the finale. A bit of "Send in the Clowns" is reprised very near the end of the show. Nothing else is heard even twice.

This suggests a trend. It has been true of the "rock musical," for the most part. It is a programmatic departure for show composers, adds something new, but works outside the show to the disadvantage of the songs that are not exposed as much as formerly. Only time can decide whether the reprise is ultimately more or less valuable. Perhaps it is only a question of taste.

G. SOME OBSERVATIONS ON STYLE

Artistic and cultural styles connote period or place—usually both—but their very mention serves to conjure up the image of particular objects or cultural products and the ages and habits of mind that created them. We speak of Baroque or Renaissance, Byzantine or Moorish, and the complex of characteristics—which is to say, style—implied by these terms becomes clearly identifiable.

Musical style—no exception—falls into classifications and subclassifications: classical, Romantic, pre-classic, Baroque, impressionistic, or twelve-tone, etc.; and beyond that, is often classifiable by country, sub-period, and various permutations of these: Italian Romantic, French Renaissance, Viennese operetta; early German Baroque, late English Renaissance, etc.

These classifications, imposed by scholars of a later time, are the natural and inevitable concomitants of a composer's own time and place. Bach, for example, is inescapably a product of the Baroque forces in Germany.

Another sense in which we characterize style—one more difficult to define—is the personal one. The work of a mature artist will bear certain characteristics, a technique, a point of view, that allow us to recognize and identify it immediately. Among the painters, for example, Rembrandt, Picasso, Klee, Gauguin, Toulouse-Lautrec, Rouault, Degas—to name only a few—succeeded in creating identifiable styles without having consciously tried to do so. The same, of course, is true of composers.

Webster defines style as "a manner of expression characteristic of an individual, a period, a school, or other identifiable group (as a nation) . . . a quality that gives distinctive excellence to something (as artistic expression) and that consists especially in the appropriateness and choiceness of the elements (as subject, medium, form) combined. . . ."

The first part of the definition concerns that aspect of style which is easily recognizable: e.g., Italian Renaissance painting. The second, dealing with "appropriateness and choiceness of the elements combined," is an aspect which, to my knowledge, has never been discussed in relation to the American musical theater.

Each of the mature theater composers has evolved his own recognizable basic style. Gershwin, Rodgers, Bernstein, Berlin, Porter, Arlen, Rome, Schwartz, Loesser, Loewe, and others have stamped themselves on their music in a way that is unmistakable. All of them are known around the world as "American" and 20th-century; also their music belongs incontrovertibly to the theater as opposed to the concert hall. All of these composers share fundamental stylistic elements in common, though their individual differences are also clearly discernible. What I should like to discuss here is not so much the personal fundamentals of these men's style as the overlay—the musical costume—applied to it in response to the particular theater material that from time to time they have treated.

The importance of this examination would become very clear

if, for example, we were to imagine an inexperienced composer attempting to score a libretto dealing with an exotic place or far-off time. He might believe that the task required scrupulous research into, and authentic use of, native themes, modes, instruments, harmonic methods, and styles. The resulting work would not be a work of art or a piece for the theater but a musicological essay. What, then, happens when a creative and experienced theater composer writes a work set in a past time or with an alien setting?

In the classical days of music-theater—i.e., opera—there was no thought of coloration to suggest time or place. In Mozart's *The Marriage of Figaro* (1786) and *Don Giovanni* (1787), both set in Seville a century before Mozart's time, nothing in the music suggests either Spain or an earlier period. Mozart must certainly have been familiar with Spanish music: Austria is only a few hundred miles from Spain. He and his contemporaries (and in fact all artists until about the mid-19th century) simply operated without consciousness of time or place. The music in these operas—like Rossini's thirty years later in *The Barber of Seville*—was exclusively the expression of the composer and his own milieu. Perhaps each of the three works paid one small obeisance to Spain in that a guitar was in evidence on the stage and was suggested orchestrally during serenade scenes.

There are hundreds of other examples. Mozart's *The Magic Flute* (1791) was set in Egypt, Beethoven's *Fidelio* (1805), in Spain again, Verdi's *La Traviata* (1853), in Paris, *Ernani* (1844), in Spain; *Masked Ball* (1859), in 17th-century Boston. Also in 1859, Gounod produced *Faust,* set in Germany. Meanwhile, Wagner's *The Flying Dutchman* (1840) had been laid in Norway; his *Tristan and Isolde* (1859), in Cornwall and its heroine was an Irish princess! Both Donizetti's *Lucia di Lammermoor* (1835) and Verdi's *Macbeth* (1847) are set in Scotland. Massenet's *Le Cid* (1885) takes place in medieval Spain, and Verdi's *Falstaff* (1893), in 15th-century England.

In none of these works is there an attempt to suggest time or place. The same holds true for all the arts—painting, drama, poetry—from the crucifixion paintings whose Holy Families are dressed in the garb of 14th-century Florentines or Venetians to

124

Shakespeare's Paduans and Venetians and Romans, who speak and behave uniformly with the inflections and postures of Elizabethan society. The awareness that different societies and historical eras produce different cultural styles, each authentic for its own time and place, is one of the crucial things that distinguishes us from our forebears.

By pointing out our own keener awareness of cultural variety and relativeness, I do not mean to argue the superiority of the contemporary artist. We are certainly not better and wiser than Mozart and Shakespeare, but we are different from them in this one respect. Our awareness stems from the growth of nationalism and the discoveries—archeological, historical, scientific—that have been increasing at a rapid rate since the middle of the last century. This awareness of the past and the faraway has been crystallized into specifics through excavations, studies of artistic antiquities of all kinds, publications in which there had previously been little or no interest, art works from opulent private collections placed on public view for the first time in history, research, restorations, etc. This general voyage of discovery in all of the arts began only about a century ago. Today, the average American high school boy has a more vivid grasp of life in ages past than the greatest scholar or artist prior to 1850. Through illustrated books, motion pictures, magazines, TV, and newspapers, he has become acquainted—whether he knows it or not—with all of the visual styles from the past. And recordings, concerts, radio programs, and live theater train his ear at least in a general way to distinguish among classical, impressionist, and Romantic music and jazz, Oriental and Occidental, cowboy songs and the folk music of Russia. These distinctions have come to be an important—if often subtle—influence on the style of music in our contemporary American theater.

The need to refer to these distinctions in works of art was of course long and slow in evolving. Verdi, who had not differentiated between the Paris of *Traviata* and the 17th-century Boston of *Masked Ball,* in composing *Aida* began for the first time to invent music that would evoke a feeling (at least for non-Egyptians like himself) of ancient Egypt. The opera, first performed in 1871, had been commissioned for the opening of the opera house in Cairo and was based on a story suggested by an Egyptologist. As W. J. Henderson, the American critic, wrote in his preface to the vocal score: "In *Aida* Verdi for the first time in his career made a deliberate attempt at local color. . . . He employed a scheme of harmony and instrumental color which keeps the Oriental locale of the opera constantly in the hearer's mind."

Aida is, to be sure, completely Italian and is written in the style of its composer. Nevertheless, Verdi did succeed in creating some suggestion of "foreign" color that—with the aid of sets and costumes—communicates Egypt to the listener. This color is sometimes to be found in the melodies (as in the Consecration Scene, with its strange vocalism), but more often in the instrumentation: in the use of harps and Oriental percussion.

Again, opera was never more French than in the works of Georges Bizet. Yet in *The Pearl Fishers* (1863), there are melodic and orchestral suggestions that, for the composer and his audience, perhaps indicate Ceylon. And in *Carmen* (1875) Spain is abundantly present to the ear. The dance rhythms, and certain melodic convolutions so peculiar to the country, are here the bases of arias and dances: "Habanera," "Seguidilla," and "Gypsy Song." These suggestions are also used in the entrance of the smugglers and the card scene; and they serve, with the use of castanets and tambourine accentuating the gypsy flavor, to impart an essence of Spain. These are relatively new, though—to any latter-day audience—requisite paraphernalia of the theater.

With *Madame Butterfly* (1904) Puccini continued in the newly found path. The use of pentatonic motifs,* along with "Eastern" percussion effects—plus Japanese scenery and cos-

* In Mosco Carner's critical biography, *Puccini,* the author lists seven Japanese songs which are integrated in *Madame Butterfly.* In actuality, they are nearly all completely pentatonic and seem therefore to lack sharp individual profiles as "tunes." Their integration into a pentatonic-suffused score is so complete that it is next to impossible to single out any one of them, and their further involvement in Puccini's personal style produces altogether an Italian opera with an Oriental flavor. While it is interesting to be told by Mr. Carner that many of the "Oriental" lines in *Madame Butterfly* can be traced to specific Japanese folk songs, the feeling which this opera has engendered in us is not affected: the music is pure Puccini.

tumes—bring us to and keep us in the Orient. This is the theatrical coloring. The opera is quite clearly Italian, just as *The Mikado,* which preceded *Butterfly* by twenty years, is English. Both clearly suggest the Orient in their music. Both are works of genius (in almost diametrically opposite ways), and the style and point of view of each belong squarely to their countries and periods of origin.

One thing mars the "coloring" of *Butterfly.* Puccini seldom miscalculated his use of coloration, but in his thematic use of "The Star-Spangled Banner" for Lt. Pinkerton, he was guilty of grossness of taste. The Japanese musical suggestion throughout is general, gentle, and integrated; but his attempt to characterize an American naval officer with such a specific device as the theme from his national anthem—impossible to integrate in this score—is mere gimmickry. It does not belong to art or theater or music but to charade. (Nor, in my opinion, did he succeed with *The Girl of the Golden West,* when he frankly imitated American-style tunes, and worse, set American colloquialisms such as "Hello, Minnie" into an otherwise Italian libretto.)

On the other hand, Giordano in *Andrea Chénier* (1896) was concerned with the French Revolution, and he employed "La Marseillaise" thematically in a thrilling way. When it is first introduced in the orchestra, an *interior* germ of the tune is heard. There is a mere suggestion; nothing is announced. It does not start at the *beginning* of the song. The small motif develops. In the last act the entire song is heard offstage—in unison voices over a low orchestral tremolando. It had been deftly planted and finally erupts—unadorned.

As opera moves into the 20th century, the examples multiply. Richard Strauss's *Salome* (1905), set in 30 A.D., with all its "modernity" achieves by some of the effects in the orchestration the atmosphere of antiquity. In his *Der Rosenkavalier* (1911), only the orchestral figure associated with Baron Ochs evokes 18th-century Vienna, where the opera is set. One could cite many other examples.

And as with opera, so, of course, with the lighter musical-theater forms. Since about the middle of the 19th century operettas and musical comedies have had their stages musically "set." In *H.M.S. Pinafore* (1879), the sea and the English Navy are concretely present. *Die Fledermaus* (1873), like many other works—such as Gershwin's *Oh, Kay!* (1926) and *Lady, Be Good* (1924)—achieved the necessary effect quite naturally; it was set in their own time and place. In the *Tales of Hoffmann* libretto (1881), Offenbach was concerned with three separate stories. The second of these is set in Venice, and the composer frames it with the "Barcarolle," with its Venetian connotation (and probable origin).

In the growing days of the American musical theater, the suggestions of time and place were abundantly present but usually corny. The names of a few American shows around the turn of the 20th century will be enough not only to illustrate the point but to bring a shudder to the imagination: *The Algerian, The Mandarin, The Wizard of the Nile, A China Doll, The Maid and the Mummy, The Man from China, The Toreador, Abyssinia, The Jewel of Asia, The Alaskan, The Rose of Algeria, The Rose of the Alhambra,* etc.

This kind of "book" show (as opposed to revue) came to be so identified with the "old-fashioned" that from about 1930 until roughly the '50's, few American shows were set in any foreign locales. It was not until around the middle of the 20th century that authors and composers in the popular musical theater began to find more subtle ways to express stylistic consciousness. At that time, composers could make full use of a sense of time and place without resorting to the naive clichés that had so marred earlier attempts at this kind of characterization. Today a knowledgeable theater writer can employ whatever coloristic variation he considers applicable to the show at hand without— and this, of course, is the point—in any way altering his own basic style.

Within a period of nine years—from 1947 to 1956—Frederick Loewe composed the scores to three shows set in widely dissimilar places: *Brigadoon* in Scotland, *Paint Your Wagon* in the gold-prospecting era of the American West, and *My Fair Lady* in London. All of the music for these three shows is unmistakably Loewe's. In *Brigadoon*, the songs *suggest* Scottish folk songs but do not either quote from or copy them. Bagpipes are

128

implied in the orchestration, and actually employed on the stage in a funeral sequence. The songs in *Paint Your Wagon* suggest the American gold rush through rhythmic patterns, typical melodic cadences, and instrumentation. *My Fair Lady* is English music-hall style. "Why Can't the English?" comes out of Gilbert and Sullivan without in the least copying them. "With a Little Bit of Luck," "I'm an Ordinary Man," "Just You Wait," "You Did It," "Get Me to the Church on Time," and "I've Grown Accustomed to Her Face" are reminiscent of the English music hall without literally *being* it.

Richard Rodgers's music is filled with similar examples. The opening song of *Pal Joey,* "A Great Big Town," belongs to the vulgar "mammy-song" school associated with Al Jolson. Its corniness characterizes the singer, Joey Evans, with pinpoint precision. "The Flower Garden of My Heart" and "That Terrific Rainbow" in the same show could not better delineate (while poking fun at the quality of) the nightclubs in which they are set, without reproducing the dullness and crudity of such places.

In *The King and I,* Rodgers uses two musical colors, each of which characterizes one of the two racial groups involved. "Mrs. Anna," the imported schoolteacher, has English-type songs: "I Whistle a Happy Tune," "Hello, Young Lovers," "Shall I Tell You What I Think of You," "Getting to Know You," and "Shall We Dance." These are Occidental in feeling, style, length of phrase, and harmony. On the other hand, "My Lord and Master" (sung by the ill-fated Tuptim) is pentatonic (Oriental) in feeling in somewhat the way Puccini employed his material in *Madame Butterfly.* The "March of the Siamese Children" seems Oriental because of its blocklike rhythmic pattern and the instrumentaion. "We Kiss in a Shadow" derives its Eastern tint from a fleeting, oft-repeated musical figure in the accompaniment. This soft, rippling effect evidently means "Oriental" to Rodgers since he used a similar effect for the same purpose in "Bali Ha'i" in *South Pacific.* He succeeds in conveying a hint of the romance of the East in a way that is conveyed by no other composer. "A Puzzlement," with its short, clipped phrases, repeated notes, square rhythm, and sparse harmony strikes Western ears as characteristic of the Orient. This is also true of "Western People Funny" and "Song of the King." It is interesting to compare the music of "Hello, Young Lovers" in *The King and I* (a tender song of remembrance) with "Blow High, Blow Low" (a song for sailors and the evil, but momentarily gay, Jigger) in *Carousel*. Both of these songs are in 6/8 time—a meter which is often identified with the sea and is particularly common to English sea chanties. As used in Anna's song, the 6/8 meter imparts a gentle and refined lilt. In the song for the sailors and Jigger, it is vigorous, bouncy, and unmistakably nautical in feeling: a single device employed for two entirely different purposes.

In an article which appeared in the Boston *Herald* the day before *Away We Go!* (subsequently renamed *Oklahoma!*) opened, the late Oscar Hammerstein II wrote: ". . . the songs Mr. Rodgers and I have written are not slavish imitations of folk ballads. They are songs which we hope may be liked for themselves, as songs of today. But the flavor of the time of our story and viewpoints of the characters who sing are maintained in all of these songs. It was our job to create this effect."

Because of this intention, so admirably realized by Rodgers and Hammerstein, it is impossible to interchange any of the songs in *Oklahoma!* (even without the lyrics) with songs in any other Rodgers and Hammerstein show. "The Surrey with the Fringe on Top" could serve neither Anna Leonowens nor Nellie Forbush nor Vera Simpson nor Carrie Pipperidge. For Anna, the song, with its barnyard-like cackle, is too American; for Nellie, it is both too long ago and too filled with the airy grace of that earlier day; for Vera, it is too simple and unsophisticated; and for Carrie, it is too far ahead of her time.

In spite of Rodgers's use of this variety of "decorations," *all* of his music is foremost and primarily *his*. The coloration contributes to the theatrical placement of character, locale, and period; nevertheless, the melodic contour and the harmonic flavor leave no doubt that this music is the work of Richard Rodgers.

Similarly with Frank Loesser. Loesser wrote "Once in Love With Amy" and "The New Ashmolean Marching Society" for *Where's Charley?* (based on *Charley's Aunt*). These songs *are*

Loesser, but strongly suggest Victorian England. The same composer, in *The Most Happy Fella*, wrote a passionately Italian "My Heart Is So Full of You" for the Italian-born Tony, and gay, festive trios for three Italian servants. In the same score, he composed "Big D," "Standing on the Corner," and "Joey" for essentially American characters. Leonard Bernstein suggested the American '30's through much of his music in *Wonderful Town*, and Puerto Ricans in "I Feel Pretty," "America," and especially in the dance music of the gymnasium scene in *West Side Story*.

In *I Can Get It for You Wholesale*, Harold Rome infused many of the songs with a Jewish inflection. This inflection, however, was not based on standard Jewish musical clichés and could not possibly have represented any character not both Jewish *and* American living at roughly the present time.

No matter how fresh, convincing, and sometimes subtle the present-day employment of these musical suggestions is, there is one danger that should be mentioned. As the characteristic materials used usually belong to a convention, it is possible that an unthinking composer might induce reactions opposite to those he intended.

For example, suppose a composer decided to make a musical out of *A Streetcar Named Desire*, which is laid in contemporary New Orleans. If he were to write a blues or dixieland song (which can well represent New Orleans) to characterize Blanche Dubois, he would destroy the character as we are intended to know her, since Blanche is at great pains to appear as a "lady" and to affect a distaste for the frivolous and the common. Although on purely musical terms and in consideration of the place and time, a blues would seem appropriate, the connotations of such a style would destroy Blanche herself.

This discussion was undertaken to show the evolution of the coloristic kind of treatment which is an integral part of the contemporary musical theater and the valuable uses to which tasteful composers have put the basic idea. It is, however, essential to understand that when Loesser suggests a Victorian flavor, or Rodgers, an Oriental one, or Loewe, a Scottish one, or Rome, an American Jewishness, he has not altered that basic style which is inescapably his own.

5

Broadway Opera

The history of opera is one of transplantation, borrowing, importation, and cross-breeding. At its very beginning, around 1600, with the Florentine Camerata's creation of monodies (as they were termed), the intention was to recreate Greek tragedy.

Italy, then, gave birth to opera and—first through court patronage and later, by enormous popular demand—nurtured the form through centuries of development. To this day, in Italy the passion for opera has persisted. Nor has its audience been limited, as in many other places, to people of wealth, rank, or education. Opera in Italy is in fact what moviegoing became in the United States about 1925: a national way of life.

Less than a century after its inception in Florence, opera had spread throughout Europe. In mid-18th-century Germany its great practitioners included Glück, Handel, and Mozart, most of whose operas were in the Italian language. Later German composers—Weber, Wagner, Richard Strauss, Berg, and Hindemith—wrote to librettos in their native language. Their music broke new paths as it went along, and the more innovative it became, the more its audience narrowed. Eventually opera in Germany came to exclude the wider public, while the popular audience in Italy still clung to the works of Donizetti, Rossini, Bellini, Verdi, and Puccini as to their flag.

In France, there were sporadic early attempts at musical theater, which at first worked quite independently of movements elsewhere. We have Adam de la Halle's *Le Jeu de Robin et Marion* (1280). After the Camerata, the French did import some Florentine works for important ceremonial occasions, but by the third quarter of the 18th century, ballet had taken root at the French court. The Italian-born Lully wrote many ballets, some of which contained vocal music, but by 1672, Lully began to write operas which became the foundations of French opera. Following were Rameau, the German Meyerbeer (who composed for Paris in the French language), Berlioz, Gounod, Bizet, Massenet, Debussy, and so forth.

During the 18th century, there began to be a split in the operatic succession: *opera buffa* in Italy and *opéra bouffe* in France. (*Singspiel* had already found its audience in Germany.) This was comic opera, which soon acquired a large family, including *opéra comique* (with spoken dialogue), operetta, ballad opera, and masque (in England), *Singspiel* in Germany, etc. Ballad opera, masque, and *Singspiel* included a variety of elements: pantomime, dance, pageantry, dialogue, songs, and choruses. Frequently these works were of a religious, national commemorative, or festive nature. *Opéra comique* could be serious (*Carmen* is an example), *buffa* (*Barber of Seville*), or *bouffe* (Offenbach's works). The developing *opéra bouffe* in France, operetta in Vienna (Strauss and Lehár), and operetta in England (Sullivan) are more closely related to musical comedy as we knew it in the first quarter of the 20th century in America than to opera.

Opera was introduced in England during the Puritan Commonwealth, when spoken plays were forbidden. Although inspired directly by the Florentine Camerata, the first English opera, *The Siege of Rhodes* (1656), had music by five different composers. Henry Purcell wrote one great opera, *Dido and Aeneas*, and some twenty years later, Handel came to London (completely under the spell of Italian opera), and wrote and performed his own (Italianate) opera, *Rinaldo* (1711). *Rinaldo* was such a success that its production established Handel as a popular exponent of this style. The Italian opera rage in London more closely resembled an epidemic than a trend.

Subsequently, as a reaction against what many staunch Englishmen felt was Italianate foppery and foolishness, the so-called ballad operas came into being. The most famous of these—and possibly the first—was John Gay's *The Beggar's Opera* (1728). Essentially, *The Beggar's Opera* was a play, interspersed with no fewer than 69 songs, dances, and choruses. The music was adapted from well-known songs written by many composers (including Handel) and a variety of folk songs. The use of musical adaptation—as opposed to newly composed scores—was one of the hallmarks of ballad opera, which was also a parody on grand opera, and the lyrics written for the songs selected were not only not Italian, but in the popular English idiom of the day. Thus in many respects *The Beggar's Opera* is an early musical comedy. From the ballad opera descended English opera—the popular form (with spoken dialogue) of grand opera, which resembled German *Singspiel* and French *opéra comique*. A popular descendant—in the popular theater sense—from English opera was Balfe's *The Bohemian Girl* (1843), written not long before the early works of Gilbert and Sullivan.

Opera was also brought from Italy to Russia as early as 1635. For nearly two centuries the Russians continued to import Italian companies, with very occasional performances of works by native composers. It was finally Glinka who wrote the first truly Russian opera, *A Life for the Tsar* (1836), and this was followed by a sudden explosion of works from great Russian composers: Rimsky-Korsakov, Mussorgsky, Borodin—and later, of course, Stravinsky, Prokofiev, and Shostakovich.

The most interesting aspect of this—and particularly noticeable in the case of Russia—is that though spawned in Italy, opera became at one point, and suddenly, a native product—thoroughly indigenous in feeling and an intrinsic part of its own time and place—and *preceded* significant music in other large forms. Composers writing opera broke new *musical* paths.

How did this happen? Why did this musical trail-blazing come about in an art which, besides music, involves plot, scenery, acting, and the other crafts peculiar to the theater? One can only surmise, of course, but I have a theory that to me seems most plausible: that this great innovation in the musical art, which became the progenitor of national musical style in each country, was born in the theater for reasons that are purely psychological.

For example—again—take the first Russian composers, all of whom wrote for the opera. Glinka (b. 1804) initially held a civil service job, as did Dargomijsky (b. 1813). Borodin (b. 1833) studied medicine and was a professor of chemistry—a career which he followed through a large part of his life. Rimsky-Korsakov (b. 1844) spent his early years as a naval officer; Cui (b. 1835) rose to the rank of general in the army and was an authority on fortifications; Mussorgsky (b. 1839) was an officer in a guard regiment; Balakirev (b. 1837) began a career in mathematics.

Several startling facts come to light here. First of all, these composers who became the fountainhead of Russian musical art were all born in the same period. All of them composed operas. All of them were—at least early in their careers—musical dilettantes. All of them began life in rural sections of Russia, where they were exposed to the rich folk music of the land.

Although several of them also composed music in other forms, it was in opera that they made their greatest and most enduring impression. Moreover, it is through their operas that they evolved the *style* which all subsequent Russian composers and all musicians throughout the world accept as *the* art music of Russia.

Nor is this curious set of circumstances unique to the founding of the Russian school. Italian operas had been imported to the French court at least as early as 1647, and there is a strong probability that other works had been performed there as early as 1605. Ballet—a French theater form—enjoyed its first real following during the reign of Louis XIII (1601–1643). Among the earliest and most notable scores composed for the ballet were those by Lully (b. 1632), a naturalized Frenchman and a distinguished feature of the French court. From ballet, Lully turned his attention to opera, a form he employed consistently until his death. Percy Scholes, in *The Oxford Companion to Music* *, says that Lully's music "is looked upon as the solid rock foundation of French Opera." His contemporary, in France, Rameau (b. 1683), was also dedicated to opera. Prior to Rameau and Lully, French music, strongly influenced by Italian polyphonists, had evolved coloristically with a native flavor, but was written chiefly in the small forms—chansons and motets—and in masses whose traditions were derived from the Italian and Netherlands polyphonic schools. But Rameau and Lully in their operas defined a genuine French style.

In Germany, after importations of Florentine examples, native composers—Keiser (b. 1674), Graun (b. 1704) at the Court of Frederick the Great, and especially Glück (b. 1714)—were setting the German style that would reach a unique climax with Mozart (b. 1756).

In Italy, the birthplace of opera, the bold musical experiments of Monteverdi (b. 1567) were revolutionary to the extreme, and their effect on all future opera everywhere, and on the formation of the Italian opera school in particular, is inestimable.

It is my considered opinion that—as I mentioned above—psychological factors were responsible in large part for the definition and development of national styles through opera. *All* of these operas written in every country (Russia excepted) were for court consumption. *All* of them constituted musical innovations of one form or other. These departures from tradition would, I believe, most likely have met with audience resistance—of the same kind that has usually greeted all other new artistic inventions—had they not been couched in, and exposed with, the other elements of theater—especially plot, costume, and scenery. Because of the multiple division of audience attention, and by the creation of a suitable excuse for the harshness of new musical expression—that it is necessitated by the exigencies and demands of the drama—the theatrical elements remove the onus from the innovative musical element.

These same conditions, I believe, have served composers in much later times. The stage works of Wagner, Strauss, Debussy, Schoenberg, Hindemith, Berg, and many others—

* Oxford University Press.

though antipathetically received at first—nevertheless came into their own more quickly because of their theatrical associations. These latter provided audiences with extra-musical involvements and, in many cases, gave them a literary reason (not necessarily intended as such by the composer) for responding to styles that would otherwise have been more difficult to accept. Music accompanying a murder, for example, is more readily forgiven for being harsh and dissonant and (to many listeners) unpleasant than the same music heard in a symphony in a formal, lighted concert hall.

The above notions all refer to the attending public. But there is also another side of the question that concerns the composer himself. I am convinced that many of the composers—past and more recent—have had their imaginations fired by the plots, characters, and settings with which they have become involved. I do not think that this has been an inconsiderable factor in the development of musical styles. The theater stimulation has been and continues to be enormously important on both sides of the footlights. The debt that *all* music owes the theater is incalculable.

Eventually opera itself in every country became divided between "grand" and "light." The three different and representative high points of the light-opera movement—Strauss, Offenbach, and Sullivan—by coincidence (always coincidence—or is it inevitability?) developed simultaneously. Together they represented a synthesis, a fruition, and a culmination. Though alike in intention, their respective works were totally dissimilar in style. In a narrow sense, despite their enormous popularity, these men produced no direct musical heirs of quality. Indirectly, however, the tradition they created was to be found most vitally developed in contemporary American musical theater. And as they had kept the seeds of opera, from which their music descended, alive in their work, so their heirs in the American musical theater were one day to create a new opera, bringing to it the fresh acquisitions of modern American idiom.

Leonard Bernstein observed in *The Joy of Music* * ". . . the American musical theater has come a long way, borrowing this

* Simon and Schuster.

from opera, that from revue, the other from operetta, something else from vaudeville—and mixing all the elements into something quite new, but something which has been steadily moving in the direction of opera." And further: "The more a show gets away from pure diversion, the more it tries to engage the interest and emotion of the audience, the closer it slides toward opera. And the more a show uses music to further its plot, the closer it moves toward the same pole." And again: "Opera is big, bigger than the spoken theater, bigger than life. And what makes it bigger? Music, sung music."

Of our model musical shows, *Carousel, The King and I, Brigadoon, My Fair Lady, Fiddler on the Roof, West Side Story,* and *A Little Night Music,* are in my opinion very close to opera as Bernstein has defined it. Perhaps they *are* the new American opera.

To be sure, the presence of opera or operetta on Broadway hardly constitutes an innovation. *The Bohemian Girl* enjoyed a run in 1844. Beginning with *Pinafore* in 1879, eleven of the Gilbert and Sullivan operettas were produced by 1899, with *The Mikado* (1885) running for 250 performances. Planquette's *The Chimes of Normandy,* Strauss's *The Queen's Lace Handkerchief* (1882) and *The Merry War* (1883) and, in the same years, Offenbach's *La Vie Parisienne* and *The Princess of Trebizonde,* Strauss's *Die Fledermaus* (1885), and many others, were successfully holding their own against the numerous extravaganzas of that time and the popular shows of Harrigan and Hart.

The American operettas of De Koven and Sousa also held the boards during the last fifteen years of the 19th century. To these, after the turn of the century, were added operettas by Edward German, Victor Herbert, Lucius Hosmer, Ludwig Englander, Lehár, more Johann Strauss, Oskar Straus, and more Sullivan. Other products of new works by nearly all of the eminent European composers continued on Broadway well into the 20th century.

Virgil Thomson's opera *4 Saints in 3 Acts* played Broadway in 1934. In 1938 Marc Blitzstein's *The Cradle Will Rock* lustily followed suit. *Carmen Jones* (based on Bizet's *Carmen*), with book and lyrics by Oscar Hammerstein II, began a run of 503 performances in 1943. Blitzstein came along again in 1949 with *Regina,* a grand opera based on Lillian Hellman's play *The Little Foxes.* Though it had far less popular appeal than *Carmen Jones,* even *Regina* ran 56 performances. Kurt Weill's *Street Scene,* based on the play by Elmer Rice, opened in 1947 and ran 148 performances. Benjamin Britten's *The Rape of Lucretia* came to the Ziegfeld Theater in 1948; and several of Gian-Carlo Menotti's operas had successful Broadway runs, beginning in 1947 with *The Medium* and *The Telephone,* followed by *The Consul* (1950), and *The Saint of Bleecker Street* (1954).

In the eighty-three years from the opening of the Metropolitan Opera House until 1966, only twenty-one operas by seventeen Americans were presented. Among the composers in this meager list are De Koven, Hadley, Herbert, Damrosch, Hagerman, Parker, Cadman, and Converse, among the older generation; and Louis Gruenberg, Deems Taylor, Howard Hanson, Bernard Rogers, Gian-Carlo Menotti, and Samuel Barber, among the younger.

Several interesting facts come to light in this connection. Out of the fourteen composers listed above, six wrote Broadway shows, and of these, three will be far better and longer remembered for their Broadway shows than for those produced in the opera house: Herbert, De Koven, and Menotti. On the other hand, of all of the operas presented as such, only two stand up today: Menotti's *Amelia Goes to the Ball* and the Menotti-Barber collaboration, *Vanessa.* None of them was given enough exposure in the Metropolitan to have made any lasting impression on anyone. Even the shortest-run of the operas on Broadway—*Regina*—with its 56 performances exceeded by at least 8 *times* the performances of *any* new opera in a single season at the Metropolitan. And *Regina* is still revived by the New York City Opera Company.

The Metropolitan seems to have produced whatever American operas it did produce under pressure. This pressure came from two sources: from some of the Met's important patrons who were dissatisfied with the way American money to support an American house had to be poured out exclusively for European impresarios, divas, conductors, and royalties; and later, from critics and from American composers themselves who were resentful about the exclusion of native works. Thus American operas produced at the Metropolitan—mostly commissions—were largely gestures of placation, and the restricted choice of works had nothing to do with considerations of merit or distinction, since nearly all of these works, being Metropolitan commissions, were firmly arranged for before a single note was put down on paper.

On the other hand, Broadway producers must know in advance what it is that they have to present, and the operas produced by them have had to stand or fall by audience response. If such operas are lacking in the qualities that make audiences care, they are out-and-out failures. They do not run. Producers, faced with the possibility of failure—and undoubtedly made uneasy by the very word "opera"—have needed to feel some confidence in the potential success of a new opera before taking the chance. For its part, the Metropolitan need only hope for approval of its American operas from the music critics; and whether or not this approval is actually forthcoming, a new opera will receive its six or eight scheduled performances, the deficit being merely an accustomed concomitant of operatic "business as usual."

Among the most successful Broadway operas there are four that I would like to discuss here. These are very different from one another, and taken together seem to me to represent a cross-section of styles in this general form in our time. They are: Gershwin's *Porgy and Bess* (1935), Blitzstein's *The Cradle Will Rock* (1937), Menotti's *The Consul* (1950), and Loesser's *The Most Happy Fella* (1956). Since I myself conducted the world premieres of the Blitzstein and Menotti works, recorded—almost completely—the Gershwin, and performed the Loesser, there might be some ground for supposing that this is why they have been singled out here. Nevertheless, in my opinion these four works are the most representative of the diversified forces at work in contemporary American opera.

In size alone, *Porgy and Bess* is the most ambitious. It was the earliest "new" opera; it contained what was for its time the most original application of native American musical material, it came the closest in outline to traditional grand opera among new works, and is, even today, the most controversial.

The printed vocal score is 559 pages as compared, for example, with *Aida's* 310. *Porgy* was a "new" American opera, because, in my opinion, the works of Charles Wakefield Cadman, Deems Taylor, Walter Damrosch, and Louis Gruenberg which had been performed at the Metropolitan Opera, were certainly *not* new. These were sincere but weak essays that had no connection with the American people, the native idioms, theater itself, or with any sense of contemporary style—even in their own time. They were imitative of grand opera as it was known everywhere else in the world, remote from home, pretentious, impotent, and self-conscious.

The musical idiom of *Porgy* was derived from Negro folk cadence and rhythm, and its harmonic texture came from the jazz makers of America—in New Orleans, New York, Chicago—during the '20's and '30's. The musical fabric of *Porgy* is like that of all Gershwin's Broadway shows, his "Rhapsody in Blue," and the rest of his works: the Negro and jazz elements also have a Jewish inflection. *Porgy* is close in outline to traditional grand opera in that it is, in Webster's definition of opera, "a drama in which music is the essential factor comprising songs with orchestral accompaniment (as recitatives, aria, chorus) and orchestral preludes and interludes."

The controversy stirred by *Porgy's* premiere in 1935 has not yet fully settled, despite the fact that it has enjoyed worldwide success and acclaim in stage revivals, motion pictures, and recordings; that its songs continue to be "treated" in all sorts of styles and arrangements; and that it contains at least six hit songs which have not in forty years shown the least sign of age. For as an opera, it still continues to annoy certain critics. It has always seemed to me that this annoyance with *Porgy* is far more the product of semantics than of anything Gershwin put into his score. It is as if just calling *Porgy* by the name "opera" serves to assail the sensibilities of those who believe that such a classification is a slur on the dignity of Wagner, Verdi, and Mozart.

Not that all or even most critics responded this way. Even at

141

its premiere, *Porgy* was hailed by reviewers—each of whom, to be sure, had his own special reservations. Brooks Atkinson, the *New York Times* drama critic, wrote: "Gershwin has contributed something glorious to the spirit of the Heywards' community legend" and "has found a personal voice that was inarticulate in the original play. The fear and the pain go deeper. . . ." However, Mr. Atkinson was disturbed by the recitatives, ". . . a deluge of casual remarks that have to be thoughtfully intoned and that amazingly impede the action."

Olin Downes, the music critic of the *Times*, complained, on the other hand, that "the treatment of the passages of recitative is seldom significant." Also, "He has not completely formed his style but here and there flashes of real contrapuntal ingenuity combine themes in a manner apposite to the grouping and action of the characters on the stage. . . . He makes effective use of spirituals, not only by harmony sometimes modal but by the dramatic combination of the massed voices and the wild exhortations of the individual singers."

John Anderson, drama critic (New York *Evening Journal*): "I found two-thirds of it mighty dull. . . . Possibly I wouldn't know a good folk opera if one walked right up and bored me to death." Burns Mantle, drama critic (New York *Daily News*) gave *Porgy* his highest accolade—four stars, his ultimate approval. Leonard Liebling, music critic (New York *American*): "The music is of our own soil and of our own days. It has tunes, harmonies, color, and rhythms to which we wholly respond. . . . What a joy for Americans to hear an opera whose every word they are able to follow, and whose comical twists come to them directly in their own tongue." Lawrence Gilman, music critic (New York *Herald Tribune*): "It was evident that Mr. Gershwin had given us something suspiciously like an authentic folk opera in an unmistakably American vein." However, Mr. Gilman, an ardent Wagnerite, loathed the "song hits . . . scattered through his score. . . . They mar it. They are its cardinal weakness. They are a blemish upon its musical integrity."

Mr. Gilman's response was that of an experienced opera-goer. He was almost the only reviewer not appalled by the presence of recitatives—the musical setting of non-lyrical speeches—in the work. His consternation was reserved for the songs, which he termed "sure-fire rubbish." Mr. John Anderson reflected the more widely held feeling about the recitative as against the opera's "hits": "When Mr. Gershwin is merely tying the narration together, he gets in the way of the movement of the whole show, but when he is decorating it with isolated compositions he enriches it marvellously."

If it is necessary to defend the use of recitative in *Porgy* at all, it must be said that Gershwin was obviously not attempting to compose a naturalistic work, but rather—as in all grand opera— one that would be bigger than nature.

Just before the entrance of Bess and Crown, there is a prosaic exchange (sung) among Serena, Porgy, and Jake:

SERENA: That gal Bess ain't fit for Gawd fearin' ladies to 'sociate with.
PORGY: Can't you keep yo' mouth off Bess. Between the Gawd fearin' ladies an' the Gawd damnin' men that gal ain't got a chance.
JAKE: Ain' I tells you Porgy sof' on her?
PORGY: No, no, brudder, Porgy ain' sof' on no woman.

This much is recitative. The music is turbulent. If it were not treated musically, the passage which follows—one of the most moving and glorious in the whole work, and *not* a developed song—would not be possible:

PORGY (*continuing, about women*):
    They pass by singin',
    They pass by cryin', always lookin'.
    They look in my do' an' they keep on movin'—
    When Gawd make cripple, he mean him to be lonely,
    Night time, day time, he got to trabble dat lonesome road,
    Night time, day time, he got to trabble dat lonesome road.*

This one passage should suffice to make my point here. In *La Bohème, Otello, Louise, Die Meistersinger,* and all the others, there are many passages of recitative that in themselves might

* PORGY AND BESS © 1935 Gershwin Publishing Corporation. Copyright Renewed. Used by Permission.

seem dull to this listener or that; but without the musical texture they create, many lyric passages that are not songs or arias would be impossible because—if there were no musical continuity—they would become small, isolated islands of music, unconnected, rootless, and even silly. They would not be an outgrowth of the always present musical texture—an essential condition for making them plausible.

In Act II of *Madame Butterfly,* there is a "conversation" between the heroine and her servant Suzuki about Butterfly's American husband:

> BUTTERFLY: And why did he provide every door in every chamber with locks, unless he meant to come back here again?
> SUZUKI: I don't know.
> BUTTERFLY: You don't know? But I can tell you. Was it not to keep outside, those plagues, my relatives, who so annoy me? And indoors, it was meant to guard his wife, and shield her—his ever faithful wife, Butterfly.*

As lines, particularly in translation, these mean very little. The music to which they are set lets us know Butterfly's anxiety and the lyrical flights her frustrated dreams take. We feel the servant's sadness at the revelation of her mistress's unrealistic fancy. The words are not real; they are set so that their delivery is unreal—larger, more emotional than such a conversation in life would be. But that is precisely the reason for the lyric recitative—to expose the insides of the characters in a manner impossible of exposition in a mere conversation. Through this device, the words simply guide the thought in an elementary way, and the music completes them—adding color and emotion. *Sung* words alone can accomplish this.

In the very same way, the recitative is a vital and essential element of *Porgy and Bess.* Critical opposition to Gershwin's use of it seems to me to stem merely from a certain state of mind: what was readily acceptable for the distant, unreal, and "exalted" characters in traditional grand opera, sung in a foreign language and set in a past time, struck many people as embar-

---

* This exchange, rendered here in my own version, is leading up to the "One Fine Day" aria.

rassing—as "put on"—when delivered by the Negro characters of a popular American-Jewish composer.

As for the individual songs, far from being blemishes upon the opera's musical integrity, as Mr. Gilman said, they are the jewels that glow in the crown. And the choral scenes with which *Porgy and Bess* abounds undoubtedly represent the most effective theatrical employment of ensemble singing and writing ever heard in any American stage work.

Moreover, Gershwin's original orchestration—long thought turgid and overwrought—will, to anyone who studies it carefully, reveal itself as a model of clarity and intelligent reflection.

As an opera, *Porgy and Bess*—and here all the drama critics concurred—intensifies the feeling, excitement, and passion of the original play. The difference between the two can be amply demonstrated with a single passage. At the very end of the play, Porgy, just out of jail, learns that Bess has gone with Sportin' Life to New York. The end of the play follows:

PORGY: Where dat dey take she?

MINGO: Noo Yo'k.

MARIA: Dat's way up Nort'.

PORGY (*pointing*): Is dat way?

MARIA: It take two days by de boat. Yo' can't find um.

PORGY: I ain't say I can find um. I say, where it is?

MARIA: Yo' can't go after she. Ain't yo' hear we say yo' can't find um.

ANNIE: Ain't yo' know Noo Yo'k mos' a t'ousand mile' from here?

PORGY: Which way dat?

LILY (*pointing*): Up Nort'—past de Custom House.

(*Porgy turns his goat and drives slowly with bowed head toward the gate*)

MARIA: Porgy, I tell you' it ain't no use!

LILY: Dat great big city. Yo' can't find um dere!

SERENA: Ain't we tells you' . . .

(*But Porgy is going on toward the gate as if he did not hear, and they cease to protest and stand motionless watching him. As Porgy reaches the gate, Scipio silently opens it. Porgy drives through and turns to left, as Lily pointed. St. Michael's chimes the quarter hour. The gate clangs shut.*)

CURTAIN *

* Reprinted with the permission of Jenifer Heyward.

145

The concluding scene from the opera, enormously elevated by the music itself as well as by the concluding choral sound, follows:

PORGY: I hear you say Noo Yo'k. Where dat?
MINGO: Most a t'ousand miles from here.
PORGY: Which way Noo Yo'k?
MARIA: It's way up Nort' pas' de Custom House.
PORGY: Bring my goat!
MARIA: What you wants wid goat, Porgy? You bes' not go any place.
PORGY: Bring my goat!
SERENA: You better stay wid yo' fren', Porgy, you'll be happy here.
PORGY: Won't nobody bring my goat?
MARIA: Ain't we tell you, you can't find her, Porgy?
SERENA: For Gawd sake, Porgy, where you goin'?
CHORUS: Where you goin', Porgy?
PORGY (*transformed and exalted*): Ain't you say Bess gone to Noo Yo'k? Dat's where I goin', I got to be wid Bess. Gawd help me to fin' her, I'm on my way. (*holds out his arms to be helped into goat cart, two men help him*)
PORGY (*with religious fervor*): Oh Lawd, I'm on my way.
PORGY AND CHORUS:
> I'm on my way to a Heav'nly Lan',
> I'll ride dat long, long road,
> If you are there to guide my han',
> Oh Lawd, I'm on my way.
> I'm on my way to a Heav'nly Lan', oh Lawd
> It's a long way, but you'll be there to take my han'.

CURTAIN.*

The play ends. The opera soars.

The story of the premiere of Marc Blitzstein's *The Cradle Will Rock* (1937) is by now a familiar one. Briefly, the opera was rehearsed for a number of months in the Federal Theatre, a branch of the WPA. Orson Welles staged it, and I conducted. There was a single preview the night before the scheduled opening. On the day of opening, the government in Washington

---

* PORGY AND BESS © 1935 Gershwin Publishing Corporation. Copyright Renewed. Used by Permission.

withheld its promised permission for the opening because of the controversial nature of the libretto. (*The Cradle Will Rock* dealt with a proposed strike against a steel-industry boss whose power was so great that he was able to buy off doctors, professors, ministers, artists, editors, gangsters—everyone except the working people themselves—to support him against the strike.) Because at performance time the theater was padlocked, the audience assembled on the sidewalk—and was taken to another theater leased for the night by John Houseman, head of the project. The actors could not gain permission from the president of Equity, the actors' union, to appear on the other stage for fear that, if they did, they might be subject to WPA dismissal. Houseman hit on the idea that the actors could sit in the audience, stand up on cue at their seats, and speak and sing. Blitzstein sat on the stage at a piano. Welles described the work and set the scenes verbally. The chorus sat in the front row with me. Thus as each scene came round, Blitzstein had no way of being sure whether the actors involved in it were going to participate. Most of them did. Often two people involved together in a scene were seated on opposite sides of the theater—a circumstance which heightened the dramatic effect. Sometimes an actor did not rise, and then Blitzstein sang and/or spoke the part from his place at the upright piano.

The evening was an event and made the front page. Within a few days the opera opened at a small theater, this time with the performers seated on the stage, without scenery or costumes, the composer at the piano. It had a run of about fourteen weeks.

In 1947 Leonard Bernstein performed the work three times with the New York Symphony Orchestra on the stage of what is now the New York City Center—again without costumes and scenery. This led to another piano-accompanied, unstaged run of about three weeks.

The first complete performance with orchestra, scenery, and costumes took place in February 1960 at the New York City Center with Tammy Grimes, Nancy Dussault, Jack Harrold, Chandler Cowles, Michael Wager, Ruth Kobart, Craig Timberlake, Frank Porretta, David Atkinson, and many others. It was staged by Howard Da Silva, had sets by David Hays, and I conducted—twenty-three years after the scheduled premiere.

The Cradle has spoken dialogue, songs, choruses, dances, and musical scenes. The French would call it *opéra comique*. It is in every sense a unique work. Its musical forefather is Kurt Weill, and its theatrical inspiration is Bertold Brecht, but its true style was distilled out of American vaudeville and minstrel shows.

The words and lyrics are as monosyllabic as possible, and the songs are, at least outwardly, as plain as folk music. From the inside, however, the music has a subtle complexity, and every melody—it abounds in melody—is full of surprises. The simplicity seems to be indicating where the music is going and what is going to happen—but not quite. It announces its intention to be banal, but this avowal is only flirtatious—the girl who leads you to her bedroom and, without warning, closes the door in your face.

The Cradle Will Rock is, of course, meant to be militant. The story's concern with the rise of unionism makes it a period piece today, but that fact in no way diminishes the work's humor, pathos, or excitement. The characters in *The Cradle* are intentionally stereotypes. Mr. Mister (the Boss) and his wife are villains. Larry Foreman, the union organizer, is heroic. The Moll, though a prostitute, is a victim of society and a kind of heroine. The Dick (cop), Reverend, Editor, Painter, Violinist, Bugs (gangster), Prexie, Mamie, and Trixie (professors) and Doctor are presented as the *real* whores who do whatever they can to please Mr. Mister in return for security and position. Ella Hammer, sister of a murdered worker, is a good girl. The Druggist, whose son is killed trying to warn a Polish worker and his girl, is weak. He has become an alcoholic because of his failure to take a stand against Mr. Mister's hired murderer. The teen-age children of Mr. Mister are comic in their stupidity and obtuseness.

The individual scenes of *The Cradle* are vignettes, like vaudeville "turns," strung together on Mr. Mister's attempt to foil the union and Larry Foreman's idiot-bright determination—triumphant in the end—to organize the workers.

The vignettes involving the "prostitutes"—Mr. Mister's unctuous aides—are all satirical in intent and funny. Those involv-

148

ing the Moll, the death of the druggist's son, and the murdered worker's sister are touching. They are unified by the device of a continual return to night court, with flashbacks and interludes.

The vaudeville-like character of the music in the comedy vignettes is intentionally "common-denominator" corny. There is a torch song, a waltz, a fox-trot, a Bach-like chorale done *a la* American Methodism, and a Hawaiian number. The title song is a forward-we-will-go march. The entrance of the violinist (Yasha) and painter (Dauber) is pure end-man minstrel show. The sunny character of the drugstore scene opening, the melodramatic gangster recitative that follows, the love duet of the Polish couple and horrifying end of the entire vignette make a startling sequence—which becomes all the more shocking by its abrupt, non-transitional segue to the ricky-ticky Yasha-Dauber minstrel show.

I should like to offer two quotations from *The Cradle*. The first is from the Drugstore Scene:

HARRY DRUGGIST (*spoken to his son*): It's a terrible world, Stevie,
And I feel fine.

And the other is from the Yasha-Dauber scene (sung). The two men enter from opposite sides, like end men in a minstrel show. They are in the lobby of a fashionable hotel.

DAUBER: Don't let me keep you, please be on your way.
    You must have many things to do.
YASHA: No, not at all, an appointment today
    Brings me to these parts.
DAUBER: Me, too.
YASHA: But the person I'm about to meet, I doubt you could have met her.
    The kind that grovels at my feet, she'd stay there if I let her.
    She's fabulously wealthy, and although that's not the reason,
    I think she can be counted on to subsidize me all next season.
DAUBER: Your lady friend does resemble a lot Someone, and that's very queer.
YASHA: So?
DAUBER: Some one who's meeting me here—

YASHA: No!
DAUBER: Is her Pierce Arrow light blue?
YASHA: Yes.
DAUBER: Not Missus Mister?
YASHA: Well, yes, Missus Mister!
DAUBER: Me too.
BOTH: Oh, there's something so damned low about the rich.
  They're fantastic, they're far-fetched, they're just funny.
  They've no impulse, no fine feeling, no great itch.
  What have they got? Money.
DAUBER (*spoken*): Stupid woman, Missus Mister.
YASHA (*spoken*): Stupid! What she doesn't know about music
  Would put Kreisler back on his feet again.
DAUBER (*spoken*): She asked me to bring El Greco to tea this sum-
  mer.*

The Cradle Will Rock is a unique work cast in a unique form. The vibrancy and sting of its humor, the genuinely colloquial quality of its music, its pathos, and its general vitality make it a milestone in American musical theater.

Of the four Broadway operas under discussion here, all of which were successful to one degree or another, Gian-Carlo Menotti's *The Consul* (1950) had the greatest financial success in its first run and today enjoys a place in the repertoires of several opera companies. It is not hard to understand why either of these things should be true. There is nothing in any way controversial about *The Consul:* the libretto is theatrical in the Sardou sense; it is dramatic and melodramatic; the characters and their problems grip the audience at the very outset. The situation in which a wife tries to get a visa in order to leave a police state; her frustration at the many delays; the similar fate of five other, all quite different, pathetic applicants; and the wife's final decision to kill herself in order to prevent her husband—wanted by the police—from returning, make for an emotionally charged libretto. Within the work there is grandeur (the "Papers" aria), pathos (the quintet at the end of Act I, the Magician's Waltz, and the Mother's Lullaby), humor (in the Magician's Scene), outraged nobility in the "Oh, Those Faces!" aria, and terror in the final surrealistic nightmare.

The emotional power and effectiveness of *The Consul* can be laid to Menotti's impeccable sense of theater. All of the characters here are prototypes. As the heroine, Magda Sorel, sings in her "Papers" aria:

> My name is woman.
> Age: still young.
> Color of hair: gray.
> Color of eyes: the color of tears.
> Occupation: waiting.*

Magda Sorel is all women in rebellion against the hopeless; her husband and mother are universal; the others—flotsam and jetsam—are all the pathetic outcasts of this world. Moreover, Menotti's characters and their story—and they have a *real* story—are his prime concern. As a composer, Menotti uses music to enforce words, and to give mood to scenes. He is not concerned that the music in any way make a display of him as composer. The style in which he wrote *The Consul* bespeaks its origins somewhere in the opera houses of Italy, but this in no way makes it less effective. The musical inflections and nuances, and above all theatricality, of *The Consul* are Menotti's, and at their best they are a great gift to our musical theater.

The final Broadway opera to be dealt with here is Frank Loesser's *The Most Happy Fella* (1956). Here the composer (as was also the case with Blitzstein and Menotti) is his own librettist. Here, too, the music displays a variety of influences, all of which come together in the hand of its composer.

One of the most remarkable achievements in *The Most Happy Fella* is Mr. Loesser's creation of the libretto out of Sidney Howard's play, *They Knew What They Wanted* (1924). Both the original play and the opera are in three acts and tell of a waitress in a small cafe who becomes the mail-order bride of a

---

* Copyright 1950 by G. Schirmer, Inc.

middle-aged Italian grape rancher in the Napa Valley, California. The man, Tony, in correspondence with the girl, sends her the photograph of his ranch foreman, who, unlike him, is young and slim and good-looking. The waitress accepts his marriage proposal and is then shocked on arriving to discover the real Tony. Tony is just then injured in a car accident and because he may die, she is persuaded to marry him. Meanwhile the bewildered waitress encounters the young man of the photograph and goes to bed with him. During Tony's long recovery, she falls genuinely in love with the older man, and just as she has succeeded in making him believe in her love, she discovers that her one-night escapade with the foreman has left her pregnant. Ultimately the situation is resolved, and the story ends happily.

In the play, all of the action takes place in Tony's farmhouse in the Napa Valley. In the opera, the action commences before that of the play in the cafe in San Francisco, moves to a street in Napa, to Tony's barn, Tony's front yard, the vineyards, and finally to a Napa railroad station. The character of the heroine (Amy in the play and Rosabella in the opera) has been altered considerably, made less tough than in the play, and warmer.

Loesser created three major new characters: a comic team— Cleo (Rosabella's friend, another waitress) and Herman (a ranch-hand and Cleo's opposite number)—and Marie, Tony's lugubrious sister. The two comedians add immeasurably to the theatrical quality of the opera, and since the heroine has a confidante, her own character has a better opportunity of being exploited. A look at the original play today makes one wonder why it was ever successful. In comparison with the libretto, it seems pale. Howard is quoted in John Gassner's introduction to *25 Best Plays of the Modern American Theater* * as claiming "only a modest role for playwriting, maintaining that the merit of a play lay in its providing good parts for acting rather than in distinction of content or writing."

The musical score is rich and varied. In fact, the only, and minor, reservation expressed by the reviewers when the opera

* Crown.

opened was that its musical variety was perhaps a little *too* great. Drama critic Walter Kerr (New York *Herald Tribune*) write: "The over-abundance is damaging. It tends to choke the movement of the action. . . ."

For me, *The Most Happy Fella* pulls together all of the best elements to be found in a superb musical show and adds to them arias of enormous emotional intensity. The lyrical and musical concepts of:

> Somebody, somewhere—
> Wants me and needs me
> Wants lonely me to smile and say "Hello"—
> Somebody, somewhere
> Wants me and needs me
> And that's very wonderful to know.*

touch the listener deeply, setting off Loesser's moving conception of Rosabella. She is no longer, as Brooks Atkinson originally characterized her, the "tired, rather commonplace waitress who is looking for a way out" but a lonely girl in need of love as well as security.

Then there is the handsome young foreman, Joey, and the song which bears his name: a song of nostalgia and dreaming and longing for an indefinable something that nobody can ever find anywhere. The style here is not opera as it has been known before, and it is also—strictly speaking—not Broadway. There are "Broadway" songs, to be sure: "Standing on the Corner" and "Big D." And there are Italian songs for Italian farmhands, "Abbondanza," "Sposalizio," and "Benvenuta." There are other, aria-like pieces: "Warm All Over," the ecstatic "My Heart Is So Full of You," and "Mamma, Mamma." There are touchingly charming songs, "How Beautiful the Days" and "Happy to Make Your Acquaintance." There are the vitriolic "I Don't Like This Dame" and "Young People." And the opening comedy song for Cleo, the second waitress, "Ooh! My Feet!"

Although Loesser has included spoken dialogue, there is also

---

* SOMEBODY, SOMEWHERE by Frank Loesser © 1956 Frank Loesser, All Rights Reserved. Used by Permission.

a great deal of recitative—without which the rich musical scenes could have degenerated into a song recital. (In this case, the press seems not to have been in the least unnerved by the recitative. John McClain, drama critic of the New York *Journal American,* commented: ". . . great musical by a guy who likes to write a lot of music and would rather have the people sing the story than talk it.")

Leonard Bernstein in *The Joy of Music* * points out about an early American musical comedy which employed American speech patterns that the characters talked like people everybody knew. In early musical comedies, such a thing was as rare as it was significant. Certainly the fact that in Loesser's "opera" characters speak and sing in the American vernacular is one of the many significant attributes that make it work so well.

CLEO, THE WAITRESS:
> Ooh my feet!
> My poor, poor feet!
> Betcha your life a waitress earns her pay.
> I've been on my feet, my poor, poor feet,
> All day long today!
> Doing my blue plate special ballet!

MARIE, THE MALICIOUS SISTER:
> You're her friend and he's my brother.
> You understand, we can talk to one another.†

Whether in song, recitative, or speech, the use of simple conversational English is so well conceived that *The Most Happy Fella* can be thoroughly meaningful—amusing and touching—to any American, regardless of his education, experience, or background.

These four operas are, each in a rather different way, products of the American musical theater—which is to say, Broadway. All of them are of high quality, and each has a continuing life. True American opera—which I feel already flourishes—has descended from Broadway. It is this American musical-theater tradition which speaks to us truly and reflects who we are.

---

* Simon and Schuster.
† © 1956 Frank Loesser, All Rights Reserved. Used by Permission.

6

A Medley

I. PIT AND THEATER

Each of the many elements of our musical theater has been evolving steadily over the past several centuries, and will hopefully continue to do so as long as there is a theater. The melody of Leonard Bernstein's "Something's Coming" is eons apart from De Koven's "Oh, Promise Me," though in actuality only seventy years separate them. The respective harmonies of Herbert and Weill set the two men in entirely different worlds. Robbins's choreography for *Fiddler on the Roof* (1964) and its integration into the action represents a style undreamed of by the dancers in *Babes in Toyland* (1903).

Equally remarkable changes have taken place in the orchestra pit and on the stage, but these have occurred so gradually and so almost imperceptibly that they are seldom mentioned. They involve a major reversal of the balance between the two interdependent musical elements: orchestra and singers. The orchestra in the pit, through the addition of new instruments and more complex contemporary orchestration, has grown busier and louder, while the singers on the stage have diminished in volume and style from opera-size to whispering crooners. But for modern-day electronic know-how, the accompaniment today would indeed annihilate the accompanied. The problems raised by such a situation seem never to have been considered seriously, as they have been dealt with only by patchwork, stop-gap methods in order to prevent catastrophe in this or that particular contingency.

The orchestra, in size, has grown very little larger from what it was three-quarters of a century ago, but the kinds of instruments and methods of orchestration have undergone vast changes. In 1905, Herbert's *Mademoiselle Modiste* in the Knickerbocker Theatre—roughly the size of the Shubert—(about 1,350 seats) was accompanied by: flute, oboe, 2 clarinets, bassoon, 2 trumpets, 1 trombone, 1 percussion, and strings—that is, between 25 and 30 players, of whom only 9 were not the quieter-playing strings. In 1926, twenty-one years later, the orchestra of Gershwin's *Oh, Kay!* at the Imperial (seating 1,650) consisted of 11 non-string instruments (plus strings) but no saxophones—the most difficult of all instruments to subdue. Kern's *Roberta* in 1933 (seven years later) at the New Amsterdam (seating 1,654) employed 10 non-strings (plus strings) and a cast of non-singers without amplification. In 1948 (fifteen years later) Porter in *Kiss Me, Kate* used 5 reeds (each playing saxophone and 1 or 2 other instruments), 2 horns, 3 trumpets, 1 trombone, percussion, harp, piano, guitar, and strings. Thus in a span of forty-three years, the 9 non-strings of *Mademoiselle Modiste* had grown to 15—more than half the size of the entire orchestra.

Rodgers in *The King and I* (1951) at the St. James (1,567 seats) employed 2 flutes, 3 clarinets, 1 oboe, 1 bassoon, 3 trumpets, 3 horns, 2 trombones, tuba, harp, 2 percussion, and strings—that is, 19 non-strings out of a total of about 33 players. Bernstein in *West Side Story* (1957) used: 5 reeds (saxophones and other woodwind "doubles"), 3 trumpets, 2 trombones, 2 percussions, guitar, piano, and strings—or 16 non-string players out of a total of about 30.

While these instrumental changes were taking place in the pit, the singers on the stage were moving in an opposite direction. Fritzi Scheff in 1905 scored a Broadway success in Victor

Herbert's *Mademoiselle Modiste*. The star had come to Broadway from the Metropolitan Opera, where she had sung in *I Pagliacci, La Bohème,* and other operas and had been audible in a theater several times larger than any on Broadway, and over an orchestra nearly four times the size of Herbert's. In *Naughty Marietta* five years later, Herbert used the Met's "Parsifal," Orville Harrold, and Emma Trentini, another refugee from opera; and Mary Ellis deserted opera for *Rose Marie* in 1924.

There have since from time to time been other illustrious operatic figures appearing on Broadway (Pinza in *South Pacific* [1949] and *Fanny* [1954] and Helen Traubel in *Pipe Dream* [1955]). Until recently the major singers employed in musical shows were large-voiced, hardy vocalists like Vivienne Segal, Dennis King, Howard Marsh, Robert Chisholm, Ray Middleton and—not least—Ethel Merman.

However, in the '40's, as musical books began to be more literate and the characters, more three-dimensional, acting became more important than singing. (A few exceptional singing-actors, notably Alfred Drake and John Raitt, were sufficiently accomplished dramatic performers to meet the new demands and were therefore continually employed.) Thus the balance began to shift. The orchestra had become louder—making use of heavier reeds (saxophones), more brass and percussion instruments, and virtuoso arrangements—and at the same time the solo singers became less vocal—first with respect to quality and then (as if to compensate for the deficiency) by the widespread adoption of new non-vocal singing styles.

The vocal ensemble also began to diminish in size and vocal quality. The initial decreases in size were usually due to rising union minimums; then the music itself began to require less vocal singing (in *West Side Story*, for instance, the ensemble contained only singing dancers); and in many recent shows ensemble singers have begun to resemble in style and quality the small-voiced, reedy principals. About this we will have more to say later.

Beginning in 1939, to prevent a total blackout of the new "soft" vocal stage by the new "hard" orchestra, microphones were introduced, and in a short time no musical was done without them. Electric amplification became a necessity even for such "vocal" performers as Ethel Merman and Alfred Drake. Six or seven microphones were spaced out evenly in the footlight troughs. Sometimes mikes were also hidden in scenery when singers had to perform at too great a distance from the fore-stage. For two decades this crude method of amplification suf-ficed. Nowadays, most principal singers wear transistor mikes strapped to their bodies under their costumes.

Sometimes the amplification is monitored. When Lena Horne played at the Imperial in *Jamaica* in 1957, a sound engineer stood at the back of the theater during performances and ma-nipulated controlling dials. As it happens, I myself conducted this particular show, having been called in to replace the origi-nal conductor, who was wrongly blamed for the orchestra's loudness. The orchestrations for Miss Horne's numbers had been done by her husband, the very able Lenny Hayton. It seemed instantly clear to me that a considerable improvement could be made by having the reed players use woodwinds in-stead of saxophones. Miss Horne, however, wanted the sound of saxophones. She was of course within her rights as an artist to have whatever made her most comfortable, but the problem of audibility could only be resolved electrically.

In *No Strings* (1962) Rodgers designed a musical requiring an orchestra of only brass, winds, and percussion playing be-hind the stage, *its* sound was piped into the theater engineered by *two* sound operators. The use of such a system was a fas-cinating experiment, and it happened to work for *No Strings*. But having the conductor remain invisible to the performers would be a limiting and even impossible practice in most other shows.*

This brings us to the one element in the theater that has not changed—the one that accounts for the conditions under which everyone working in musical theater, as well as every ticket holder, must suffer: the theater itself. The building, the rela-tionships of stage, orchestra pit, and auditorium remain pre-

---

* This method was again employed in *I Do! I Do!* (1966).

cisely as they were several centuries ago. The proportions have not been altered, and new acoustical problems have not been studied; nor, when a new theater has been built, have the people who must work in it been consulted.

Perhaps the most striking example of this non-communication is that of the Forrest Theatre in Philadelphia—completed before anyone discovered that it contained no dressing rooms! When I conducted *Goldilocks*, the first musical to be presented in the then-new Lunt-Fontanne Theater (1958), I was asked by producer Robert Whitehead to examine the orchestra pit prior to our pre-Broadway tour. I found that the new pit could seat no more than ten performing musicians, whereas the minimum number employed in any show is twenty-five! So in that almost completed theater, a row of seats bordering the pit had to be removed. The concrete floor had to be drilled out to make the additional space flush with the existing pit. Both ends of the pit had to be drilled out. The back brick wall under the stage had to be removed and replaced several feet farther back under the stage.

What distresses every person on stage and in the audience is the faulty balance between pit and stage. Many members of that unknowing public who buy seats in the first couple of rows in the orchestra, or the first couple of rows in the first and second balconies, write letters to producers or newspapers complaining that the orchestra is too loud. What really happens is that the sound spreads only for a row or two on the main floor, but goes straight up, as through a horn, to the edges of the balconies.

On the other hand, in most theaters the orchestra—especially to listeners who care for a complete sound (lows and highs and middles)—is nearly inaudible from about the eighth orchestra row to the back. In the Forty-Sixth Street Theatre, for example, the orchestra pit is so low that listeners on the main floor hear little more than the first trumpet, piccolo (which always penetrates), and drums. Nearly everything else is lost. Artistic orchestrators feel suicidal. Composers tend to resign themselves; their greatest fear is of antagonizing the critics by overshadowing the stage. The experienced producer usually pays no

159

attention to the complaining letters, having learned that they are inevitable and that circumstances which produce them are irremediable.

Most New York theaters today are very well maintained—especially that part which is visible to the audience. It is therefore difficult to believe that the present Imperial Theatre housed Youmans's *Mary Jane McKane* in 1923—thirty-three years ago. The following year it boasted *Rose Marie* with Dennis King and Mary Ellis, both of whom had big voices. The orchestrations by today's standards were small and primitive. And twenty-three years later, in 1946, Berlin's *Annie Get Your Gun* opened at the same Imperial Theatre. Not only did five saxophones and an extra trumpet make an enormous 'difference in the sound volume, but the style of scoring in *Annie*—the style of a raucous 1946 musical comedy (with the limitless voices of Ethel Merman and Ray Middleton easily rising above the din)—was several light-years beyond that of *Rose Marie*.

The Shubert housed the tiny *Maytime* in 1917, Harold Arlen's *Bloomer Girl* in 1944, and Jule Styne's *Bells Are Ringing* in 1956. A fifty-two-year-old house, the Shubert is still the pride of the "alley." The lighting equipment has been improved a number of times; the old seats have been replaced by new ones. At one time the pit was lowered disastrously about six feet, making coordination between stage and orchestra impossible and causing the accompaniment to all but disappear. The pit has now been nearly restored. Lights, seats, paint, new carpeting, etc., have all been considerably updated, but acoustics remain a matter of basic structure.

Once at the old Metropolitan Opera House I sat in a box at about the middle of the auditorium. An orchestra of some eighty musicians accompanied the singers without ever "covering" them. It seemed to me that the explanation for this lay in the vast empty air-space between the stage and the boxes and high-reaching balconies. The orchestra's sound could indeed rise straight up overhead without assailing a single listener, because seats (in the upper floors) began about twenty-eight rows in front of the stage.

The would-be Broadway acoustical "experts" invariably cite

the pit at the old Metropolitan, which was very low, as a model. They fail, however, to mention the fact that the Metropolitan pit extended out nearly sixteen feet in front of the stage, or to what would be about the sixth row in any theater. This placed the conductor so far from the stage (rather than immediately *under* it) that he was clearly visible to every stage performer and to everyone in the orchestra, which sat far enough away to see him without having to look heavenward.

Today's treatment of acoustical problems in the Broadway theater is a primitive patchwork. Since amplification is applied only to the singers, does this not create a dichotomy in sound quality between stage and pit? Does not the listener have to blend in his own ear a mechanical sound with a real one? While so crude a system may help the small-voiced singer to surmount the orchestral maelstrom, it does nothing (and means to do nothing) to alleviate the listener's burden of trying to accommodate himself comfortably to the big sound in acoustically live spots in a small theater.

If it is a fault to attempt to "mix" a mechanical quality with a real one—and I believe that it is—and if it is necessary for the singers to be amplified—which it certainly is—then it would seem to follow that the solution lies in amplifying both stage *and* orchestra. In this way the balance between them could be controlled, and they could be mixed together satisfactorily—something that is at least attempted today in television.

If, for instance, the orchestra were enclosed within a soundproof pit, the upper part of the conductor surrounded by a connecting glass bubble large enough to allow him to move, see the stage and be seen by the performers, it would be possible to channel the orchestral sound and mix it proportionately with the amplified voices. In this way, all sound would be of a unified quality and would emanate from speakers pointing in desirable directions. There would be no front-row problems, and never any interference with stage performers. The limited number of strings in the average pit orchestra could be amplified so that the existing imbalance between strings and the brass-reed-drum-heavy orchestra could be corrected. In such a setup the stage singing would be piped into the pit so that the players would have the opportunity to accompany—an impossibility if they were to hear only themselves. With this setup it would even be possible to revive earlier shows with their original orchestrations. This is never done in first-class revivals under today's conditions because the old sound (by our standards) seems too thin.

John S. Wilson, writing in *Theatre Arts* Magazine in 1962, pointed out two acoustical factors involving current-day theater which have long been familiar to me. One is the changing style of acting, which has led to such "intense" introspection that the vocal sound emitted is frequently "introspective" to the point of inaudibility. This same method eschews the study of voice and speech as injurious to the "reality" of performances. When things go this far—and they often do—nothing would seem to serve but a microphone attached to the soul!

A most unfortunate second factor concerns the general public, which in increasing numbers "participate" in their passive way in television performances. Prior to TV, the same people had radios. They also have records and phonographs. The users know that all of these media *can be controlled.* Hordes of people keep radios playing from breakfast to bed. Against this music and spiel, they telephone, talk with visitors, read, write, and even sleep—all of which means that they have become inured to whatever meaning sound conveys.

To the TV watchers, every word or sigh—important or trivial—is effortlessly comprehensible. The background or accompaniment to a vocalist is always safely engineered *under* speech and song. It never assails or interferes, and it doesn't seem to matter to anyone that an orchestra of ninety could as well be only a string quartet when the mixers finish giving the living-room potentates what is more comfortable but frequently less effective.

The effects of these media on live contemporary theater are unfortunate and real. They are unfortunate because the listener is a hundred times more accustomed to his home set, complete with dinner, beer, a reclining chair—and all at no extra cost—than to being inside a live theater. He is used to the one, harassed by the other, and unable to conceive of them as different. And he expressed his dissatisfaction in letters to the producer or the Sunday *Times*.

In addition, because the TV viewer has control of his set and knows full well that he can see and hear the program he has selected but cannot be seen or heard by the performer, he thoughtlessly brings these identical conditions with him on his infrequent journey to the live theater. As a result, he talks at will during the live performance, noisily opens a cellophane package of candy, and indulges in many other personal practices which annoy fellow members of the audience. He even reacts belligerently to critical glares and "sshs." The same person attending an opera becomes so thrilled at the sight of a real and elaborate stage set that he mindlessly applauds it regardless of the ongoing musical performance.

The TV viewers' failure to recognize desirable behavioral differences between home and public performances is, I fear, one sign of the changing times and mores. While this condition is new, theatrical architecture, at least in New York, has not been altered in any way.

One can only hope that theater owners will become increasingly aware of today's real problems and stop relying on hasty, expensive adjustments which will not resolve them. But the resolution—in whatever form it takes—must not be attempted without consulting the people who have worked as performers and know, from a practical point of view, the needs that no amount of theoretical and dogmatic folderol alone can take into account.

II. THE ENSEMBLE . . .
SIC TRANSIT GLORIA MUNDI

Of all the evolving elements in our musical theater, none has undergone so many and such radical changes as the group of girls and boys known as The Ensemble. In operetta days, it was a fair-sized gathering of strong-voiced singers. Their music taxed their vocal ranges. Since they were used at important dramatic moments, it was necessary for them to give out a powerful sound. Their number was very often in excess of fifty. And

163

as dancers were also required, a show would generally have a corps de ballet, featuring a male and female principal.

Around the turn of the century the ensemble for the newer musical comedy—in keeping with the simpler music—came to be a single group. The chorus was frequently not divided into parts—soprano, alto, tenor, and bass—but sang only in unison.

The nature of these musical shows made pulchritude the principal qualification for membership in the ensemble—with imaginable consequences to its vocal quality.

After beauty, this single ensemble had to fulfill a minimal requirement in both singing and dancing. The vocal ranges were not demanding, and the choreography consisted of simple steps and kicks which became standard season after season and were only too well known by everybody. This continued until the late '30's.

When *Pal Joey* was first produced in 1940, the ensemble consisted of seventeen girls and nine boys—all dancers (including Van Johnson, the movie star, and Stanley Donen, the movie director and producer). There were no singers as such. There was no part-singing.

Only three years later, with the production of *Oklahoma!*, all this was drastically changed. Agnes de Mille created exacting choreography for *Oklahoma!* which required well-trained dancers, and Jay Blackton, the musical director, made vocal arrangements in multiple parts. There were sixteen singers, and eighteen dancers. The ensemble was once again divided—as in the good old days of operetta—into two groups, and the performers had to be trained craftsmen.

In *South Pacific* (1949), the ensemble reverted to a single unit. For one thing, *South Pacific* had no real "dances" as such. No choreographer's name appears in the list of credits, although there was some "movement" that could be called dancing. Second, there was no part-singing. A single ensemble group, able to sing a bit and move a bit, sufficed. But with *The King and I* (1951) Rodgers and Hammerstein once again created a show requiring two separate units which oftentimes functioned together. Jerome Robbins created a notable and important ballet for this show, "The Small House of Uncle Thomas," which

164

required highly skilled dancers. Singing was also needed but—as in *South Pacific*—it was not divided nor was it complex. Some singers simply served to strengthen the vocal sound, which was nearly adequately created by dancers.

The same Jerome Robbins was responsible six years later for *West Side Story.* Here the dancing was of prime importance throughout, and while singing was necessary, the music required no vocal "quality" and was written for unison voices. This show employed *only* accomplished dancers who could also sing.

There is, inevitably, an economic side to the uses of the ensemble. Over the last decade, the minimum salary of an ensemble performer has risen 33% for the five-week rehearsal period and 50% for performances. While a producer can find excellent singers who are willing to work for minimum salary, good dancers are fewer and can, being in greater demand, usually get 20% or more above scale. An effective vocal ensemble consists of from twelve to eighteen singers (depending on the style of the show's music and the precise results desired). The size of the dance ensemble—also dependent upon the requirements of the show—can vary from about sixteen to twenty.* Supposing that we figure the smallest number of singers and dancers, *all* of them engaged at minimum scale: twenty-eight ensemble performers today would add more than $8,000 to the show's weekly budget. In addition, at least twenty-eight—and probably at least four times that many—costumes, which are astronomically expensive, would have to be made and serviced each week. All of this adds up to a major budgetary item (based only on minimum numbers and minimum salaries), one which has in recent years occasioned considerable rethinking in production planning.

This economic consideration has undoubtedly caused certain artistic changes; nevertheless, as it has necessitated a more sober kind of thinking and planning, it has largely resulted in artistic benefit. Let me explain. The hiring of singers for shows has often been a result of habit. One does a musical show; naturally there must be a vocal ensemble. If, however, this group, no

---

* In *Company,* there was a single dancer. In *A Little Night Music,* there is a "chorus" of five singers, and no dance ensemble.

matter how potentially effective, has little opportunity to function within the framework of the show, its engagement is wasteful.

Librettos—and directors—have been responsible for the current trend, which is to use dancers who can sing adequately but dance expertly, and then either reinforce ensemble singing with a few opulent voices (if necessary) or get enough vocally from the dancers themselves to satisfy the show's needs. The librettos have contributed to this practice in that the best of them more nearly resemble plays than spectacles—once the trademark of musicals. In a play, since we are involved principally with the problems of a few people, the action is usually limited in space and offers little opportunity to bring on a group of "merry villagers."

Many of the best directors have arrived at directing through careers that began with dancing, moved on to choreography, and culminated in directing. One need only mention the names of Jerome Robbins, Gower Champion, Bob Fosse, and Michael Kidd. Through the years these men have had considerable experience working alongside or with singers. They know what everyone in the theater knows, that *as a group* singers move awkwardly, speak the simplest lines as though they were declaiming a recitative in a Handel oratorio, and seldom remember (after direction) whether they should begin moving with their left or right foot! This is possibly attributable to their exclusive concern with production of "pear-shaped" tones.

Two other factors in the curtailment of singers should be mentioned. One of them concerns much of today's musical style. If the score of a show is "jazzy" or rock, nobody will want to hear edgeless, rounded—perhaps otherwise glorious—voices; sharpness of attack, rhythm, and what we have come to feel is a modern "flat" (unvibrated) sound are more appropriate. Most of today's shows will prefer non-singer singers to the other kind, and it therefore works best when highly skilled dancers are able also to contribute a vocal quality and a color that suits today's shows.

Further, I believe that much of the non-use of singing

choruses as such can still be attributed to a reaction against operettas. In these, "merry villagers" were an inevitable part of the production. Every opening number and every finale was designed to feature them. They sang well, and since that was what they were engaged to do, they more than fulfilled their obligation. They did not move. They were often more than a bit overweight and frequently less than juvenile. These facts, understood within the convention of the genre, were apparently not disturbing. Choruses always came in wholesale "lots." Their costumes were usually identical in design though occasionally varied in color. In the opening scene of *The Red Mill*, for example, perhaps sixteen girls were dressed as artists' models and sixteen men as "artists," with tams, palettes, etc. In *The Student Prince,* the men were uniformed university students replete with beer mugs. In *No, No, Nanette* the girls were identical flappers, each with an identically gay boyfriend. Even as late as *Brigadoon* in 1947, the ensemble were "merry villagers."

It is interesting to note that in all musical comedies prior to about 1935, few people were identified in the cast lists by name: in *Rose Marie* there were ten out of a cast of perhaps sixty; in *Naughty Marietta* there were twenty-one listed; in *The Desert Song* there were seventeen "principals" in a cast that included ninety-seven others!

In *Bells Are Ringing,* produced in 1956, twenty-nine names were in the cast. Out of this, fifteen were members of the ensemble—singing or dancing—and only twenty others filled out the total ensemble *without* character names. There were thirty-five names in the cast of *South Pacific* and only six other performers left unidentified. Out of a singing and dancing ensemble totalling thirty-six in *My Fair Lady,* only nineteen (about one half) were not named as characters in the cast. The entire cast of *West Side Story* numbered thirty-nine; *Man of La Mancha* contained twenty-four; *1776* employed twenty-seven. Every member of each played a part!

Because of the present-day movement away from "merry villagers" and toward individually identified characters, costumes are varied to help break the visual monotony, staging is "broken

167

up" to do away with the straight line or perfect half-moon surrounding the stage, and many ensemble people play small parts which are *named* in the cast list.

For one or another of a whole combination of reasons—artistic, economic, directorial, or psychological—the singing chorus, that once inhabited the musical theater by divine right, today totters, or is altogether obliterated from it. This is a matter of fact. If the elaborate ensemble were ever to find its way home again, it would be as the result of an honest, functional theatrical need for it. The chorus that held sway so long as convention was not questioned, and the cost was incidental. Now that convention has been examined and rejected: who needs it? The quality of the music, once requiring stentorian singing voices, has undergone a metamorphosis. The libretto says that every person on stage is an identifiable character with an acting function. The cost today of a singing chorus is high, in keeping with everything else. When a commodity is no longer essential, it begins to collect dust on any shelf.

III. OVERTURE

While the style, content, form, and originality of today's best musicals have continued to go forward, one aspect of the show has lagged deplorably behind. This is the overture. The general neglect of the overture is particularly regrettable, for the musical opportunities it affords are unlimited. It is, moreover, a form which boasts a long and superb tradition, but conditions in the contemporary theater have somehow arrested its development.

Nothing in grand opera—and perhaps little in all of music—can surpass the power, expressiveness, and perfection of form of the overture to Mozart's *Don Giovanni*. Here the composer created a masterpiece. We are told that this overture was written in exactly the way overtures are almost invariably written for our theater today: the night before the premiere. Nor does the similarity end here; for much of the overture's material was taken from a section of the opera itself—specifically, from its final act. Alas, however, the comparisons end here. What Mozart wrote was a formal piece with symphonic proportions and it became a profound work of art.

In Italian operas of the early 19th century, overtures came somewhat closer to those of current Broadway shows in that they usually consisted of entire "tunes" or arias strung loosely together. Offenbach and Sullivan often followed the same procedure, though Offenbach sometimes injected a drama into his developed preludes while Sullivan was usually content to offer quotations.

The Wagnerian music dramas contain developed preludes which stand by themselves in the symphonic repertoire. In these, Wagner, too, often not only quoted lengthy passages from the operas themselves, but also described his characters and elaborated on the motifs to create excitement about what was to come. Within many of Wagner's preludes, the drama which is to follow is presented almost completely in musical capsule.

Verdi often began with only a short introduction, as in *Il Trovatore* and in *Otello,* which opens with only a brief *agitato* to set up a raging storm; and in the same year, for *La Traviata,* he wrote a short mood piece (based on an aria) to introduce the opera, and a second version of the same material to open the final act.

The Puccini operas, being more purely theatrical than the earlier Italian models, also used "preludes" or orchestral introductions rather than extended overtures. The ominous chords that announce *Tosca,* the scurrying Oriental-type figures that introduce *Madame Butterfly,* the histrionic *scherzo* which takes up the curtain on *La Bohème* are a marked departure from the tradition which preceded Verdi and Puccini. In the same year which saw the debut of *Bohème,* Giordano produced *Andrea Chénier.* Here the act introductions are cut to a minimum: with the first notes of the orchestra, the curtain rises and the opera is in motion. Offenbach, on the other hand, in his overture to *Orpheus in the Underworld,* and Johann Strauss, in his overture to *Die Fledermaus,* like Mozart, created what are in their own ways masterpieces of the extended form. These examples—there are many others—are merely meant to sketch the vast range and variety of overture possibilities open to a composer, depending on his intention.

All of the music referred to above was composed for sizeable orchestras and for use in theaters where audiences normally *attend quietly* to whatever is presented. Unfortunately, however, the contemporary American musical theater provides neither of these conditions: the orchestras are about one-third to one-fourth the size, and audiences listen to nothing until the curtain has risen and stars have made their entrances.

The problems are rather like the proverbial chicken and the egg: it is impossible to know whether the dull overtures have bred audience inattention, or vice versa. I myself suspect that the audience behavior with respect to overtures is extra-musical and has by now become such a firmly rooted convention that it may never be wholly corrected.

The extra-musical factors I refer to are billing, lighting, and acoustics, and the first two are closely related. Seldom is a conductor commented on by a critic—let alone listed in the show credits accompanying the review—unless it is to say that the orchestra is too loud. Musical style, pacing, tempo, and ensemble work generally go unattended. And as they are ignored in print, conductor and orchestra are ignored further by the audience which, except on opening nights, rarely even bothers to note the conductor's name.

Customary theater-lighting practices contribute to the audience's lack of interest. On opening night, the auditorium lights may be dimmed before the conductor appears, and he is allowed to walk into a spotlight; the effect of this is to prepare attention. If, on the other hand, the auditorium lights are on when the conductor enters the pit, and the music commences without warning, audiences simply talk louder in order to be heard. In addition, Americans at the theater generally tend to feel that while songs may be intended for listening, orchestral music primarily serves as "background." In movies, for instance, this function of music is intentional. At home, when TV and radio are turned on, the listener is in control: he can turn the music off or down, talk over it, or ignore it altogether.

The third factor, acoustics, has been discussed in the preceding chapter. As we have pointed out, the twenty-five man orchestra minimum required by the Musicians' Union can only barely be seated in most pits. In shows by Rodgers and Loewe particularly, where the orchestra is extended often to thirty-three and thirty-four players, the pits have to be chosen carefully and sometimes enlarged. The orchestrations themselves are invariably discussed by composer-arranger-choreographer-conductor in advance of "freezing" the precise instrumentation. These discussions include: do we need one or two drummers (choreographers today feel that two are a bare essential); how many brass and reeds; do we use harp, guitar, piano. If we need six brass, five reeds, two percussion, piano, harp, and guitar, then we may use only nine more players to complete the minimum complement. We must have one double bass. The remaining eight players will constitute the poverty-stricken string section, divided into violins, violas, and cellos.

In today's lower pit, passages for four or five violins (it is most natural to write passages for violins alone in any symphony or opera, but then there are thirty to forty players) are inaudible especially in competition with conversation (which, of course, they must be). Flutes, clarinets, and bassoons are also easily outtalked. As a result, for purposes of audibility and attention, overtures are written to be especially loud. When a quiet passage occurs (the lips of brass players need *occasional* rest), the audience tends to resume its conversation, and the thread of the overture—such as it is—is lost and never regained.

Because of the lack of importance attached to them, overtures have not changed commensurately with the general musical-theater development. With few exceptions, most of them are merely "compiled" at the last minute and consist of a simple threading together of tunes in a programmatic way: fast-slow-fast, or loud-soft-loud. The compilation is then framed by a big introduction and a bigger ending.

The exceptions to this are few indeed. *Carousel* begins with a waltz suite during which the curtain opens to the pantomimed prologue. *The Most Happy Fella* has a thematic introduction which works similarly to the beginnings of the Puccini operas. *Candide* actually has an overture with a beginning, middle, and an end! *Fiddler on the Roof* employs only a single violin cadenza for the taking up of the curtain. An innovation is to be found at the beginning of Sondheim's *A Little Night Music*, which commences on the stage with an introductory ensemble number performed by a chorus of five singers who appear, costumed individually in evening attire at the start. What they sing is billed on the program as "Overture."

The vast majority of show overtures are potpourris of songs contained in the show. Once in a while, an arranger devises an especially effective one. The overtures to *Wonderful Town* and *Fanny* are examples of old theater practice executed unusually well.

At present, unlike as in opera, no theater composer orchestrates his own show. For one thing, the pressure of time during the rehearsal period does not permit it; the composer is of necessity occupied with other matters. This means more often than not that the arranger (with suggestions from the composer) has the job of laying out an overture that will include four or five of the show's songs literally transcribed for instruments. The choice of songs is generally based on a notion of which of them may prove to be "hits." They should be "plugged" for the sake of the show, the composer, the publisher, and the record companies. The selected tunes are then placed in a sequence which permits the greatest contrast.

In keeping with the lack of importance given to the overture in the overall production, it gets orchestrated only after everything else is finished. The job, then, has to be done in great haste. (Realistically, too, the show *can* go on with a temporary overture, but not without song accompaniments.) Also, as the overture represents a considerable expense in scoring and copying, producers are understandably concerned about the possibility that if it is written too early, it might contain song material which may be dropped from the show; they are also loath to spend money for rewriting. A temporary overture is therefore usually pasted hastily together, and before the show opens on Broadway, it is occasionally repented and rewritten.

There is small cause for wonder, then, that under the circumstances, a minimum of time, interest, creativity, and money should be spent on so unattended an element in today's shows. So long as nobody cares and nobody listens, why bother?

Pity.

IV. THE CRITIC AND THE PRODUCER IN THE CHANGING MUSICAL THEATER

Webster defines a critic as "one who expresses a reasoned opinion on any matter involving a judgment of its value, truth, or righteousness, an appreciation of its beauty or technique, or an interpretation." This definition contains no mention of how one becomes qualified to express such an opinion. In the New York *Sunday News* of September 5, 1965, that paper's drama critic, John Chapman, wrote: "In answer to a hypothetical question 'what are the requirements of being a drama critic?' I answer: 'Well, the main one is experience in going to the theater. One way of getting this start is paying for it at the box office. I often did.'" In some sense, then, every theatergoer is a critic.

What distinguishes critics from ordinary theatergoers is that, in the process of being exposed consistently over the years to all kinds of shows, they are obligated to form and articulate their opinions. Those are necessarily influenced by personal taste. However, since critics attend most productions over a period of many years, they are given the opportunity to achieve a broader frame of reference—a wider standard of comparison—than people who attend the theater sporadically. The fact that a critic cannot possibly become intimately versed in all of the technical problems of musical-theater craft does not, in my opinion, undermine his right to have a personal view which he then expresses personally.

The past few years have witnessed famous feuds between certain producers and critics. Each of these feuds has been occasioned by a piece of adverse criticism. It is an understandably frustrating experience for the producer who opens a new show when, for example, Walter Kerr (once with the New York *Herald Tribune*) writes favorably about his production, while Stanley Kauffmann (once with the more influential *New York Times*) writes adversely. Moreover, the adverse criticism comes near to causing the producer apoplexy when it turns out to be the *only* negative comment, all the other critics having reacted favorably. It seems to him then that, let us say, the *Times* critic is either a villain or a fool. The irate producer becomes threatening, abusive, and vociferous, and the resultant publicity has the effect of making the lone adverse reviewer more famous than he previously was.

Much of the current discussion about the "power of the critics" seems foolish. Certainly as regards the very best shows of the past forty years, critical opinion of the time almost unanimously concurred with the later judgment of history. Since the '20's, most of the shows which we have come to regard as our most lasting achievements were received without a serious dissenting critical voice and enjoyed excellent runs. These include *Show Boat, Oklahoma!, Carousel, Brigadoon, Annie Get Your Gun, Kiss Me, Kate, Guys and Dolls, The King and I, West Side Story, My Fair Lady,* and many others.

On the other hand, many shows managed to run successfully with little or no critical acclaim—the while suffering from an indisputable artistic poverty. Among these latter were *A Night in Paris* (335 performances), *Five O'Clock Girl* (280), *Good Boy* (253), *May Wine* (213), *Hellzapoppin'* (1404), *Leave It to Me* (307), *Sons O'Fun* (742), and others.

Still other shows received a preponderantly ecstatic press when in my opinion they were stereotypes. In this category are *The Music Man, Funny Girl, Skyscraper, Milk and Honey, Hello, Dolly!,* and *Mame.* Each of these had something to commend it—frequently an impressive star performance, or the genius of a virtuoso director; but on the whole, in these cases the critics' enthusiasm should have been regarded by quarrelsome producers as an unearned bonus.

Though the critics have had a record for having certified our best shows, they have often curtailed the lives of other shows which have had a real, but flawed, distinction. Criticism seems to lack the kind of language that would allow an expression of dissatisfaction with this or that very real shortcoming without at the same time damning the entire show. Particularly does this seem true of more artistically ambitious shows. The higher the

174

aspiration, the more difficult its perfect realization; and reviewers generally have proved their inability to communicate to the public that although they regard a show as imperfect, it ought nevertheless be seen for the unusual qualities it does possess. Unusual productions have been unable to survive for a length of time commensurate with their unique, though perhaps incomplete, values. Examples: *Candide, The Golden Apple, Lost in the Stars, Street Scene, Regina,* and *Anyone Can Whistle.* All of them had problems, but they were adventurous, arresting, and fresh. They were not given enough time and exposure to make the impression they deserved to make. The more venturesome theater public, given encouragement, would have supported these shows and come in varying degrees to treasure them.

It seems strange to us now to look back and consider shows that were once hailed by public and critics and reaped rich box-office harvests. Herbert's *The Country Girl* outlived by 64 performances his *Naughty Marietta,* with its distinguished score; George M. Cohan's *The Little Millionaire,* which ran for 192 performances, and *The Merry Malones,* which ran for 208; Rudolf Friml's *High Jinks* (213) and *Sometime* (283); Sigmund Romberg's *The Blue Paradise* (356) and *Maytime* (492); Jerome Kern's *Very Good Eddie* (341) and *Oh, Boy!* (463); George Gershwin's *Song of the Flame* (219); Vincent Youmans's *Wildflower* (477); Cole Porter's *Mexican Hayride* (481)—to name but a few. It is easy to explain many of the above successes, and others like them, by saying that times and tastes have changed. However, such a notion in no way accounts for the fact that these same writers in the same period wrote other shows which the passing of time has crowned with honor.

It is inevitable that, on some special occasions, the passage of time would make this or that even very understandable critical *faux pas* amusing. Certainly the history of music is filled with many such examples. The opening of *Show Boat,* on December 27, 1927, constitutes a very special one in American musical theater. The pre-Broadway tour of *Show Boat* had been so successful that the advance ticket sale in New York was enormous if not unparalleled. (It must be remembered that musical shows at that time enjoyed little genuine critical esteem, despite the fact that reviewers could nevertheless be enthusiastic about one musical or another by applying standards different from those used in measuring more "serious" theater.) On that night in December 1927 when *Show Boat* was to make history, the highly esteemed Philip Barry was also unveiling a new play, *Paris Bound*. The first-string critics attended the Barry play; it was their assistants who were left to rave about *Show Boat*. *Paris Bound* ran 234 performances (with favorable notices) while *Show Boat* initially ran 575. After a successful tour, it ran 181 performances in 1932, 418 in 1946, has had four more recent revivals in New York, was converted into a successful motion picture, and never in a single year goes unperformed somewhere in the United States.

If it can be said that standards of durability have not been fundamentally altered, there have been changes both in the critical approach to shows and in producers' practices in relation to the critics. And both of these changes have had a significant influence on the public and therefore on the theater itself.

In earlier times the best of the critics seem to have been beguiled first and foremost by the stars, the costumes, the scenery, and the dancing. The book was never taken seriously, the music and lyrics, seldom mentioned. Director and musical director were ignored. The cast and physical production occupied the primary place in reviews, while the creative aspects of a show were either only alluded to or passed over entirely.

When *Rose Marie* opened in 1924, Charles Belmont Davis, reviewing it in the New York *Herald Tribune,* failed to mention a single song; the songs are, of course, solely responsible for the fact that the show today remains popular throughout the United States. Mary Ellis, the female star, received Mr. Davis's most extensive consideration, including: "Even when she tried to follow the chorus girls in some simple dance steps and failed she was still appealing, at least to us she was." Later he added ". . . that long line of deep-chested, red-blooded chorus men in their uniforms with their ringing voices were a novelty and a delight." The play was definitely not the thing.

Nor did the drama critic of the New York *World* mention any songs, although he did take some cognizance of the book: "The production is one of those singularly rare subjects, a musical melodrama." Deems Taylor, the music critic, also writing in the *World*, commented: "Being good American comedy stuff, it is of course vastly more attractive and infinitely more sophisticated [sic!] and amusing than some of the more trying Italian operas in the Metropolitan's repertoire—*The Barber* and *William Tell*, for instance."

Exactly three months after *Rose Marie*, Gershwin's *Lady, Be Good* opened. The score, containing such celebrated songs as "So Am I," "Fascinating Rhythm," "Oh, Lady Be Good," and "The Man I Love," was scarcely mentioned by reviewers in the *New York Times, World,* or *American*. For these men the main attractions of the show were the charm of Adele Astaire and the comic ability of Walter Catlett. Of the book by Guy Bolton and Fred Thompson, the *Times* reviewer remarked that the show ". . . contained just enough story to call Miss Astaire on the stage at frequent intervals."

In 1925, Youmans's *No, No, Nanette* was a smash hit. Of the seven New York dailies whose reviews of the show I have read, all commented favorably on "Tea for Two" and "I Want to be Happy"—an attention to the music doubtless attributable to the fact that these songs had become well known *before* the show opened in New York. Mr. Davis, once more writing in the *Herald Tribune*, shed some light on criticism itself: "The laughter and the tears of an audience are the only critics—the only signs worth heeding." M. L. in the *Daily News* said: "The plot of *No, No, Nanette*—but why ask foolish questions?" On the other hand, the reviewer on the *Evening Post* remarked, "The piece has—strange to say—a plot which remains in sight."

Less than one week after the opening of *No, No, Nanette*, Rudolf Friml's operetta *The Vagabond King* was given its premiere. The reviews of the time were highly enthusiastic; they were also—even in the perspective of more than forty years later—rather accurate, emphasizing the virtues of the score, on which whatever has survived depends.

It is also interesting to note some of the critical response to the comedy material of those days. As I remarked earlier, musical-theater comedy used to consist largely of topical material or interpolated jokes, and its datedness, therefore, is the chief cause of its unfunniness today. The truth, however, is that it did not fare much better among its contemporaries. The critic on the *World* once remarked: "The comedian [was] as amusing as possible under the circumstances."

Roughly one year after *The Vagabond King,* Romberg's *The Desert Song* opened. This show is more enduring today than *The Vagabond King* but ran 40 performances fewer in its initial stand. *The Desert Song* was also unanimously approved, but this time it was the music that received the most critical attention. The *Sun,* however, reported that *The Desert Song* "is no ordinary operetta hung on a pleasant thread of story. . . ." and ". . . . the songs gave little promise of general approval as played in free or ballad rhythm, but 'One Alone' and 'I Want a Kiss' (one of the weak songs of this unusually rich score) may yet become time-worn."

Richard Watts, Jr. wrote in the *Herald Tribune:* "The question of how simple-minded the book of a musical comedy can be was debated on the stage of the Casino last night and the verdict arrived at was 'no end.' " Of the score, Mr. Watts added that "though never violently original or strikingly distinguished, [it] yet manages to be generally tuneful and effective. . . ." And of the leading comedian he said, "He was not greatly aided in his work last night by the authors."

A month earlier, Gershwin's *Oh, Kay!* had been presented. Nearly all the reviews dealt first and mainly with Gertrude Lawrence, but they also carried favorable comment on the show. Stephen Rathburn's piece in the *Sun* quoted from the show, "Never criticize a bootlegger's English if his Scotch is all right," and commented, unfortunately: "But much of the humor was not as good as that example." Rathburn also observed that "the person who designed the unusually attractive costumes for the chorus deserves to have his or her name printed on the program."

A Mr. J. Brooks Atkinson wrote the review in the *Times* and made one of the earliest references I have found anywhere to the staging of a show. He labeled Bolton and Wodehouse's book "serviceable" and Gershwin's score "rich." He called the comedy writing "as scurvy a lot of bad puns as ever scuttled a rum-runner." Of Victor Moore he wrote that he "totters languidly through a long roulade of indiscriminate comedy, unseemly impertinence and a constant rattle of amusing 'gags.' " Mr. Atkinson also possessed the perspicacity to name in admiration all of the marvelous and enduring songs in the score.

Thus far, I have been at some pain to demonstrate several points relating to critics of musical shows of our past—the shows which time tells us are our native "classics." In a general sense, these "big" shows, *Rose Marie* and *Lady, Be Good* in 1924, *No, No, Nanette* and *The Vagabond King* in 1925, and *The Desert Song* and *Oh, Kay!* in 1926, are representative of a most important era in the American musical theater, for in these works the style of native musical theater was being crystallized.

The critics of the period greeted all of these shows with only minor reservations. While at first they were primarily concerned with stars and tinsel, eventually their reviews came to give primary attention to the scores, then to the books, lyrics, and productions—and lastly to the players (with the exceptions of *Rose Marie,* in which enthusiasm for Mary Ellis got so out of hand that no songs were even mentioned, and *Lady, Be Good,* in which Adele Astaire's appearance precluded any consideration of the show itself).

The reviewers as a whole did not approve of the librettos but found so many attractive qualities in the productions that the shortcomings of the books were taken as almost incidental to the otherwise happy occasions. But the fact that there *was* general discontent with the books seems now to have been a clear harbinger of things to come.

To be sure, among the reviews one finds quite a lot of shocking ignorance, as well as much silly writing. For instance, Alan Dale, in the *American,* made the following observation: "Anything quaintly orchestrated can be exquisite." And, "Personally orchestrations 'obsess' me, I seldom find any worthwhile." Of *No, No, Nanette* he said: "Bless your heart, I can't say any more, can I? If I announced that *No, No, Nanette* was not worth waiting for as long as we waited, you'd say 'the grapes are sour,' or something acidulated of that ilk." Of *Oh, Kay!:* "Always the artist, always delightful, humorous, piquant, and other adjectives of equal import, Miss [Gertrude] Lawrence scarcely lent herself to the constant interruptions of chorus, funny men, plot, and the other accessories of the unchanging entertainment 'with music.' " Of *Lady, Be Good,* he remarked that the music was "redeemed from the usual by the *orchestrations* of George Gershwin. His ditties are not extraordinary, but his orchestration is masterly" (italics mine). Of course Gershwin did not orchestrate *Lady, Be Good,* and the "ditties" *are* "masterly" in musical-theater history. Then there was Charles Belmont Davis in the *Herald Tribune:* "To us Miss Groody seems to fairly exclude [sic!] virtue from every pore. When her golden slipper is poised at the highest point above her head we cannot down the thought that it should be resting on the rocker of a cradle."

Still it would be absurd after forty years to quarrel with the judgments of the critics—even the silly ones. They usually put their approval on the best products of the period and often succeeded in singling out that part of the whole which was the most important. That the critics in this period made any contribution to the theater by the astuteness of their analyses is not the case, but neither did they damage it with the rejection of its newer trends.

They were also able to achieve in their reviews that kind of natural balance which made it possible for them, despite their complaints, to communicate to the public the experience of pleasure or enjoyment. Take the example of *Lady, Be Good:* within one article, which pointed out that the book was nonexistent, the comedy was poor, and a principal singer hadn't much voice, the reader was still persuaded convincingly that the show was enjoyable! Surely we would agree today that Gershwin's *Lady, Be Good* was an event in history. It marked the first collaboration of the two Gershwin brothers. It had the Astaires, Walter Catlett (considered by many the funniest comedian of his time), and Cliff Edwards *plus* his ukelele.

The crucial factor in creating the role of the critic today has been the producers. The producers of the mid-'20's were different: they had all been born into, or very early apprenticed to, the theater. Today's producers chiefly are businessmen who learn by experience if they survive long enough. Lew Fields, who presented the early Rodgers and Hart *The Girl Friend* and *Peggy Ann* (both with books by his son, Herbert) had spent a lifetime as a celebrated performer in the team of Weber and Fields. He had been a theater owner and operator as well as a performing artist before he turned producer. In 1927 Fields produced *Hit the Deck* and *Connecticut Yankee,* also with books by his son. H. H. Frazee, who produced *No, No, Nanette,* had been an advance theatrical agent, produced his first show at twenty-two, and built theaters (including the Cort in Chicago and the Lyceum in New York). Russell Janney, a Yale graduate, had had various theater jobs as a young man. His first production was in 1908 at the age of twenty-four. As a result of financial reverses, he took jobs from time to time in a number of different theatrical enterprises: publicist for Beerbohm Tree, founder of the Russell Janney Players, publicist for Theda Bara at 20th Century Fox, advance man for George Arliss and Laurette Taylor, etc. Then in 1924 he produced his first major show, *The Vagabond King,* which was an enormous hit. Arthur Hammerstein, the son of Oscar Hammerstein I, grew up in a theatrical environment. He was involved in "construction and decoration," managed his father's grand-opera interests, produced opera himself, and in 1910, began a Broadway producing career with Herbert's *Naughty Marietta,* followed by Friml's *The Firefly* (1912) reaching a climax with *Rose Marie* in 1924. Vinton Freedley (who co-produced with Alex Aarons) was a graduate in law from Harvard and the University of Pennsylvania, after which he spent five years acting in stock and road companies. His association with Aarons began in 1924, with Gershwin's *Lady, Be Good.* Schwab and Mandel, who also teamed together as producers, served apprenticeships as critics and then became playwrights.

These men, and others like them, had worked in the theater as novices, had learned through experience what they needed to know, and had finally become producers, having already been baptized in and dedicated to the Unholy Temple.

The producer of today is almost invariably a businessman first. David Merrick, the most prolific of present-day entrepreneurs, began life as a lawyer, served a one-man apprenticeship as general manager for Herman Shumlin, then launched a theatrical career for himself which has been unequalled, in respect at least to quantity of productions, by any other producer in history: in the course of eleven years (1954 to 1965), Merrick presented fifty shows. From the start, he set himself the task of learning his new trade in his own way. He accepted as little as possible from prior practice, and constantly questioned the desirability of following old procedures just because everybody else had followed them. From time to time, he employed exploitation methods that would have put P. T. Barnum to shame; he has often found ways and means of curtailing scenic and costume costs; he has on occasion denied certain critics admittance to a new show; he has often stood up successfully against certain union practices which he felt were unfair. Over many years, he retained a kind of permanent staff of stagehands, electricians, carpenters, office workers, etc. He often fired people in key positions within his organization and then rehired them. All of his practices are unpredictable, personal, unique, and often produce successful and distinguished shows.

Moreover, forty years ago producers constituted a small circle of men. Today each new season turns up new and different producers—few of whom are able to survive the hardships of inexperience, poor judgment, and the increasing difficulties of financing expensive new shows. And the competition is keen: fewer than half of the theaters operating forty years ago are presently standing or available for legitimate shows. Whether the producer is himself chiefly a businessman or simply in competition with other businessmen, today the *business* of theater has to be judiciously handled or there will be no show at all.

This change in the character and origins of producers took place during a period which also witnessed a changing position for the theater critic, and the relation between these two developments is not an accidental one. It is my belief that the new breed of producers was directly responsible for the present power and position of the contemporary critics.

For it is a fact that nowadays a bad press means no run for a new show, a mixed reception usually means a short run, and a favorable set of notices generally produces a long run. When and how and why did this happen? What have the new "business" producers to do with it? What, if any, are the exceptions—the long runs that take place in the teeth of bad reviews? *

Generally a show which enjoys a long run despite adverse or tepid reviews features a star whose reputation is so powerful—whose audience is so oblivious to the opinions of critics and so large and so faithful to the star—that failure is impossible. This kind of success is possible today only with stars and/or recordings. A *theater* star as such is no longer a star in the box-office sense without a highly regarded show. Mary Martin in *Jenny* (a bad press) lasted only ten weeks. Bert Lahr in *Foxy* (a bad press) lasted about nine weeks. Alfred Drake in *Kean* (a bad press) lasted about eleven weeks. This also works in reverse. When Rosalind Russell left a smash hit, *Wonderful Town,* after a capacity fourteen months, she was replaced by Carol Channing. In spite of Carol Channing's excellent performance, it was clear to the world that THE STAR had left; attendance dwindled through about twelve more weeks in New York. The same Carol Channing opened the following year in an inadequate new musical, *The Vamp,* which, owing to adverse criticism of the show itself, had a short run; but when she returned to Broadway nine years later in *Hello, Dolly!,* both she and the show were given rave reviews, and Channing became the big new Broadway star.

One of the important questions to be answered about the power of criticism is that of the relationship between the new-style "businessmen-producers" and the enormous new influence of the critics.

About sixty years ago, producers began to use favorable quotations culled from the reviews in their advertisements. At first, these were small quotes in small ads. Little by little, these ads grew—until, as at the present time, it became a usual thing to find in the *Times* a full-page ad consisting of excerpts from all quotable reviews. Short quoted phrases appear in lights on the-

---

* Most recently, a favorable press cannot be relied on to assure a long run.

ater marquees, and longer excerpts are reproduced on full-size sign boards in front of the theater and on large billboards, not only in New York but in cities and airports throughout the United States. These practices have become so widespread and are so much a part of the public's expectation ("we'll wait and see") that it is necessary now for all producers to follow the procedure or be unable to compete successfully.

The producers themselves have made the critics famous. It is they who have said, in effect: "Look at Atkinson's rave"—or Kerr's, or anybody else's. The feuds between the producers (who have received adverse notices) and the damning critics have led to newspaper and magazine articles, TV and radio debates, and all sorts of attendant publicity. And the net result, particularly over the last ten years, has been the enhancement of the importance of men who once upon a time were merely people doing the work for which they had been hired. If certain producers indeed regard certain critics as monsters, it is they themselves who have created the Golem that threatens them.

Another, and a more fundamental, factor in the current power of the critics is economics. Since the price of theater tickets has more than doubled during the past fifteen years, and since virtually everyone in the United States has access to a TV set, the average theatergoer will wait before spending his $30.00 (or more) for a pair of seats until he has had reasonable assurance from the critics that his time, trouble, and money will be well spent.

Today's high ticket prices are not the result of the whimsical impositions of producers but are necessitated by the sharp rise in production costs. A musical show today often costs $1,000,000 as compared with perhaps $80,000 thirty years ago. The operating budget has more than trebled during the same period. Producers—under strict legal surveillance—can collect *no* profit until all of the backers have been reimbursed, and this recouping of so large an investment is usually impossible unless the show receives a great press and has a near-capacity audience for nearly two years.

The critics, then, do now exercise a life-and-death power over most productions. But this power is no more an arbitrary thing

184

than the price of tickets. If the critics can kill a show, their reasons can more often than not be laid to the poverty of the show itself. And the show's failure must also be laid to the producer, who may in the first place have been mistaken in his assessment of its value or in his choice of director and/or star. The late George Jean Nathan once said that he had never read a script that he felt had genuine merit which remained unproduced. I find Nathan's observation just as valid for the musical theater today.

Of the shows selected for study in this book, *all* received superb reviews, *all* drew audiences which paid off their investments, and all continue to flourish in community theaters.

On the other hand, in my opinion, most current musical-theater failures deserve their fate. Sometimes even the best writers and composers can go astray. Only twice in my own experience have there been really good shows which were so new to their time that in one way or another they were treated with less than complete enthusiasm. These were *Pal Joey* and *Porgy and Bess*. However, even in these cases, their revivals (*Pal Joey,* eleven years after the original production, and *Porgy and Bess,* seven years later) were received warmly by press and public.

So basically new a show as *West Side Story*—which many people had feared in advance would be "caviar to the general"— was called by Brooks Atkinson in the *Times:* ". . . one of those occasions when theater people, engrossed in an original project, are all in top form."

Most of the rest of the press followed suit:

The *Mirror*'s headline (Robert Coleman): *"West Side Story* a Sensational Hit!"

Journal-American's headline (John McClain): "Music Magnificent in Overwhelming Hit."

New York World-Telegram and Sun's headline (Frank Aston): "Love and Hate Make Beauty."

Daily News's headline (John Chapman): *"West Side Story* a Splendid and Super-Modern Musical Drama."

Only Walter Kerr (*Herald Tribune*) felt that the show was "almost never emotionally affecting."

West Side Story through the intervening years has been a success in theaters the world over, in motion pictures, for record companies, and for publishers—of books, sheet music, and musical scores. Walter Kerr's difference of opinion, honest as it was, in no way dimmed the public's ardor. The other reviewers' enthusiasm undoubtedly helped the project to get off the ground at the outset. But the fact remains that *West Side Story* is built on a compelling idea, has a dramatic book fashioned from *Romeo and Juliet*, has fresh lyrics and music, and was excitingly conceived and staged. Its great success—like that of *Rose Marie* at a time when critics had no power (or, for that matter, of *My Fair Lady, Oklahoma!, Carousel, Guys and Dolls, Kiss Me, Kate, South Pacific, The King and I, Annie Get Your Gun, Brigadoon*, and ultimately *Pal Joey*—at a time when critics did)—was in the end the result of superb creativity.

I do not know a single work of *unqualified* distinction that (contrary to the views of many producers) was not acclaimed by the critics. On the other hand, it is a too-simple matter to list a number of successes—successes by critical and (at the time) audience choice—which are best forgotten in yesterday's light drizzle.

V. THE PRE-BROADWAY TOUR

The future of almost any show on Broadway is fairly predictable the morning after its opening. Occasionally, some special circumstance may alter the prediction. Let us take the case of a hypothetical show, which we shall call *Magna*. If *Magna* has a star who is currently popular in motion pictures, TV, or recordings, it will have a large advance sale. Consequently, a poor reception from the critics will not have any immediate ill effect on the show's run. Sometimes a show's composer-lyricist team becomes its "star." When *Camelot* was announced, the fact that its authors, Alan Jay Lerner and Frederick Loewe, had previously written *My Fair Lady* brought the new production a tremendous advance sale. The presence of Richard Burton,

Julie Andrews, and Robert Goulet in the cast—though they were less famous then than now—also did not harm, and thus the tepid critical response to *Camelot* had little effect.

Without some sort of star image, however, the show's future existence is 99% dependent on the critics. This proposition must be further broken down. The *New York Times* and the New York *Daily News* have between them a majority of the city's newspaper audience; furthermore, each of them represents a different and diametrically opposite class of theatergoers. If these two papers publish adverse reviews of *Magna*—regardless of what the other critics say—there is little likelihood that all the king's men can put *Magna* together again—or at least for very long.

One other thing might save the show in the face of an unfriendly press: if its cost of operation is low, if there is enough favorable quotable material in the reviews, and if its subject matter is attractive enough to appeal to the mass appetite, a resolute producer with money may (and often does) launch an expensive advertising and publicity campaign in newspapers, radio, and TV which may eventually pay off. Sometimes, too, a big hit song can go a long way toward giving successful first aid.

In any case, the day after *Magna*'s opening in New York is a momentous one for all concerned. If things have turned out well, there will be a long local run followed by successful tours for this company or several companies running simultaneously in Chicago, the West Coast, London, and other places. There will be a movie sale. There will be secondary rights: release of *Magna* for productions in thousands of professional summer theaters, stock companies, amateur or semiprofessional community theaters, colleges, high schools, etc., which, in the course of many years, produce annual incomes totaling millions of dollars.* All these in turn spark recordings and vocal score, book

* According to *Variety*, as quoted by Alvin Toffler in *The Culture Consumers*, there are 5,000 non-professional theater groups in the United States, plus about the same number of college theaters, and perhaps 15,000 more groups in clubs, churches, and schools, and perhaps 500,000 amateur productions which run up an attendance of about one hundred million each year.

and sheet music sales, and bring in additional revenues from performing-rights societies (ASCAP or BMI) for radio and TV licensing of songs from the show or for a TV production of the entire show. That morning after *Magna*'s opening, the possibilities of very high stakes are to be determined.

In an effort to prepare new shows well for their fateful Broadway reception, producers for many years have been taking them on a pre-Broadway tour. Before this tour, the show has been rehearsed in studios and/or bare theaters in New York for four weeks, then rehearsed with scenery, costumes, props, lights, and orchestra out of town—Boston, New Haven, Philadelphia are the most usual locations—for a week. Normally there are a couple of previews to accustom the newly-brought-in stagehands and musicians to the running order, and the actors to the reactions of an audience. After the previews there is the out-of-town opening. Let us say that *Magna* opens in Boston. The morning after the opening, reviews will appear in five daily papers. There will be a *Variety* review during the week and newspaper essays on the following Sunday.

During *Magna*'s three-week run in Boston, the company rehearses every day. On Sunday—the only day when there is no performance—rehearsals last ten hours. After every performance the authors, director, producer, choreographer, musical director, and sometimes the stars, visiting agents—and often some outside director or author called in for advice—meet together for many hours to dissect the current state of *Magna*. There will be arguments, accusations, and threats; every detail of the production will be analyzed microscopically, berated, defended; perhaps the gathering will reach enough of a consensus to warrant some new trial action.

The discussions at such meetings center around three factors: the attitude of the Boston press, the reaction of the Boston audience, and the personal assessments of those present. All these factors weigh in deciding what to do or not to do in the future. For example, it is the consensus that the librettist needs to cut the length of several scenes, rewrite two others, strengthen the dramatic tension of the first-act finale, and perhaps cut out a character altogether. It will be found that one song does not work with the audience, that none of the critics mentioned another, that the star needs a comedy song near the end of the show. It may be agreed that one of *Magna*'s principals is incorrectly cast and must be replaced. Two orchestrations are found to be too "busy" or noisy for the singers. The dance numbers invariably need trimming. One set is too drab and needs repainting. A set of chorus costumes is too inflexible for dancing. The lighting—oh, the lighting!—well, a musical comedy should not be played in the dark.

The discussions go on endlessly night after night. Work is done immediately—often all night—on the agreed-to changes. At each day's rehearsal the performers are likely to be given dialogue and music cuts plus a few pages of new material which must be rehearsed, then memorized so they can be tried out during that evening's performance. New songs are rehearsed, orchestrated, and tried out. Some first-act songs go into Act II, and vice versa. Dances are shortened, costumes changed, lighting reset, running order of scenes altered.

By no means will all of these changes be permanent. Some of them will stand for one or two performances and then be altered again. Backstage and onstage, confusion is enormous, with everyone becoming increasingly fatigued and irritable.

After three interminable weeks in Boston, *Magna* now moves to Philadelphia. A new orchestra and new stagehands are rehearsed. Again there is an opening. Again there are reviews the morning after, though only three this time. Again there are meetings, now concerned with the reactions of Philadelphia's critics and audiences, both of which groups may be at wide variance with their brethren in Boston. Revisions continue on an almost daily basis, but because of too many faulty trials and the growing awareness of New York only just around the corner, hysteria is a frequent guest. After two more weeks, *Magna* entrains for New York, where still a third set of musicians and stagehands are rehearsed. Again a few previews help acquaint new personnel with the show and accustom the now edgy cast to new acoustics and new stage and auditorium dimensions. Then comes the opening which will determine *Magna*'s future.

This, in brief, is the routine—presented without many of the inside stories of blood and tears from the beginning of rehearsals to *the* opening night.

It would be interesting here to appraise the effects of pre-Broadway tours on certain particular musical shows. I have picked ten, which will be designated by letters. The one effect all ten suffered in common—though the shows subsequently came to different ends—was a substantial pre-Broadway loss of money *in addition* to the initial production costs:

"A"—which was eventually a flop in New York—had mixed notices in Philadelphia; it had a star, but lost $26,000 during three weeks.

"B" was also a flop—before and on Broadway. It had no major star and lost $67,000 during four weeks in Philadelphia.

"C," which ultimately ran ten weeks in New York, spent six weeks between Detroit and Toronto, changed directors in midstream, and lost $18,000.

"A," "B," and "C" were all total losses in the end—almost half a million dollars each.

"D" was a very heavy musical which also had a star. It was a success everywhere, including Broadway, but its seven weeks in Boston and Philadelphia lost $32,000.

"E" was a great success everywhere. It also had a star and did sellout business for four weeks in Philadelphia but spent $3,000 more than it earned—and at capacity.

"F" had a modest New York success (little interest afterward on the road) and lost $21,122 during four weeks out of town.

"G," one of the biggest hits, made a profit of only $4,655 in seven weeks during which little was changed in the show.

"H" was a flop in New York, but had a star who has a particularly adoring out-of-town public. In five weeks it earned a profit of $14,500 all of which—and more—it lost in New York.

"I" lost in three weeks $54,500 (in addition to production costs) and was not brought into New York at all.

"J" played nine weeks in three stands before Broadway. It received poor notices on its tour as well as on Broadway. It lost $83,000 in tryout (in addition to all production costs) and despite much tinkering, was never satisfactory.

The cost of transporting the scenery, costumes, lights, and personnel (about 100 people to each place and back to New York); the cost of hauling, hanging, taking down, rehauling, reshipping, and rehanging, etc., of scenery; hanging, focusing, and re-focusing of lights; advertising in each place; per diems averaging about $40 (for every day of seven weeks) to roughly twenty people: producer(s), company manager, press agent(s), orchestrator(s), copyist(s), composer, lyricist, author(s), scene designer, costume designer, director, choreographer, musical director, stars and various assistants and secretaries whose contracts so stipulate—plus the enormous costs of making out-of-town revisions—all add up, even for successful shows, to a loss. This loss, I emphasize again, is over and above the original investment in scenery, costumes, rehearsals, orchestration, copying, etc.

Many of the costs, to be sure, apply to all touring shows, even those post-Broadway tours of hit shows that bring great profits. There are two important differences, however, between pre- and post-Broadway tours. The post-Broadway tour comes to audiences prepared, by word of mouth and publicity, to rush to see the show; a successful show usually plays to enthusiastic capacity audiences everywhere. And second, in a tryout, there are the extra high expenses of revision: the cost of new orchestrations (with resultant extra orchestra rehearsals) and copying, new scene painting, transportation and alteration of new costumes—all done at the sharply increased scales that craftsmen operating away from New York City command.

But financial loss entailed in the pre-Broadway tour is by no means the greatest problem it creates for the life of a show (and if the show becomes a hit, this loss becomes a minor detail). In addition to the strain (fatigue and discontent) placed on the show's personnel en route to Broadway, there are the effects of the out-of-town reviews and the reactions of audiences—both of which are often at odds with the reception the show will be accorded in New York. Whether out-of-town audiences react favorably or unfavorably is beside the point. In either case, the response can wreak havoc with the future of a new show by misleading the producer, authors, and directors and by confusing the basis for their decisions. To change, or not to change. . . .

The purpose of a pre-Broadway tour is to gain time and experience before the Broadway opening. The show as an entity is to be tested: to see how it works, what there is in it that does not work, what needs cutting or rewriting, substituting, trimming, redirecting, re-orchestrating, re-choreographing, re-designing, and recasting. This takes time. After the Broadway opening major revisions are given no opportunity to produce any major effect on critics or audience. 'Pre-opening performances, whether in or out of New York, are for the purpose of being allowed time—which is the opportunity to work.

But the out-of-town tour actually works *against* time. Suppose *Magna* plays three weeks each in Boston and Philadelphia, then has two New York previews before opening. At the end of the Boston run—a Saturday night—the show closes and moves to Philadelphia. On that Sunday morning, the company entrains and arrives in Philadelphia perhaps about 6:00 P.M. A rehearsal call before 8:00 P.M. is not permissible and is usually omitted because of cast fatigue and lack of adjustment to a new city. Had the move not taken place, the company would have had *ten* hours of work—an important bonus.

The following day—Monday—the theater is a noisy madhouse with hanging scenery, focusing and hanging lights, carrying in costumes and props, etc. The company is having a rehearsal in some hotel ballroom. Having played the show for three weeks with costumes, orchestra, scenery, lights, and an audience, this kind of rehearsal is a letdown. It can seldom be used to achieve performance level. More often it permits the director to give notes, make cuts, and distribute new speeches or scenes.

While this sort of day can have its small uses, much of the time is wasted. People are treading water. The feeling of the company members is diffused. We're in a new town, in a strange hall. How's your hotel? Mine stinks! Think we can go to a movie tonight? (There is usually no Monday performance in the first week in a new city. The stage is not yet completely set up.) Why does he insist on rehearsing this scene? I get confused here out of the set, etc.

The next day, Tuesday (usually the day of the new opening), the company is called to the theater in the afternoon. The vast beehive of activity on stage has gone on most of the night and is still not completed. The company is waiting so that there can be even a two-hour rehearsal on stage when the setup has been completed. *This* rehearsal is essential solely *because* of the move. The cast must try the new acoustics, sing with the new orchestra, and allow the new stagehands to practice scene changing. The rehearsal is not for the cast (except for acoustical testing) but for the new personnel, who will once again be obsolete in three weeks.

The day after opening is Wednesday, when there will probably be a matinee, and so no rehearsals will take place before Thursday at 11:00 or 12:00 A.M.

To total this: because of the Boston-to-Philadelphia move, there will have been some token rehearsals adding up to a potential *maximum* of eleven hours after the Friday rehearsal in Boston and until the Thursday one in Philadelphia! Without the move, there would have been twenty concentrated hours.

This same schedule interruption recurs when the company departs from Philadelphia for New York. During the six-weeks-plus-two-days prior to the first New York preview, there may be a total of 146 rehearsal hours. Had the show remained in New York and played six weeks of previews, the company could have rehearsed 180 hours—an important difference to everyone involved in the project. These out-of-town moves lose rather than gain time—undermining the chief purpose of all pre-opening activity.

Another purpose of the tryout is to provide the performers with experience: opportunity to grow in their roles, to further their "ensemble" relationship with other performers, to become accustomed to the many physical problems they necessarily encounter—quick costume changes, difficult entrances and exits in relation to scenery, etc.—and accustomed to working with the orchestra, and to feel out audience reaction.

193

It is my belief, however, that time and experience—both of them of incalculable benefit—can far better be gained by staying in New York City. In the best shows of the fairly recent past, very little was accomplished by their out-of-town runs. *Oklahoma!*, for instance, first opened in Boston—under the title of *Away We Go!* Elliot Norton, powerful critic of the Boston *Post*, found fault only with its length. (As did Cyrus Durgin of the *Globe* and Elinor Hughes of the *Herald*. The show was subsequently shortened, but excessive length is a common fault of all new shows at their first opening.) Everyone raved about the music, lyrics, and dancing. The critic on the *Christian Science Monitor* liked the show but remarked that it "contains too much rural humor and homely sentiment." He also gave his highest praise, among a cast which included Alfred Drake, Celeste Holm, Howard da Silva, and Lee Dixon, to Joseph Buloff in the subsidiary role of Ali Hakim, the Peddler! He objected to the death of Jud near the end of the show and commented, "It is true that a tragic note was struck in *Yeomen of the Guard*, but *Yeomen of the Guard* is not musical comedy and Mr. Rodgers is not Sir Arthur Sullivan." The same critic also wrote, "The best song in the show is a satiric duet called 'Pore Jud Is Daid.' " Fortunately in this case—but it is not always so—these opinions had no effect on the show.

The reception of *Porgy and Bess* in Boston was almost identical to that given subsequently in New York. Elinor Hughes liked it but was puzzled by the translation of the play to opera: "Does it gain enough through amplification of sound and fury to compensate for what it loses in realism?" Edwin F. Melvin in the Boston *Evening Transcript* was favorable. No suggestions were made, no real criticisms offered, and no real enthusiasm felt.

On the other hand, *South Pacific* elicited raves from both Norton and Hughes—the two most influential of Boston's reviewers at that time. Norton's only two minor reservations, in an unusually long and rhapsodic notice, were complaints of length (usual, usually justified, and usually corrected) and the show's not taking "even fuller advantage" of Pinza's voice. *My Fair Lady* was received ecstatically in both Philadelphia and Boston.

No show ever opened to a more perfect press. Sensenderfer in the Philadelphia *Evening Bulletin* observed, ". . . and lyrics by Alan Jay Lerner . . . actually enhance in rhymes Shaw's own barbed arrows." Frank Loesser's opera, *The Most Happy Fella,* also enjoyed marvelous receptions both in Boston and Philadelphia.

Thus we can see that the best shows have only needed time to arrive at their proper length, to improve details, and crystallize performances at their highest potential level. But a majority of writers are not masters, nor are all producers and directors fully experienced; and the differences of opinion encountered in the show's formative stage—especially in print—can drive already harassed and hysterical show people helter-skelter down blind alleys in uncoordinated, directionless efforts to "correct."

For shows—naturally they are the majority—that fall anywhere below greatness, then, the first press reception and audience reaction, whether warm or hostile, are bound to exert a disproportionate influence on their final shaping. Directors, authors, and producers have to be inhumanly strong-minded and clearheaded to be able to maintain their perspective, especially in the face of published opposition. Also, if the guiding force of a show (usually the producer and/or director) remains steady in his intention to override the reactions of out-of-town critics, it is impossible for anyone with a different opinion to be sure whether he is acting from "better judgment" or mere stubbornness. The obverse of the unwarranted pre-Broadway criticism leading to misplaced revisions is also true.

Take the case of the revue, *Bless You All.* In 1950 the show opened in Philadelphia to unqualified hurrahs. The cast, headed by Mary McCarty, Pearl Bailey, Jules Munshin, Valerie Bettis, and Byron Palmer, was accounted "brilliant." Harold Rome's songs and Arnold Auerbach's sketches were found to be above reproach. In Philadelphia, therefore, no real work was done. The show was a smash; even standing room was sold out. In New York, *Bless You All* was coolly received by everyone and closed after six weeks.

In 1963 Noel Coward's *The Girl Who Came to Supper* played

Boston for five weeks, then moved to Philadelphia for more practice before New York. Elinor Hughes was favorable but restrained. *Variety*'s Boston notice began, "This show rates a great big bouquet in all departments." The *Christian Science Monitor* was reserved and pointed to a "warning signal . . . the applause an audience showers on a bit player (Tessie O'Shea) who manages by uncanny showmanship to inject momentary life into a dawdling production." Five weeks later, in Philadelphia, the reviews were ecstatic. New York's reception was poor, and the expensive show folded in a short while.

Take Me Along (1959), a musical based on O'Neill's *Ah, Wilderness!*, starred Jackie Gleason, Walter Pidgeon, Eileen Herlie, Robert Morse, and Una Merkel. In Boston it received raves, Elliot Norton using such words as "memorable," "ranking with the great ones," "lively and entertaining," "fresh and stimulating," and Elinor Hughes prophesying "right now that it should have as long a run as its original." Philadelphia critics were just as enthusiastic and no more constructive.

In New York the press was mixed. Brooks Atkinson in the *Times* summarized his response with, "If the producers of *Take Me Along* decide to play the 2nd act twice, they will have this department's full endorsement." On the other hand, Frank Aston in the *World Telegram* observed: "Musicals like this one . . . are all too rare in terms of its opening half. The second portion suffers from anemia. . . ." In his first paragraph in the *Herald Tribune,* Walter Kerr wrote: "The new musical . . . takes place in the . . . sunlit world of 1910, when everybody had a gay old morning at the Fourth of July picnic, came home to a hearty dinner, and then went to sleep for the rest of the afternoon. The show sort of does that too."

Behind the scenes of this show—where I happen to have been—two significant changes did, and then finally didn't, take place during the pre-Broadway tour. The first of these was the firing of the choreographer and his replacement with another. The new choreographer demanded new music, scenery, and costumes, and the dancers had to rehearse incessantly to learn new ballets. This was in Boston. After the show opened in Philadelphia, the new choreographer, dances, music, costumes, and scenery were discarded; the original choreographer returned and rehearsed the original dances for New York.

The second change was that Jackie Gleason wanted a solo comedy song near the end of the show. It was not generally agreed that he needed one, but Bob Merrill, the composer-lyricist, tried several times to come up with such a song. Nothing seemed to work. A well known TV writer was secretly called in. For two days he worked around the clock. Gleason quite properly didn't like the result of his work, and so matters were left—as they had been in the case of the dances—exactly where they began.

Take Me Along ran on Broadway for roughly a year. A few weeks after Gleason left (at the end of a one-year contract), the show closed.

One final example—and another in which I personally figured—was the American production of a show which had played to packed houses in Paris for three years: *La Grosse Valise*. In its American incarnation the show played for two-and-a-half weeks in Boston prior to New York previews, and closed in New York at the end of its first week of regular performances.

When I saw the first run-through of *La Grosse Valise*, it was obvious to me that the show had great possibilities. It was a tiny show with little dialogue, much music and dancing. Its star was the scenery; and the actors who moved in front of this scenery—chiefly in the person of one man—would have to perform pantomime of the highest order. Very little dialogue was written in the script, but there were vast numbers of pages describing action and sight gags.

After several days of rehearsal, it became clear that the English actor assigned this principal part was neither a comic nor a pantomimist—and in fact had little gift for, nor any experience with, these sorts of things. He was an actor.

The French actor who had created the role (I was told) was a great comic artist. At staff meetings in Boston several of us attempted to convince the producer and the original French director, Robert Dhery, of the need to replace the leading man. The producer did not feel strongly about it; the director said that he thought he could get a proper performance out of the present actor. (Whether he really believed this or just preferred to be relieved of the chore of beginning again with a new actor can perhaps be surmised from the fact that M. Dhery wished to return to Paris *before* our New York opening to complete a movie commitment of which our producer was obviously unaware.) In any case, up to the opening night in Boston, a deep pessimism had been spreading among the entire staff. At the final meeting before this opening, the producer had finally become convinced that a new leading man was probably essential. M. Dhery had been "persuaded" to stay on a while longer, but he was noncommittal.

The morning after opening night, the scene in the producer's suite was straight out of a 1930's movie about a great stock-market bonanza. The Boston press had been enthusiastic, *especially* about the leading man; the producer and his sidemen were congratulating themselves in the manner of tycoons at the phones yelling, "Get me New York," "Get it in the press," "I'll take ten thousand," "Sell a million," etc.

The Boston reception was to prove to be *La Grosse Valise*'s kiss of death; for afterwards, there were few discussions about changes in the show although most of us felt the need for them even more strongly. As we said before, the Boston (or Philadelphia or Detroit or Washington) audience is *not* like the New York audience. During the performance of *La Grosse Valise* one heard considerable—if somewhat muted—merriment in the Boston theater. And because of this, some members of the staff who had feared disaster suddenly became confident of the show's ultimate success.

In Boston, nothing of any significance was done to *La Grosse Valise*. There were a few changes, including a new song (the show ran half an hour less than the average musical), and very few dance rehearsals.

In New York we went through the usual motions, which had little meaning. There were about ten preview performances. The audiences did not laugh. The audiences did not applaud. Then the producer began to be acutely concerned. As the days went by, he was to become increasingly so. It was too late.

Nothing could be done. *La Grosse Valise* closed after a single week of performances following a catastrophic New York opening that received a totally unfavorable press.

As stated earlier, the purpose of the pre-Broadway tour is to gain time for work on the weaknesses of a new show, to give the performers experience in playing before audiences, and an opportunity to grow in and refine their roles. But to continue with this particular tradition (which has been used less and less lately in the production of new *plays*) adds a sizeable extra financial burden to today's alarming costs of production. Furthermore, and more important, the out-of-town reception can be disastrously confusing and misleading.

The few great shows have always fared well critically out-of-town, though it seems impossible to believe that all of them would not have done at least as well had they remained in New York with seven weeks of previews at *reduced prices*. (The audience should not be asked to pay full price for an unfinished show.) The advantages of New York tryouts are manifold. First of all, the financial savings would be considerable: there would not be three orchestras, but one; not three advertising campaigns, but one; not three sets of stagehands, but one. There would be no travel expenses, and no per diems. Previews at reduced prices would constitute no hardship, since in any case the scale of prices in other cities is several dollars below that in New York.

Another advantage of trying out in New York is that in this way, producers submit the show to the reactions of heterogeneous groups of New Yorkers, rather than to the one-class audiences that attend benefits. Moreover, since *no* reviews will appear until the producer has designated an official opening, no one involved in creating or performing the show will be afforded the opportunity to get into that state of self-deceptive, false security.

While a truly good show will always succeed, a not-so-good one may, if worked on properly, succeed well enough to get by; and time and experience are invaluable necessities for every new show. But it is a fact—obscured by the tradition of out-of-town patching and fixing—that only good shows, those incorporating the known "principles" in the elements of books, lyrics, and music, ought ever to be placed in rehearsal in the first place. Until a show has been brought to a high point of excellence on paper, it ought to remain *only* on paper, where it can be rethought and rewritten time and again without the loss of anything but the creator's effort. If this were to become the standard approach to musical production, any discussion of the pre-Broadway tour would be only academic.

Certainly the pre-Broadway tours of the good shows of the past did not produce changes that could not and would not have been made here, there, or anywhere; and the out-of-town critics have usually agreed on these shows' merits. But the shows with problems to begin with have most often had such problems compounded in the pre-Broadway tour, and a clear resolution of them has probably never been found. An uncertain musical show should simply not go into production except as a tryout in a summer or community theater. The pre-Broadway tour will not provide, or even help to find, the resolution to basic problems.

One rebuttal to the professional people who argue that one purpose of getting out of the city is to be removed from New York colleagues who would—if they saw a show before it was ready to be judged—spread damaging adverse reports. This argument could only stand up in stagecoach days: not only is Boston less than an hour from New York by air, but there has not been a new show in either Boston or Philadelphia in twenty-five years that has not been packed with New York theater people—agents, authors, directors, producers, actors, and office boys. Their tales have included nothing less than, for instance, the imminent demise of *South Pacific* in Boston. Few people pay attention any longer to these delicious rumors; they are expected.

One distinguished composer-lyricist-author-producer with whom I discussed this subject felt that he might agree with me—that a new show could play previews only in New York—except in the case of comedy. He felt that the jokes would get around and therefore seem stale at the eventual New York opening.

I have mentioned his conversation here in fairness, but I do not agree with him, especially in light of the fact that comedy in today's best shows does not any longer stem from jokes. For example, one of the many big laughs in *Fiddler on the Roof* occurs after Tevye has given his consent (the first one) for his eldest daughter to marry the poor tailor whom she loves instead of the wealthy butcher—a previously arranged match. At the end of this scene, Tevye is struck as if by lightning when he remembers his wife! He says, "What'll I tell Golde?"

This brings a huge laugh because it is properly set up in the show. For it to be repeated outside the theater would mean nothing. It is my feeling, as I have said, that today's humor is not extractable and therefore cannot damage the show by outside repetition.

I can find no argument in favor of out-of-town pre-Broadway tours. The non-musical theater has increasingly come around to the use of the Broadway preview. In every case that I am aware of, a previewed play has opened in a condition and to a reception which would not have been altered simply because a company trouped to another city. Time—the opportunity to observe and to work—and audiences are the only necessities for every author, director, and performer before he can say "This is it!" Geography has nothing to do with the problem.

VI. RECORDINGS AND THE MUSICAL THEATER

Since the beginning of the record industry, excerpts from works of the musical stage have been recorded. The sales of these early recordings were pegged largely on the reputations of classical artists. Stars of the opera in particular "waxed" famous arias, which occupied one side of a 78-RPM disc; the reverse side was left blank. Although most of these early records featured singers, there was also some recording of violinists, pianists, and orchestras.

It would be an understatement to describe recording conditions in those days as primitive. The idea was new, equipment was crude, and little or no engineering technique existed. Soloists would bellow into box-like microphones, and the supporting orchestral sound filtered in weakly.

As the record industry grew and more people bought phonographs, the library of recorded music grew in volume and variety. There was something to please every taste. (When I was a child, we had a limited record library, but it included, besides Alma Gluck, Caruso, McCormack, Melba, and Paderewski, an old classic called "Wang Wang Blues.") Before 1920, dance orchestras were recording pop songs.

It was inevitable, once popular music was found to be recordworthy, that popular stars would be appropriately utilized. Since many of these were theater performers, it followed that they would record songs from shows they were currently identified with. Gradually, the interest of record companies and audiences shifted from stars to material. After the premiere of *Porgy and Bess* in 1935 (recording, by then, was no longer in its infancy), Decca issued three double-side, ten-inch records of "hits" from the opera sung by members of the cast and conducted by Alexander Smallens, musical director of the production. There were no "name" performers. The records could be bought individually, or together in an album—which cost fifty cents extra. Gertrude Lawrence recorded some songs from *Lady in the Dark* (1941); Ray Bolger did "Once in Love With Amy" from *Where's Charley?* (1948), etc.

Throughout this period, making records was an arduous task. In America the companies used discs made of acetate or wax. The latter had to be stored in the control booth in an oven until needed for immediate use. When mistakes occurred—and they always do—a new disc had to be put in place (a process which in itself was time-consuming) and the selection had to be performed again from the beginning. Not infrequently it was necessary to make six or seven "takes" of a number before a recording even approaching satisfactory was cut.

In the meanwhile, various valuable technical advances were being made. Engineers were designing and developing consoles which allowed them to make adjustments in the sound balance mechanically. A large number of microphones began to be used simultaneously in the studio, with one each for soloists, strings, brass, winds, percussion, harp, bass, etc., and it was possible for the engineer to bring all of the separate sounds together in a desirable relationship.

In Europe, especially in Hitler's Germany, during the early 1940's, recordings were being made on very heavy—almost unliftable—steel tapes. These allowed an infinitely longer continuous amount of sound to be set down without interruption. Ten-inch discs held only about three minutes on one side; twelve-inch discs permitted a maximum of five minutes. Tapes could accommodate a nearly unlimited time span.

The unwieldy steel tapes had set a new idea in motion. From steel there was a changeover to wire. Various other materials were experimented with, and finally plastic tape was developed in America and put into general use here about 1950.

(The question of sound quality which is constantly being improved, and the use of stereo sound systems—three-dimensional, as opposed to monaural, or one-dimensional—are matters that do not concern us here.)

Tapes represented an enormous improvement over discs. First of all—quality aside—the task of recording has been made far less painful than formerly. Now when errors are made—a studio noise occurs, a singer or instrumentalist "fluffs" a note, or a word in a lyric is sung incorrectly—it is no longer necessary to do a remake from the beginning. A single correct musical phrase can be spliced in to replace the faulty one. Even a single note can be used artfully to replace one that was off pitch or of inferior quality.

As to music itself, and theater music in particular, it was in 1943 that Decca made the first original cast recording of a "complete" show. This was of course *Oklahoma!* David Kapp of Decca first produced six double-sided, ten-inch records of songs from the show. As with *Porgy and Bess,* these records could be bought separately or in an album. So successful was this original album that Kapp subsequently recorded two more ten-inch records; and with Volumes I and II, this first *Oklahoma!* recording was practically complete. The undertaking proved to be one of historic importance, setting a precedent that was to have far-reaching effects not only on the record industry but on musical theater itself.

The most important technological advance apart from tapes, and particularly for show albums, was the advent of long-playing records—which came into general use between 1951 and 1952. The obvious advantage of the long-playing record was that about twenty minutes of music could be presented (uninterruptedly, as in the case of symphonies and operas) on a twelve-inch side—or a total of about forty minutes-plus on both sides of a single disc. But in order to manufacture these records, factory equipment had to be altered drastically.

At first, most new records were issued at both 78 and 33⅓ speeds. Little by little, new records came to be made exclusively at the new speed, and older records that were still in demand were re-recorded for playing at the new speed. The new records were also made of unbreakable material.

Original-cast recordings of shows became established practice. For about twenty years, no musical show—on or off Broadway—opened without some kind of recording contract. When a show was a big hit, not only was the original-cast album made but other recordings appeared in varying numbers and treatments—produced by any and all other companies.

Usually the contract with a new show *allowed* the recording company, under a number of different conditions, to record the show, but without requiring that it do so. Thus after the Broadway opening, if the show seemed to be fairly stable, the cast album would be done. If the show had a negative reception, the records would not be made. This was not invariably the case, however. Columbia Records, for instance, had a contract for Leonard Bernstein's *Candide*. Despite the fact that *Candide* lasted only seventy-three performances in 1956, Goddard Lieberson, then president of Columbia Records, recorded it, because the score was unique and special, and the album has had a consistently good sale. *Anya* was recorded *before* the New York opening (a rare practice), and despite the show's unqualified failure and hasty demise, the records were released. On the other hand, the cast of *Bonanza Bound* came to New York from

Philadelphia during the pre-Broadway tour and made its album. The show closed permanently one week later—still in Philadelphia—and the records were never issued. Ordinarily the taping of a show is scheduled for the first Sunday after the Broadway opening. Often the album is on sale in the shops and played on radio programs four days later! This kind of one-day recording schedule is extremely exhausting, especially for conductor, orchestra, and engineering staff, but it becomes obligatory under the rules of Actors Equity Association, which state that "the actors engaged therein [recording] shall be paid a minimum of one week's salary for each day or part thereof" and "a day's recording session shall be limited to nine consecutive hours, inclusive of one hour allowed for meals."

Because of these restrictions, and the huge investment involved in a cast recording, the one-day schedule has to be carefully planned and scrupulously adhered to. The orchestra generally commences at 10:00 A.M. and finishes about midnight, with two *possible* one-hour intermissions for meals! All performers, including the chorus, are scheduled so that all work involving any one performer is completed within the time Equity allows.

Since cast albums began to be produced only in 1943—and even then not consistently—there was already a vast repertory of works from the American musical theater that had never been put on records. Accordingly, in the late 1940's Goddard Lieberson, then Executive Vice-President of Columbia Records, initiated—with me as conductor—a series of albums of previously unrecorded shows. We used the original orchestrations, and, in some cases, members of the original cast, and put out a number of shows in an attempt to fill some of the gaps in the recorded-show library. Among the shows we taped were *Pal Joey*, a 3-LP *Porgy and Bess*, *Girl Crazy*, *Roberta*, *Babes in Arms*, *The Boys From Syracuse*, *On Your Toes*, and many others.

The recording of *Pal Joey* with Vivienne Segal and Harold Lang led to the very successful revival of the show featuring the same two stars. The *Porgy and Bess* recording, made with the original and unedited Gershwin orchestrations, is still the most

205

complete of the many recordings which appeared especially after the release of the motion picture.

The difference in cost between an original-cast album and one simply organized by a studio is enormous. Since Equity requires a minimum of a week's salary for each member of the cast employed, the ensemble singers (for example) receive at least $210.00 each, and sixteen to twenty of them may be employed. At a non-cast-album recording, where youth and beauty are not considerations, a group of sometimes better voices and invariably superior musicians can be organized at $53 each for a three-hour session. This one session generally will suffice for chorus rehearsal and recording, and a group of possibly ten singers, all with enormous microphone experience, will do the job professionally. Particularly minor principals, who may be used only in a single song, will be paid far less than a stage performer, whose weekly theater salary is based on a sizeable acting part and perhaps some dancing.

What is not generally known is that arrangers and copyists of a show score are paid their original fees again when their material is used in a cast album. Also inasmuch as the string section of theater orchestras is necessarily limited in size, it is enlarged for the recording sessions by perhaps twelve or more extra players.

The artistic and historical meanings of the original-cast albums are strongly related. These albums are invariably done in the presence and with the approval of the composers. They are made after five weeks of rehearsal and perhaps nine weeks of performance. The performing style has been meticulously set so that, on records, the style is permanently and indisputably defined. The record of an important show will be of artistic and historical significance to all future generations. Future generations will be able to comprehend precisely what our shows were, how they were performed, and what our orchestras and arrangements sounded like. We know, for instance, the mechanics of Caruso's vocal production. From some old recordings with the composer at the piano, we know precisely how Debussy meant his songs to be performed. We are, however, left to argue about the performance style of all music written prior to the era of record making.

In our own time, these albums serve another artistic purpose. I had said earlier that "when a show is a big hit, not only the original-cast album is made but other recordings appear in varying number and treatments." This means that when songs in a new show become popular, they are hastily "arranged" in a wide range of styles that will be purposely different from the original. Some are made for dancing with totally changed rhythms, altered melodic lines, and harmonies whose purpose, it would seem, is to carry the particular piece as far from the original as possible.

Then too, there are the singers, the "stylists," who—expressing themselves—set out to "improve" what is already successful. The new song is the wet concrete on which these "artists" must leave an imprint. With very few exceptions, these stars consistently alter melody and rhythm and, sometimes, even lyrics as well. Their orchestrations do everything possible to disavow any connection with the song as it was conceived.

Now these recordings of single songs made by the reigning favorites of TV, nightclubs, and records are heard, adored, and imitated by many more people at any given time than are influenced by the cast album. They lend an indelible and almost inescapable coloration to the existence of their respective songs, especially among the young. Usually they go out of style quickly. The cast album, however, remains—and, in the long run, prevails.

When, as is common practice, successful Broadway shows are released for performance by amateurs, community theaters, colleges, and high schools, it is the original-cast album that exerts the strongest influence. The young amateur performer must replace his TV memory of each song with a definite sense of the show's real style—not to mention the correct notes and tempos. The cast album also provides some guidance to those directors who were unable, because of distance from New York or lack of means, to see the original production—or to those who, if they did see the original, nevertheless need careful reminding. As we can see, the educational value of cast recordings coincides with the artistic and historical ones.

Last in this discussion, but by no means least, is the economic importance of recordings for the production and potential success of contemporary musical theater. From the beginning of cast recordings and through about 1946, theater producers assumed that the public-relations and advertising value of records to the success of any show were such that the recording companies were not required to pay anything for the premiere rights. Beginning about 1947, however, the business transactions took on a new and significant aspect. Because the record companies had come to recognize the great potential of hit-show cast albums, they began regularly to audition new shows in advance of production, read the scripts, and try to assess the merits and the additional assets promised by the star's, the director's, and the producer's capabilities. As a result, the companies began to bid competitively for the shows. When the property was "hot" enough, they would offer not only producer royalties, but guarantees of "singles" (apart from the cast album) by various pop artists under contract to the particular company, a program of advertising sometimes also tied in with TV and radio shows, and finally (sometimes enormous) cash investment in the show itself.

Each of these factors has on occasion proved to be of importance to everyone involved in the project. Pop "singles" in our time are often released weeks in advance of the show's Broadway opening (something which had once been thought detrimental), and this new practice has often resulted in so much popularity for one or two of a show's songs (the audience comes *into* the theater whistling the songs) that at the Broadway premiere, the audience has spontaneously applauded a number which was being *introduced* in the overture! The availability of these "singles" in advance (providing the songs are of hit quality) permits plugs for the shows during their pre-Broadway, out-of-town tour and has sometimes nearly saturated the general New York public in advance of opening.

When *Wish You Were Here* opened to a less than enthusiastic press, Harold Rome's title song was heard on the air constantly, and the success of this song contributed enormously to the eventual success (nearly 600 performances) of the show itself (which was revised after the opening). Ervin Drake's song, "A Room Without Windows," recorded in advance by Steve Lawrence, helped considerably to lengthen the run of *What Makes Sammy Run?*

A record company's investment in a production can be a decisive factor to a producer who is having difficulty raising the necessary capital. Sometimes the investment will be a token $10,000 to 50,000, which—in view of the present-day $1,000,000 production costs—is not a significant sum. Sometimes the amount will be considerably greater. A famous example of record company-producer relations—the first of its kind—was Columbia's supplying the entire capital for *My Fair Lady*. Since then, other companies have taken similar plunges—some successfully—though none as yet with such enormous success as *My Fair Lady*.

What I must not fail to mention is that while all of the benefits listed above are of inestimable value to a show and its production, the composer and lyricist also reap their own additional rewards. These begin with royalties from the sale of records. And further, since records are played again and again on radio shows and are "logged" for air-performance credit, the composers and lyricists are paid by performing-rights societies (ASCAP or BMI) who license these broadcasts.

Altogether, the role played by recording companies in the careers of producers, composers, and lyricists is unique and was an essential and integral part of the life of contemporary musical theater.

Unfortunately, within the past five years the recording company-theater production relationship has changed considerably. Several quite different factors have brought about the change.

The sudden popularity of rock (in all forms) has resulted in astronomical sales of record singles—many different recordings sold in enormous quantities, each during a fairly restricted period of time. The turnover is highly profitable despite the limited life-span during which any one record may be in demand.

The cost of making these recordings is infinitely less than the cost of the enormous organization required to make a cast album. There may be one principal vocalist, sometimes backed by a small ensemble or an instrumental combo of from four to fourteen players.

Musical-theater albums with their high production costs are not bought in such quantities as they were in the '50's and '60's. Theater production costs have soared so high and the gamble on success has become so chancy that record companies seldom want to risk investment in the show itself, especially when they are unenthusiastic about the remote possibility of cutting its album.

What I have written fairly accurately describes today's record company-theater production conditions. That there will be some reversion to former practice is a possibility so remote at this time that I would be reluctant to make any prediction.

As long as cast-album production costs remain so high and the purchasing demand so low, there will certainly be no change. The reality of the situation should stimulate more creative thinking on the part of people responsible for these increased costs. Without some extensive revisions—depressing as it is to believe—the cast-album, for two decades an important certainty, will go down in history as a primitive practice.

VII. POSTSCRIPT:
PERFORMERS IN THE THEATER

No discussion of musical theater would be complete without mention of the stage performer's role and obligation. Since our contemporary musical is descended from grand opera via operetta, I can think of no simpler approach to such a discussion than through the performer's evolution in these media.

The musical desires and directions of a composer, especially at premieres of new operas, operettas, or musical shows (where, unless dead, he will be distinctly present), have always been law. And every composer I have ever known or heard about wants absolute adherence to what he has committed to paper. Until about twenty-five or thirty years ago, it would have been unthinkable for a singer to deviate from notation—at least in the composer's presence. Occasionally—even almost traditionally—a prima donna at a climax has sung a note higher than the one the composer wrote (probably because nobody else could have reached it), or due to weak-minded taste, she has held a note incredibly overlong. These are minor, if incorrigible, deviations that came with time to be thought of as "traditional." Most of them were not.

I remember the late Ezio Pinza, who was unable to read music, saying to me that one of the things he found "interesting" about Toscanini, with whom he frequently worked, was that the latter required *everyone* to sing *all* notes precisely as written. To Pinza, this was abnormal and strange!

The battles between composers and temperamental prima donnas in opera and operetta have been engraved in blood on the pages of history. Usually, the final victory could be claimed by the composer.

In contemporary musical theater the situation is vaguely similar, especially when the composer is well established, experienced, and—above everything else—famous. Such a man will set the tempos of all of his songs for the conductor. Usually these are slower than one would imagine. He will be explicit with the arranger as to instrumental coloring, musical figures, and the style he means to have employed. He will supervise the singers—especially the principals—in their performance of every detail of every song, and during the endless pre-Broadway trek, he will take nightly notes of even slight deviations and insist on their correction. When the show has opened, it becomes the conductor's responsibility to act as watchdog and prevent lapses and changes. Occasionally during the show's run, the composer will drop in at a performance and will (usually) pull down the tempos which may have been unconsciously speeded up; make corrections involving a performer's perhaps unintentional change in attitude toward a song, or simply remind defectors that they are beginning to re-compose what he had set down.

But today—because of the enormous popularity of radio, TV, and records—one or two or three big hit songs in a show will have been recorded hundreds of times by "artists" outside of the show itself. These recordings will exploit primarily the style and personality of the recording star. The orchestral arrangement will be a deliberate departure from the original. New rhythms will sometimes seem to create an entire new song. Or the singer will perform only variations on the melody, without having first exposed the original; some lyrics may even default their creator's version.

These records are in turn dinned into the ears of an entire generation through the home phonograph and/or radio disc jockeys. Similar "star renderings" will be heard on major TV programs. Often the motion-picture version will also authorize departures from, and "improvements" on, the original.

These recorded, TV, and motion-picture versions are, for good or ill, of incalculable value to the fame and prestige of the show (if it is still running) and to the composer and lyricist, whose pockets will have become stuffed with the delicious gold that these most commercial of enterprises produce.

In fact, so far as I can see, the chief harm that results from the musical deviations is the way in which they become indelibly impressed on the public's consciousness. When the show—a great success—is finally produced live in thousands of outlying theaters, the new performers will automatically emulate the pop recordings that they know. The musical director may be in no position to prevent this. And when this happens, the concept of the show's style is violated.

This kind of corruption is as unpreventable as it is unfortunate, especially when these treatments of songs are brought back into the theater, where they never originated and will never belong. And the performer in the theater has an obligation to adhere faithfully to the original, because to do so not only fulfills the composer's intention, but constitutes the very essence of the style of musical theater.

7

Rock and Non-Plot*

*To try to belong to one's own
time is already to be out of date.*
—EUGÈNE IONESCO
(translated by Donald Watson)

One of the many hallmarks of current rock non-theater musicals is the employment of non-plot, which many critics have accepted with incredible equanimity as though a musical without a plot is a perfectly usual state.

But is this really true?

Unusual it is without doubt. Impossible, I would say, *unless* it had extremely well-defined characters. For with such characters peopling the stage, certain relationships, animosities, attractions, revulsions, differences—situations—would of necessity begin to germinate and develop, and the result would have to be a kind of drama that might conceivably substitute for plot. If we are allowed to know the people, we would automatically be supplied with some sense of feeling, of caring. We would sense conflicts and affinities, struggles to associate or be rid of, efforts to charm, to repel, to love, or to hate. These are at least primitive

---

* This chapter is taken from *Words with Music* also by Lehman Engel (Macmillan, 1972).

213

foundations for or surrogates in lieu of a plot. They are at least situations. But characters defined sharply and identifiably would have to exist and with the greatest of clarity.

Professor George Pierce Baker of Harvard published his famous *Dramatic Technique* in 1919. I would like to quote some lines that seem relevant here:

Some plays depend almost wholly upon mere bustle and rapidly shifting movement, much of it wholly unnecessary to the plot. Large portions of many recent musical comedies illustrate this.

Not a single one of these—many successful at the time—only 50 years later, is alive.

Characterization, preceding and accompanying action, creates sympathy or repulsion for the figure or figures involved. This sympathy or repulsion in turn converts mere interest into emotional response of the keenest kind. . . . no higher form can develop till characterization appears to explain and interpret action.

While action is popularly held to be central in drama, emotion is really the essential. . . .

Accurately conveyed emotion is the fundamental in all good drama.

It would seem, then, that a musical minus all of the elements of story, premise, characters, conflict, development would wind up as a revue, but the non-plot shows are *not* revues. There is no recognizable start or stop to the "happening" as a whole, no well-defined units, no sketches, no dance, no connecting thread. What is it then that such a theatrical "happening" has left? The complete answer usually can only be that it has "songs." No matter how good the songs are—and often they are excellent—they must lack the all-important theatrical ingredient of having been born of some recognizable theatrical situation and made for a specific identifiable character reacting in it. Without such motivations, the songs become generalized, will not arouse audience empathy, will occur in unconnected and therefore meaningless sequence. The audience may as well arrive and/or depart at will without having missed anything. This theater is today's equivalent of vaudeville, or minstrel show, or, at best, *Ziegfeld Follies,* although the latter nearly always contained literate amusing sketches which added up in a slight but complete denouement because characters within situations were developed swiftly to a (sometimes illogical) conclusion but with an ending which caused the audience to explode with laughter.

It is also true that the songs in most of the shows are (because of plotlessness) not going anywhere, not exposing anything or anybody. They are simply numbers which give themselves only a single opportunity of succeeding. Are they *that* interesting? Certainly these unmotivated separate songs can be equated to those very old non-working songs that occurred in the revues of the '20's when the sudden restlessness and apathy of the audiences was all too embarrassingly apparent. Lastly— about the songs—for a reason which I cannot comprehend, they never end. They merely stop, or, as in many pop records, they fade away. That is as about as atheatrical as a theater song can be.

The non-plot musicals have eschewed an important motivating theatrical element in being plotless and characterless because they have failed to furnish the audience with the sense of caring. They can no longer motivate any desire to see how anything will turn out since there is nothing to turn out, nothing impending—in fact, in this sense, nothing at all. There is nobody to root for because there is nobody, only (usually) a stage full of people, as full as the budget allows, one occasionally distinguishable from another physically by size, shape, or kind of hair. No one bears a clear-cut relationship to another so that there is no loving union to hope for, no mystery, little to laugh about unless generalized, naïve and, already well-known puerile jokes fired at religion, family, the Establishment, draft evasion and the like are capable of provoking it.

Another thing. Since time and place occupy no part of the proceedings there can be little if any sense of unified style. Costumes and scenery—if they exist at all—must be non-specific, which is not the same as being abstract. In the good abstract there is recognizable style and form. In the non-specific there is only negativism. We are careful to suggest nothing and to relate to nothing.

What remains is often considerable youthful vigor, ear splitting sound volume, sometimes mesmerizing rhythm, music composed of childishly simple and limited melody, narrowly prescribed harmony, and the rhythm of incessant and unrelieved repetition. The latter two qualities also often apply to the lyrics.

On the other hand, the knowing use of non-plot recognizes special thinking on the part of the writers who have been steeped in tradition and in most cases have blasted off from such distinguished earlier writers as Chekhov, Ibsen, and even Büchner. However, the application of non-plot here refers to those inexperienced, immature, and thoughtless writers who merely suggest non-plot because of an inability to come up with a good, simple, and non-cliché plot. What residue remains suggests a story line that is derelict in being absent—a poor shaved-down plot in lieu of one that should be better defined and more original.

Certainly this kind of non-plot is due to three conditions: nonknowledge born of insufficient education and experience, an overwhelming desire particularly on the part of many young "creative" people to rush quickly into a situation in which they may (and frequently do) have a quick if temporary success, and very real reaction against the poor, threadbare, overused, noncreative librettos written and produced during the past two decades.

The latter condition has, I believe, corroded the judgment of many critics who have admittedly been bored with a large part of what they have had to tolerate during these some twenty years. They have obviously reacted favorably to almost everything that was different, that provided a change from their nearly unendurable nightly chores. But in being able to accept without the slightest queasiness the non-plot, directionless, characterless new musicals, these same critics have incubated a kind of kinetic non-musical which threatens to destroy and to a large extent discourage more serious, better based creativity. This non-plot, etc., musical is at most and at best a transitional groping toward something newer than anything which has existed for some time, but transitional it is and the eventual main event will unquestionably be spawned by more knowledgeable creative people who also eschew the thread-bare trappings of the more recent past without disclaiming the very foundations of musical theater. These foundations include, among other things, at least characters.

In the turn-of-the-century musical the book existed only to string the songs together. I believe that this accurately describes the "books" *Hair, Promenade,* and *Salvation.* However, there were songs galore in those early musicals which were so good that they exist and are reused today even by the most avant-garde singers and electric combos. The books dropped dead in their own day. Today the principal difference is that the music also drops dead rather instantly.

It was after that period in the '20's that our writers learned much about libretto-writing. Now today some people find it unnecessary to have books. To lay the blame on the foolish books of the past fifteen years and conclude that no book is better than a bad one seems somehow silly. Why don't the writers bother to learn their craft so that they can *extend* what has been accomplished and make it today's?

I said earlier that "the non-plot aspect is due to . . . non-knowledge born of insufficient education or experience." In precisely the same way the music in these shows, and most of the others in their category, is limited to a frozen, narrow, circumscribed bailiwick. The harmonies consist of three, four, or five simple chords in any one song and in almost all songs of this style, and the melody seldom rises, falls, or cadences above or below a tiny limited range. Also most of the melodies are extremely old and predictable, while their harmonic welding was standard in turn-of-the-century hymnology. Does this non-book, narrow-gauge music seem to comprise a liberation? I doubt it. Rather it is like a corset, the stays of which are only too clearly visible.

However, there is one thing that this movement may in the end accomplish. Not monumental or memorable shows or music that will become cherished either for their own quality or as a beacon to future writers. It is quite possible—possible—that just the break-away in and of itself may constitute a revolution against what was and what was tenaciously holding on to its own superior progenitor as its only claim to being. If a non-book is to be considered superior to a poor book, this must be a fallacy and I strenuously object to it as a point of view. But a book has been an integral part of musical theater, and the characters it has engendered (or vice versa), and the progress of a plot could be noted along the way, and the caring that these—plot and characters—bred in the audience. These constituted musical theater at its best (*all* theater, for that matter) along with music that stirred by its freshness and warmth—not its overnoisiness and its incessant, persistent percussive drive that would do credit to primitive man and was undoubtedly all that he had recourse to in his earliest stage.

Non-plot to me is a possibility in all kinds of theater but at its best it is more sophisticated and requires more know-how than the old plot usage did. Non-plot does not exist successfully by default but is consciously made by design. Its creation has to be the work of knowledgeable craftsmen who know how to apply it and what to use as replacement for the plot, which, in non-existence, will leave a void.

Actually a most serious moral ought to be pointed out here. Musical theater pieces from our past have evaporated—poof!— largely because they have been so tightly connected to their own times exclusively. *No, No, Nanette* (1925) by Vincent Youmans had some brilliant songs that lie around like those columns which once belonged to a majestic temple in ancient Delphi: nothing else remains. *This* was a flapper musical and once so very contemporary.* The first Pulitzer Prize for a musical went to the Gershwins' *Of Thee I Sing* (1931), a political

* The 1971 successful revival of *No, No, Nanette* does not invalidate the above statement. In fact, it has nothing to do with it. The recent revival has a nearly 90 percent new book by Burt Shevelove, and it not only works well as a tasteful "entertainment," but as the characters are left two-dimensional as originally drawn, their songs—though enormously charming—are also two-dimensional and could therefore easily be inserted into a new book. Also as this musical comedy has no pretensions to emotional depth (who ever thought of such a thing in 1925?), character depth and situation depth are not even to be considered.

lampoon. Today this work is a ruin because it was stapled into its own time and situations which nowadays we have to ask Great-grandpa or an archaeologist (nearly synonymous) to explain.

Think of the embarrassment that lies ahead. Vietnam, which is indeed a disgrace, will surely end one way or another. "Pot" is almost certain to become legalized, and those who are extolling it now will then be as amusing and as interesting as Carry Nation. The discovery and freeing of sex is about as new as liquor was to me (I had French grandparents in Mississippi) when my college classmates to whom it had been denied first discovered it during—of course—Prohibition. And it's utter poppycock (I am anticipating a silly suggestion) to entertain any idea whatsoever that *Hair, Salvation* or any of the others will have exerted any pressures on our futures as once did *Uncle Tom's Cabin.* Think about it. The reasons for the failures of the first as a social force and the success of the latter are all too apparent.

The aforementioned Dr. Baker also wrote: "The permanent value of a play, however, rests on its characterization." I do agree, Dr. Baker, but suppose there are *no* characters, as in *Hair;* what then? And with no characters there can be no plot, and we are back where we started with non-plot. With no plot, the audience is cheated of any experiencing and are given in its place some "sensing." The first of these words suggests feeling, encounter, undergoing, actual living through an event, while the latter connects with sensuous perception, instinctive reactions, and many other things the precise effects of which cannot be calculated and require neither art, knowledge, discipline, or experience.

As Galsworthy suggested, "character is situation," and when characters are defined, set up, respond or react, they have to create some line which may very well involve the audience, even if this line is not, in essence, a plot. Among recent plays there are the very talented David Storey's two, *The Contractor* and *Home,* which, in lieu of plots, nevertheless have such clearly defined characters that the audience is made to care— plot or no plot.

However, *Hair,* the most successful of all the new non-plot rock shows, despite program assignments, lacks even characters. All the people are pretty much alike and indistinguishable, one from another.

The evening is non-dramatic because of the sketchy relationships between people and poor identification of most of them.

Hair throbs and excites like a parade—any parade: circus, Labor Day, Nazi, St. Patrick's Day, or any other. It is noisier than any parade. It is less disciplined. It is not a theater piece—neither "show" nor revue. Plotless, humorless, self-conscious, stale, largely lyricless in spite of many excellent tunes, characterless, and without development—except that Sheila will and won't and will and does go to bed with Claude, and the latter will and won't and will and must go to Vietnam. *Hair* is a *thing*, and it attempts to destroy what is, without a care, but fails to offer something new in its place.

I am glad that it has happened. It was inevitable. It may have opened an important door to something new. Hopefully that will be good—and good and interesting theater with a shape and characters to care about. *Hair* itself is none of these things.

Surely we have progressed further along in history, in time. Surely it is abundantly clear to everyone that shows like *Henry, Sweet Henry, Minnie's Boys, Jimmy, George M!, Dear World, Coco, Her First Roman, Zorba, Maggie Flynn, Darling of the Day*, and many more like these with their impossibly bad books and music that is supposed to make us nostalgic are not indeed the progeny of *Carousel, West Side Story*, and *Fiddler on the Roof*. But by burning the bridges of our heritage, by now knowing what it emerged from, we will never build something worthily new. It is easy to negate, to destroy, to turn the back on what was good, and very difficult on the other hand to pick up some connection and continue to build in a fresh new direction. But it can be done, and with all the pros and cons, the rantings and ravings, it *will* be done. But this interim vacillation is not even a small part of doing it. Non-books, non-scores, and the endlessly reiterated narrow subject matter—pot, four-letter words, free sex, Vietnam, draft-card burnings, etc.—are all too tiresome. What existed in Greece, in the sixth century before

Christ and then again and differently in the medieval music-plays, and later in new clothes in Shakespeare—love, hate, factional differences, ambition, and more—as they are eternal in life, so they are and always will be in the theater.

Experimentation ought to be characterized as a noble word. Webster says it is "a trial made to confirm or disprove something doubtful; an operation undertaken to discover some unknown principle or effect, or to test some suggested truth, or to demonstrate some known truth." Implicit in all parts of these definitions is some kind of knowledge or truth-finding from which or upon which some *orderly* test is to be made.

Experimentation implies progress, a going from some specific place to another in an approach toward the future.

Today "experimentation" is so disorderly and unconnected that most of those who pride themselves on being a part of it are surely not going anywhere. They seize on popular trends, often achieve fame and fortune for a brief time, know nothing to begin with and end up really giving out nothing. Waste. And experimentation becomes a dirty word indicating a hodge-podge of ice cream, catsup, bean soup, and salt. No taste. No reason. All of the ingredients readily at hand but adding up to nothing when meaninglessly put together. Genuine laziness, foolishness, and a large amount of arrogance. *Promenade* and *Salvation* were theater frauds. At least *Little Mary Sunshine* and *The Boy Friend* had the virtue of consistency when they employed the musical and stage style of the '20's and stayed with it for a full evening of fun and games. *Promenade,* however, was not a score but a crazy quilt. It lacked sense of style. It was so disjointed that it belonged to no one, no time, no place, and certainly to no theater. The plot—as nearly as one could be discerned—was also a pretentious conglomeration. The lyrics grew in no direction and were largely meaningless. The many musical styles hashed together had to have been the work of an amateur.

In the musical theater of the '20's and '30's there was (and there is today) a clearly detectable evolution at work. The new young men were broadening their harmonic palettes with more sophisticated colors, molding their melodies into shapes hitherto undreamed of in theater and popular music although these had already been explored earlier in "serious" music. They were also beginning to use rhythmic patterns from the songs and dances of the folk art of the entire recently discovered world.

The lyricists were quickly going away from the clichés of the past toward original, particular images which they found our language to be filled with, images waiting only to be recognized and utilized. The librettists were finding that characters might be three-dimensional and that plots could be literate. All of these processes were proceeding simultaneously, and they erupted simultaneously from a number of different people into our universally respected and relished musical theater of the '40's, '50's, and early '60's.

I believe that now again everyone recognizes the need for change, but in the meanwhile we have been jolted into many things that do not and will not fit into the musical theater. None of these things are new, and they cannot develop because they have long ago been integrated as useful or bypassed as childish. The "new" theater music is actually quite old. Basically it is rhythm 'n' blues, revivalist or a pale imitation of 16th-century madrigals. In writing of the beginnings of rock 'n' roll, Nik Cohn in his book *Rock* (Stein and Day) wrote that it "was very simple music. All that mattered was the noise it made, its drive, its aggression, its newness. All that was taboo was boredom. . . . The lyrics were mostly non-existent, simply slogans one step away from gibberish."

Rock in its many guises has gone in many directions since the above-defined style of the '50's, but it has not, thus far, really found a style that is for the theater. Its tunes are too limited, the rhythms too unchanging. There are too few contrasts. It is meant for something abstract like records and large dollar earnings. It seldom characterizes the individual in either music or lyrics, and this latter—particularization—and the musical contrasts are essential musical-theater concomitants.

Experimentation, when it is real, when it takes advantage of history and quite rightly eschews the immediate past in favor of something new and authentic, will always be about to take our hands and help us up the steep, tortuous steps that lead on to

what is solidly new. The rest is only a happening, a puny fireworks, a pale scream in the night which no one need worry
about since it lacks credibility and direction. It will attract and it
will also fade away.

CODA

And on the pedestal these words appear:
"My name is Ozymandias, king of kings:
Look on my works, ye Mighty, and despair!"
Nothing beside remains.

—SHELLEY

And so this book must end, though I am reluctant to leave it because it is necessarily unfinished. For every time there is a new show—for good or ill—there is something more to be learned.

At this particular moment in our history, American theater in general is going through a period of transition. In non-musical theater, lately, a whole series of slight and highly ephemeral comedies have achieved enormous popularity. Most of these comedies, so far as style, content, and method are concerned, in fact belong within a tradition that held sway in the American theater approximately a quarter of a century ago. They neither add nor pretend to add anything new; they run on and on, are constructed to entertain a large, but hardly discriminating, audience, and only in their own time. Although crafted expertly, they have nothing at all to do with theater art. They are—to me—on this account deadly dull and will inevitably pass into oblivion. Lest I be misunderstood, I am not arguing for the necessity of seriousness or grandeur of theme to a lasting theater. I also like to laugh, but I do feel frustrated, as I believe many others must, by the absence of style and substance. The comedies of Oscar Wilde and Shaw—to name only two—have both style and substance; and the French comedies and farces of the 18th and 19th centuries had, at the very least, style.

Among the most talented writers for our serious non-musical theater, there are several who are attempting to explore new paths in drama. These writers command our respect and gratitude for their intention to do so. Eventually, perhaps, they will succeed in bringing a currently uncertain theater to something new and real. For the moment, however, most of these writers seem to be laboring under two major hindering, self-imposed constraints: first, a conscious and harmful avoidance of emotion; and second, a preoccupation with experience of a very special, and, indeed, often almost clinically pathological nature. Both of these constraints act to keep them from achieving works of enduring and universal quality.

Many new plays in this category enjoy enormous success, but often for the wrong reason: the shock implicit in their adventurousness. Many other plays consciously involved in the exploration of new techniques and styles fail immediately and do not get the chance to have the wider hearing they deserve; today's costs of theater production being so staggering, critical dissent will almost certainly bring a play to an abrupt end. Critical dissatisfaction has often been operating on a kind of double standard. An ambitious play is judged inadequate because it has not attained fully its self-appointed destination and is not recognized as a commendable and interesting effort, while formula plays—achieving their restricted goals with a degree of perfection—a perfection of nothingness—are praised. One fails; the other succeeds.

Musicals, on the other hand—and despite an inordinate annual number of costly failures—today enjoy the greatest success, appeal to the widest audience, and, at their very best, stay around indefinitely. When *Carousel,* for example, was revived at the New York City Center, Dan Sullivan, the *New York Times* critic, wrote (in agreement with most of the others):

How does it stand up after twenty-one years? How do the pyramids stand up? . . . But in another twenty-one years, how will what's happening, baby, look? Not half so well, I'd guess, as *Carousel* does.

Unfortunately, however, the majority of our newest musicals (*Fiddler on the Roof* and *A Little Night Music* being notable exceptions), though enormously successful, seem to have little more than empty interiors, sometimes adroitly concealed behind colorful and swiftly changing facades. The material around which most of the books, characters, music, and lyrics are built tends to be perfunctory; indeed, it generally does not even attempt to be anything more. What this material, and the shows it spawns, lacks chiefly, is *feeling,* the precise element which makes it possible for audiences, year after year, to go on caring about the show.

It is this lack of feeling that makes most of the current new—and, I hope, transitional—musicals blood brothers of those talented (and successful) but empty plays that we are being offered. Empty musicals, like empty plays, can often enjoy great box-office popularity, entertaining audiences as they do more adroitly by means of the added elements: song, dance, and a seemingly endless, kaleidoscopic, swift-moving array of scenery and costumes. While the mind and heart are left uninvolved, the eye, at least, can be fascinated, and the ear, on occasion, nearly satisfied, when it is not totally deafened.

The acclaim currently being accorded new musicals in this category inevitably makes itself felt at the box office; the "take" on these shows is record-breaking. Such momentary success is hardly new: each succeeding season in the history of musical theater has turned up at least one world-beater whose title, music, and even the names of whose authors now molder in obscurity in some statistical file.

The issue of survival cannot be overemphasized. The shows that I believe to be empty I also believe will die from malnutrition—their innards simply do not function—and they will remain dead forever. Even in terms of money—playing to capacity audiences as all of them do, and for an impressive period—without the universality born of depth and authenticity of feeling, they cannot have an after-life. They will not tour extensively. Their revival potential will be small and limited. Their indefinite recording future will also be most doubtful. Lacking the

226

qualities of the distinguished shows, they will, in the end, even fall short of these in terms of revenue.

The distinguished shows I refer to are not necessarily serious in tone or character. But even if they are comedies, their material is nearly timeless, and their characters can be identified with by ordinary human beings, who are made to care that there be a satisfactory resolution of the problem presented.

One more word on this point. Perhaps no notion is more unfair to the practitioners of any of the public-entertainment arts—certainly, no idea is more harmful to their standards—than that which divides the arts into "high" and "low," reserving the power to endure to the former and a passing ephemerality to the latter. Both grow out of their own times, and greatness, for both, resides in their ability to speak afresh to each of the generations that comes after. Because Mozart's *Don Giovanni* is a great work of musical-theater art, it does not follow that the best works of Gilbert and Sullivan, Johann Strauss, Richard Rodgers and many others are not also significant and lasting works in their own way. What is more important, it does not follow that those who work in a "lighter vein," must not submit to high standards applicable to their own sort of creativity.

One cannot say that a tin of fresh beluga caviar is superior to a bunch of Malaga grapes. Both are savored, each for its own distinct qualities, and they are incomparable.

E. E. Cummings wrote:

> since feeling is first
> who pays any attention
> to the syntax of things
> will never wholly kiss you

These brilliant lines sum up the most important thing to be said about creativity in the musical theater: the absence of *feeling first* prevents an audience from becoming involved with a show. So many of the glittering, successful, and even—in some respects—brilliant shows of today's theater are never to be loved. They occupy an audience's slack time; they faintly amuse and fade away.

227

This book, then, has tried to examine the masterpieces of musical theater. And it is my hope that it might just possibly contribute in some way toward the extension of that special line which has evolved slowly and painfully, and which now fully represents us, our time and place, our way of life. New writers who try to create seriously in this direction must not be discouraged by the success of many of today's vapid substitutes for the possible, and, indeed, already demonstrated goal. *Abie's Irish Rose* was, in its own way, also a great success: in its day, it earned millions of dollars. Period. Does anyone believe *Abie's Irish Rose* was a great, or even a distinguished, or even, really, a good play?

I have not been writing about the *Abie's Irish Rose*'s of our musical theater. There cannot be any precise method for accomplishing what works of this kind achieve; one can neither calculate the means nor predict the results. I firmly believe, on the other hand, that the creation of a distinguished show is calculable. Certainly, the principles exist and are present to be learned. One cannot, of course, calculate talent. But if existing knowledge is combined with real talent, and employed with taste, I believe deeply that the results must be satisfying, profitable in every way, and that the best of these works will come alive and be treasured indefinitely and everywhere.

APPENDIX I

Discography

The following list of show recordings (including some revues) is as complete as I could make it. I have not listed recordings of shows (since this volume relates to the American musical theater) that were not made in this country. *The Girl Who Came to Supper* has music and lyrics by Noel Coward, who was, of course, English, but the show was a new one, conceived and produced here. It is a local product, while *Oliver!* for example, was not.

I have made no effort to list a number of single records that were—at the time—the sole recorded excerpts from a new show of a past time. One very good reason for this omission is the fact that these records have been unavailable for a long time.

Sometimes I have listed two recordings of a show, usually when an original cast album was not made. Sometimes I have listed "excerpts" in lieu of a complete recording when, to my knowledge, none has ever been made.

None of these recordings is actually complete. Because of disc space limitations, there have invariably been interior cuts and whole excisions. Ordinarily these latter consist of dance music (not written by the show's composer, but based on the composer's themes), incidental music (underscoring), and in some cases, the least important songs.

The abbreviations following each listing refer to the names of recording companies: Col. (Columbia), RCA-Vic. (RCA-Victor), Cap. (Capitol), Dec. (Decca).

ALL AMERICAN. Lyrics by Lee Adams. Music by Charles Strouse. Col.

ALL IN LOVE. Lyrics by Bruce Geller. Music by Jacques Urbont. Mer.

ALLEGRO. Lyrics by Oscar Hammerstein II. Music by Richard Rodgers. RCA-Vic.

ANKLES AWEIGH. Lyrics by Dan Shapiro. Music by Sammy Fain. Dec.

ANNIE GET YOUR GUN. Lyrics and music by Irving Berlin. Dec.

ANYA. Music and lyrics by Wright and Forrest, based on melodies by Rachmaninoff. United Artists.

ANYONE CAN WHISTLE. Lyrics and music by Stephen Sondheim. Col.

ANYTHING GOES. Lyrics and music by Cole Porter. Epic.

APPLAUSE. Music by Charles Strouse. Lyrics by Lee Adams. ABC.

APPLE TREE. Music by Jerry Bock. Lyrics by Sheldon Harnick. Col.

ARMS AND THE GIRL. Lyrics by Dorothy Fields. Music by Morton Gould. Dec.

ATHENIAN TOUCH, THE. Lyrics by David Eddy. Music by Willard Straight. Broadway East Records.

BAJOUR. Music and lyrics by Walter Marks. Col.

BAKER STREET. Music and lyrics by Marian Grudeff and Raymond Jessel. MGM.

BELLS ARE RINGING. Lyrics by Betty Comden and Adolph Green. Music by Jule Styne. Col.

BEN FRANKLIN IN PARIS. Music by Mark Sandrich, Jr. Lyrics by Sidney Michaels. Cap.

BEST FOOT FORWARD. Lyrics and music by Hugh Martin and Ralph Blane. Cadence.

BLOOMER GIRL. Lyrics by E. Y. Harburg. Music by Harold Arlen. Dec.

BOYS FROM SYRACUSE, THE. Lyrics by Lorenz Hart. Music by Richard Rodgers. Col. (Also in new arrangements from the Revival. Cap.)

BRAVO GIOVANNI. Lyrics by Ronny Graham. Music by Milton Schafer. Col.

BRIGADOON. Lyrics by Alan Jay Lerner. Music by Frederick Loewe. RCA-Vic. (Modern Recording, Col.)

BY JUPITER. Music by Richard Rodgers. Lyrics by Lorenz Hart. RCA.

BY THE BEAUTIFUL SEA. Lyrics by Dorothy Fields. Music by Arthur Schwartz. Cap.

BYE BYE BIRDIE. Lyrics by Lee Adams. Music by Charles Strouse. Col.

CABARET. Music by John Kander. Lyrics by Fred Ebb. Col.

CABIN IN THE SKY. Lyrics by John Latouche. Music by Vernon Duke. Cap.

CALL ME MADAM. Lyrics and music by Irving Berlin. Dec.

CALL ME MISTER. Lyrics and music by Harold Rome. Dec.

CAMELOT. Lyrics by Alan Jay Lerner. Music by Frederick Loewe. Col.

CAN-CAN. Lyrics and music by Cole Porter. Cap.

CANDIDE. Lyrics by Richard Wilbur, John Latouche, and Dorothy Parker. Music by Leonard Bernstein. Col.

CARNIVAL! Lyrics and music by Bob Merrill. MGM.

CAROUSEL. Lyrics by Oscar Hammerstein II. Music by Richard Rodgers. Dec.

CELEBRATION. Music by Harvey Schmidt. Lyrics by Tom Jones. Cap.

CHRISTINE. Lyrics by Paul Francis Webster. Music by Sammy Fain. Col.

Coco. Music by André Previn. Lyrics by Alan Jay Lerner. Paramount.

COMPANY. Lyrics and music by Stephen Sondheim. Col.

CONNECTICUT YANKEE, A. Lyrics by Lorenz Hart. Music by Richard Rodgers. Dec.

CONSUL, THE. Libretto and score by Gian-Carlo Menotti. Dec.

DAMN YANKEES. Lyrics and music by Richard Adler and Jerry Ross. Vic.

DARLING OF THE DAY. Music by Jule Styne. Lyrics by E. Y. Harburg. RCA.

DEAR WORLD. Lyrics and music by Jerry Herman. RCA.

DESERT SONG, THE. Lyrics by Otto Harbach, Oscar Hammerstein II, and Frank Mandel. Music by Sigmund Romberg. RCA-Vic.

DESTRY RIDES AGAIN. Lyrics and music by Harold Rome. Dec.

DO I HEAR A WALTZ? Lyrics by Stephen Sondheim. Music by Richard Rodgers. Col.

DONNEYBROOK! Lyrics and music by Johnny Burke. Kapp.

DON'T BOTHER ME, I CAN'T COPE. Lyrics and music by Micki Grant. Polydor.

DO RE MI. Lyrics by Betty Comden and Adolph Green. Music by Jule Styne. Vic.

ERNEST IN LOVE. Lyrics by Anne Croswell. Music by Lee Pockriss. Col.

FADE OUT-FADE IN. Lyrics by Betty Comden and Adolph Green. Music by Jule Styne. ABC-Paramount.

FAMILY AFFAIR, A. Lyrics and music by James Goldman, John Kander and William Goldman. United Artists.

FANNY. Lyrics and music by Harold Rome. RCA-Vic.

FANTASTICKS, THE. Lyrics by Tom Jones. Music by Harvey Schmidt. MGM.

FIDDLER ON THE ROOF. Lyrics by Sheldon Harnick. Music by Jerry Bock. RCA-Vic.

FINIAN'S RAINBOW. Lyrics by E. Y. Harburg. Music by Burton Lane. Col.

FIORELLO! Lyrics by Sheldon Harnick. Music by Jerry Bock. Cap.

FIRST IMPRESSIONS. Lyrics and music by Robert Goldman, Glenn Paxton, and George Weiss. Col.

FLAHOOLEY. Lyrics by E. Y. Harburg. Music by Sammy Fain. Cap.

FLORA, THE RED MENACE. Lyrics by Fred Ebb. Music by John Kander. RCA-Vic.

FLOWER DRUM SONG. Lyrics by Oscar Hammerstein II. Music by Richard Rodgers. Col.

FLY BLACKBIRD. Lyrics by C. Jackson and James Hatch. Music by C. Jackson. Mer.

FOLLIES. Lyrics and music by Stephen Sondheim. Cap.

FUNNY GIRL. Lyrics by Bob Merrill. Music by Jule Styne. Cap.

FUNNY THING HAPPENED ON THE WAY TO THE FORUM, A. Lyrics and music by Stephen Sondheim. Cap.

GAY LIFE, THE. Lyrics by Howard Dietz. Music by Arthur Schwartz. Cap.

GENTLEMEN PREFER BLONDES. Lyrics by Leo Robin. Music by Jule Styne. Col.

GIRL CRAZY. Lyrics by Ira Gershwin. Music by George Gershwin. Col.

GIRL IN PINK TIGHTS, THE. Lyrics by Leo Robin. Music by Sigmund Romberg. Col.

GIRL WHO CAME TO SUPPER, THE. Lyrics and music by Noel Coward. Col.

GODSPELL. Lyrics and music by Stephen Schwartz. Bell.

GOLDEN APPLE, THE. Lyrics by John Latouche. Music by Jerome Moross. Elektra.

GOLDEN BOY. Lyrics by Lee Adams. Music by Charles Strouse. Cap.

GOLDEN RAINBOW. Lyrics and music by Walter Marks. Calendar.

GOLDILOCKS. Lyrics by Joan Ford, Walter and Jean Kerr. Music by Leroy Anderson. Col.

GREASE. Lyrics and music by Jim Jacobs and Warren Casey. MGM.

GREENWICH VILLAGE, U.S.A. Lyrics by Jeanne Bargy, Frank Gehrecke, and Herb Corey. Music by Jeanne Bargy. 20th Cent. Fox.

GREENWILLOW. Lyrics and music by Frank Loesser. RCA-Vic.

GUYS AND DOLLS. Lyrics and music by Frank Loesser. Dec.

GYPSY. Lyrics by Stephen Sondheim. Music by Jule Styne. Col.

HAIR. Lyrics and music by Gerome Ragni and James Rado. RCA.

233

HAPPIEST GIRL IN THE WORLD, THE. Lyrics by E. Y. Harburg. Music by Jacques Offenbach. Col.

HAPPY HUNTING. Lyrics by Matt Dubey. Music by Harold Karr. RCA-Vic.

HAPPY TIME, THE. Music by John Kander. Lyrics by Fred Ebb. RCA.

HAZEL FLAGG. Lyrics by Bob Hilliard. Music by Jule Styne. RCA-Vic.

HELLO, DOLLY! Lyrics and music by Jerry Herman. RCA-Vic.

HERE'S LOVE. Lyrics and music by Meredith Willson. Col.

HIGH BUTTON SHOES. Lyrics by Sammy Cahn. Music by Jule Styne. Camden.

HIGH SPIRITS. Lyrics and music by Hugh Martin and Timothy Gray. ABC-Paramount.

HIT THE DECK. Lyrics by Clifford Grey and Leo Robin. Music by Vincent Youmans. MGM.

HOUSE OF FLOWERS. Lyrics by Truman Capote and Harold Arlen. Music by Harold Arlen. Col.

HOW TO SUCCEED IN BUSINESS WITHOUT REALLY TRYING. Lyrics and music by Frank Loesser. RCA-Vic.

I CAN GET IT FOR YOU WHOLESALE. Lyrics and music by Harold Rome. Col.

I HAD A BALL. Lyrics and music by Jack Lawrence and Stan Freeman. Mer.

IRENE. Music by Harry Tierney. Lyrics by Joseph McCarthy. Col.

JAMAICA. Lyrics by E. Y. Harburg. Music by Harold Arlen. RCA-Vic.

JENNIE. Lyrics by Howard Dietz. Music by Arthur Schwartz. RCA-Vic.

JUNO. Lyrics and music by Marc Blitzstein. Col.

KEAN. Lyrics and music by Robert Wright and George Forrest. Col.

KING AND I, THE. Lyrics by Oscar Hammerstein II. Music by Richard Rodgers. Dec.

KISMET. Music and lyrics by Robert Wright and George Forrest. Music based on Borodin. Col.

KISS ME, KATE. Lyrics and music by Cole Porter. Col.

KWAMINA. Lyrics and music by Richard Adler. Cap.

LADY IN THE DARK. Lyrics by Ira Gershwin. Music by Kurt Weill. Col.

LAST SWEET DAYS OF ISAAC, THE. Lyrics by Gretchen Cryer. Music by Nancy Ford.

LEAVE IT TO JANE. Lyrics by P. G. Wodehouse. Music by Jerome Kern. Strand.

LET IT RIDE. Lyrics and music by Jay Livingston and Ray Evans. RCA-Vic.

LI'L ABNER. Lyrics by Johnny Mercer. Music by Gene de Paul. Col.

LITTLE MARY SUNSHINE. Lyrics and music by Rick Besoyan. Cap.

LITTLE ME. Lyrics by Carolyn Leigh. Music by Cy Coleman. RCA-Vic.

LITTLE NIGHT MUSIC, A. Lyrics and music by Stephen Sondheim. Col.

LOOK, MA, I'M DANCIN'! Lyrics and music by Hugh Martin. Dec.

LOST IN THE STARS. Lyrics by Maxwell Anderson. Music by Kurt Weill. Dec.

LUTE SONG. Lyrics by Bernard Hanighen. Music by Raymond Scott. Dec.

MAKE A WISH. Lyrics and music by Hugh Martin. RCA-Vic.

MAME. Music and lyrics by Jerry Herman. Col.

MAN OF LA MANCHA. Lyrics by Joe Darien. Music by Mitch Leigh. Kapp.

ME AND JULIET. Lyrics by Oscar Hammerstein II. Music by Richard Rodgers. RCA-Vic.

ME NOBODY KNOWS, THE. Music by Gary William Friedman. Lyrics by Will Holt. Atlantic.

MEDIUM, THE. Libretto and score by Gian-Carlo Menotti. Col.

MEXICAN HAYRIDE. Lyrics and music by Cole Porter. Dec.

MILK AND HONEY. Lyrics and music by Jerry Herman. RCA-Vic.

MISS LIBERTY. Lyrics and music by Irving Berlin. Col.

MOST HAPPY FELLA, THE. Lyrics and music by Frank Loesser. Col.

MR. PRESIDENT. Lyrics and music by Irving Berlin. Col.

MR. WONDERFUL. Lyrics and music by Jerry Bock, Larry Holofcener and George Weiss. Dec.

MRS. PATTERSON. Lyrics and music by James Shelton. RCA-Vic.

MUSIC MAN, THE. Lyrics and music by Meredith Willson. Cap.

MY FAIR LADY. Lyrics by Alan Jay Lerner. Music by Frederick Loewe. Col.

NAUGHTY MARIETTA. Lyrics by Rita Johnson Young. Music by Victor Herbert. Cap.

NERVOUS SET, THE. Lyrics by Fran Landesman. Music by Tommy Wolf. Col.

NEW FACES OF 1952. Music and lyrics by various composers. RCA-Vic.

NEW GIRL IN TOWN. Lyrics and music by Bob Merrill. RCA-Vic.

NEW MOON. Lyrics by Lawrence Schwab. Music by Sigmund Romberg. (White Horse Inn, Excerpts). Cap.

NO, NO, NANETTE. Music by Vincent Youmans. Lyrics by Irving Caesar and Otto Harbach. Col.

NO STRINGS. Lyrics and music by Richard Rodgers. Cap.

OF THEE I SING. Lyrics by Ira Gershwin. Music by George Gershwin. Cap.

OH CAPTAIN! Lyrics and music by Jay Livingston and Ray Evans. Col.

OH, KAY! Lyrics by Ira Gershwin. Music by George Gershwin. Col.

OH SAY CAN YOU SEE. Lyrics by Bill Conklin and Bob Miller. Music by Jack Holmes. Grenville Co.

OKLAHOMA! Lyrics by Oscar Hammerstein II. Music by Richard Rodgers. Dec.

ON A CLEAR DAY YOU CAN SEE FOREVER. Lyrics by Alan Jay Lerner. Music by Burton Lane. RCA-Vic.

ON THE TOWN. Lyrics by Betty Comden and Adolph Green. Music by Leonard Bernstein. Col.

236

ON YOUR TOES. Lyrics by Lorenz Hart. Music by Richard Rodgers. Col.

ONCE UPON A MATTRESS. Lyrics by Marshall Barer. Music by Mary Rodgers. Kapp.

110 IN THE SHADE. Lyrics by Tom Jones. Music by Harvey Schmidt. RCA-Vic.

ONE TOUCH OF VENUS. Lyrics by Ogden Nash. Music by Kurt Weill. Dec.

OUT OF THIS WORLD. Lyrics and music by Cole Porter. Col.

PAINT YOUR WAGON. Lyrics by Alan Jay Lerner. Music by Frederick Loewe. RCA-Vic.

PAJAMA GAME. Lyrics and music by Richard Adler and Jerry Ross. Col.

PAL JOEY. Lyrics by Lorenz Hart. Music by Richard Rodgers. Col.

PARADE. Music and lyrics by Jerry Herman. Kapp.

PETER PAN. Lyrics by Carolyn Leigh, Betty Comden, and Adolph Green. Music by Mark Charlap and Jule Styne. RCA-Vic.

PINS AND NEEDLES. Music and lyrics by Harold Rome. Col.

PIPE DREAM. Lyrics by Oscar Hammerstein II. Music by Richard Rodgers. RCA-Vic.

PLAIN AND FANCY. Lyrics by Arnold Horwitt. Music by Albert Hague. Cap.

PORGY AND BESS. Lyrics by Ira Gershwin. Music by George Gershwin. Col.

PRINCE AND THE PAUPER, THE. Lyrics by Verna Tomasson. Music by George Fischoff. Lon.

PROMENADE. Lyrics by Maria Irene Fornes. Music by Al Carmines. RCA.

PROMISES, PROMISES. Music by Burt Bacharach. Lyrics by Hal David. U.A.

RAISIN. Music by Judd Woldin. Lyrics by Robert Brittan. Col.

REDHEAD. Lyrics by Dorothy Fields. Music by Albert Hague. RCA-Vic.

RIVERWIND. Lyrics and music by John Jennings. Lon.

ROBERTA. Lyrics by Otto Harbach, Oscar Hammerstein II, Dorothy Fields, Jimmy McHugh. Music by Jerome Kern. Col.

ROSE MARIE. Lyrics by Otto Harbach and Oscar Hammerstein II. Music by Rudolf Friml and Herbert Stothart. RCA-Vic.

ROTHSCHILDS, THE. Music by Jerry Bock. Lyrics by Sheldon Harnick. Col.

SAIL AWAY. Lyrics and music by Noel Coward. Cap.

SAINT OF BLEECKER STREET, THE. Libretto and score by Gian-Carlo Menotti. RCA-Vic.

SALVATION. Music and lyrics by Peter Link and C. C. Courtney. Cap.

SANDHOG. Lyrics by Waldo Salt. Music by Earl Robinson. Van.

SARATOGA. Lyrics by Johnny Mercer. Music by Harold Arlen. RCA-Vic.

SAY, DARLING. Lyrics by Betty Comden and Adolph Green. Music by Jule Styne. RCA-Vic.

SECRET LIFE OF WALTER MITTY, THE. Lyrics by Earl Shuman. Music by Leon Carr. Col.

SEESAW. Music by Cy Coleman. Lyrics by Dorothy Fields. Buddah.

SEVENTEEN. Lyrics by Kim Gannon. Music by Walter Kent. RCA-Vic.

1776. Music and lyrics by Sherman Edwards. Col.

SEVENTH HEAVEN. Lyrics by Stella Unger. Music by Victor Young. Dec.

SEVENTY GIRLS SEVENTY. Music by John Kander. Lyrics by Fred Ebb. Col.

SHE LOVES ME. Lyrics by Sheldon Harnick. Music by Jerry Bock. MGM.

SHOWBOAT. Lyrics by Oscar Hammerstein II. Music by Jerome Kern. Both Col. and RCA-Vic.

SHOW GIRL. Lyrics and music by Charles Gaynor. Forum.

SILK STOCKINGS. Lyrics and music by Cole Porter. RCA-Vic.

SKYSCRAPER. Lyrics by Sammy Cahn. Music by James Van Heusen. Cap.

SONG OF NORWAY. Music and lyrics by Wright and Forrest. Based on music by Grieg. Col.

SOUND OF MUSIC, THE. Lyrics by Oscar Hammerstein II. Music by Richard Rodgers. Col.

SOUTH PACIFIC. Lyrics by Oscar Hammerstein II. Music by Richard Rodgers. Col.

ST. LOUIS WOMAN. Lyrics by Johnny Mercer. Music by Harold Arlen. Cap.

STREET SCENE. Lyrics by Langston Hughes. Music by Kurt Weill. Col.

STUDENT PRINCE, THE. Lyrics by Dorothy Donnelly. Music by Sigmund Romberg. Col.

SUBWAYS ARE FOR SLEEPING. Lyrics by Betty Comden and Adolph Green. Music by Jule Styne. Col.

SUGAR. Music by Jule Styne. Lyrics by Bob Merrill. U.A.

SUPERMAN. Music by Charles Strouse. Lyrics by Lee Adams. Col.

SWEET CHARITY. Lyrics by Dorothy Fields. Music by Cy Coleman. Col.

TAKE ME ALONG. Lyrics and music by Bob Merrill. Vic.

TELEPHONE, THE. Libretto and score by Gian-Carlo Menotti. Col.

TENDERLOIN. Lyrics by Sheldon Harnick. Music by Jerry Bock. Cap.

TEXAS, LI'L DARLIN'. Lyrics by Johnny Mercer. Music by Robert Emmett Dolan. Dec.

THREE WISHES FOR JAMIE. Lyrics and music by Ralph Blane. Cap.

TOP BANANA. Lyrics and music by Johnny Mercer. Cap.

TOVARICH. Lyrics by Anne Croswell. Music by Lee Pockriss. Cap.

TREE GROWS IN BROOKLYN, A. Lyrics by Dorothy Fields. Music by Arthur Schwartz. Col.

TWO BY TWO. Music by Richard Rodgers. Lyrics by Martin Charnin. Col.

TWO GENTLEMEN OF VERONA. Music by Galt MacDermot. Lyrics by John Guare. ABC.

UNSINKABLE MOLLY BROWN, THE. Lyrics and music by Meredith Willson. Cap.

UP IN CENTRAL PARK. Lyrics by Herbert and Dorothy Fields. Music by Sigmund Romberg. Dec.

VAGABOND KING, THE. Lyrics by Brian Hooker. Music by Rudolf Friml. Vic.

WALKING HAPPY. Music by James Van Heusen. Lyrics by Sammy Cahn. Cap.

WEST SIDE STORY. Lyrics by Stephen Sondheim. Music by Leonard Bernstein. Col.

WHAT MAKES SAMMY RUN. Lyrics and music by Ervin Drake. Col.

WHERE'S CHARLEY? Lyrics and music by Frank Loesser. Manmouth-Evergreen.

WHOOP-UP. Lyrics by Norman Gimbel. Music by Moose Charlap. MGM.

WILDCAT. Lyrics by Carolyn Leigh. Music by Cy Coleman. RCA-Vic.

WISH YOU WERE HERE. Lyrics and music by Harold Rome. Camden.

WONDERFUL TOWN. Lyrics by Betty Comden and Adolph Green. Music by Leonard Bernstein. Dec.

YOUNG ABE LINCOLN. Lyrics by Joan Javits. Music by Victor Ziskin. Golden LP.

YOU'RE A GOOD MAN, CHARLIE BROWN. Lyrics and music by Clark Gesner. MGM.

YOUR OWN THING. Music and lyrics by Hal Hester and Danny Apolinar. RCA.

ZORBA. Music by John Kander. Lyrics by Fred Ebb. Cap.

MUSICAL SHOWS RECORDED IN EXCERPTS

BABES IN ARMS, JUMBO. Lyrics by Lorenz Hart. Music by Richard Rodgers. RCA-Vic.

BABES IN TOYLAND. Lyrics by Glen MacDonough. Music by Victor Herbert. Dec.

BANDWAGON, THE, LITTLE SHOWS, THE. Lyrics by Howard Dietz. Music by Arthur Schwartz. RCA-Vic.

GIRL FRIEND, THE. Lyrics by Lorenz Hart. Music by Richard Rodgers. Epic.

LUTE SONG. Lyrics by Bernard Hanighen. Music by Raymond Scott. Dec.

NAUGHTY MARIETTA. Lyrics by Rida Johnson Young. Music by Victor Herbert. Cap.

NEW MOON, THE. Lyrics by Lawrence Schwab. Music by Sigmund Romberg. Epic.

ON THE TOWN. Lyrics by Betty Comden and Adolph Green. Music By Leonard Bernstein. Dec.

RED MILL, THE. Lyrics by Henry Blossom. Music by Victor Herbert. Cap.

RED MILL, THE. Lyrics by Henry Blossom. Music by Victor Herbert. Dec.

RED MILL, UP IN CENTRAL PARK. Lyrics by Herbert Fields. Music by Sigmund Romberg. Dec.

WHITE HORSE INN. Lyrics by Irving Caesar. Music by Ralph Benatsky. Epic.

APPENDIX 2

Published Librettos

ANNIE GET YOUR GUN, by Herbert and Dorothy Fields (Rodgers & Hammerstein Library Edition)

APPLAUSE, by Betty Comden and Adolph Green (Random House)

APPLE TREE, THE, by Sheldon Harnick and Jerry Bock with Jerome Coopersmith (Random House)

BAKER STREET, by Jerome Coopersmith (Doubleday)

BELLS ARE RINGING, by Betty Comden and Adolph Green (Random House)

BRIGADOON, book and lyrics by Alan Jay Lerner (Random House)

CABARET, by Joe Masteroff (Random House)

CAMELOT, by Alan Jay Lerner (Dell)

CANDIDE, by Lillian Hellman (based on Voltaire), lyrics by Richard Wilbur, John Latouche and Dorothy Parker (Random House)

CARNIVAL, by Michael Stewart (DBS Publications, Inc.)

COMPANY, by George Furth (Random House)

EDUCATION OF HYMAN KAPLAN, THE, by Benjamin Zavin (Drama Publ. Co.)

FANNY, by S. N. Behrman and Joshua Logan (Random House)

FANTASTICKS, THE, by Tom Jones and Harvey Schmidt (Drama Book Shop)

FIDDLER ON THE ROOF, by Joseph Stein (Pocket Books)

FIORELLO!, by Jerome Weidman and George Abbott (Random House/Popular Giant)

FIRST IMPRESSIONS, by Abe Burrows (Samuel French)

FOLLIES, by James Goldman (Random House)

FUNNY THING HAPPENED ON THE WAY TO THE FORUM, A, by Burt Shevelove (Dodd, Mead)

GOLDEN BOY, by Clifford Odets and William Gibson (Bantam Books)

GOLDILOCKS, by Jean and Walter Kerr (Crest Books)

GREASE, by Jacobs & Casey (Winter House)

GUYS AND DOLLS, book by Jo Swerling and Abe Burrows (Based on a story and characters by Damon Runyan), in FROM THE AMERICAN DRAMA, Volume 4, edited by Eric Bentley (A Doubleday Anchor Book)

GYPSY, book by Arthur Laurents, suggested by the memoirs of Gypsy Rose Lee (Random House)

HAPPY HUNTING, by Howard Lindsay and Russell Crouse (Random House)

HAPPY TIME, THE, by N. Richard Nash (Drama Publ. Co.)

HELLO, DOLLY! by Michael Stewart (Drama Book Shop)

HOUSE OF FLOWERS, by Truman Capote (Random House)

How NOW, DOW JONES, by Max Shulman (Samuel French)

I CAN GET IT FOR YOU WHOLESALE, book by Jerome Weidman (Random House)

KISMET, by Charles Lederer and Luther Davis (Random House)

LADY IN THE DARK, by Moss Hart (Dramatic Play Service)

LITTLE NIGHT MUSIC, A, by Hugh Wheeler (Dodd, Mead)

MAME, by Jerome Lawrence and Robert E. Lee (Random House)

MAN OF LA MANCHA, by Dale Wasserman (Random House)

ME NOBODY KNOWS, THE, edited by Stephen M. Joseph (Avon)

MUSIC MAN, THE, book by Meredith Willson (Putnam)

MY FAIR LADY, by Alan Jay Lerner, adapted from George Bernard Shaw's PYGMALION (Coward-McCann)

NEW GIRL IN TOWN, by George Abbott (Random House)

OF THEE I SING, by Kaufman and Ryskind (Samuel French)

ON A CLEAR DAY YOU CAN SEE FOREVER, by Alan Jay Lerner (Random House)

PAINT YOUR WAGON, by Alan Jay Lerner (Chappell & Co.)

PAJAMA GAME, THE, by Abbott and Bissell (Music Theatre Inc.)

PLAIN AND FANCY, by Joseph Stein and Will Glickman (Samuel French)

PORGY AND BESS, by Du Bose Heyward (Gershwin Publishing Co.)

PROMISES, PROMISES, by Neil Simon (Random House)

PURLIE, by Davis-Rose-Udell (Samuel French)

Six plays by Rodgers and Hammerstein (OKLAHOMA!, CAROUSEL, ALLEGRO, SOUTH PACIFIC, THE KING AND I, ME AND JULIET) (Modern Library)

1776, by Peter Stone (Viking Press)

SHOW BOAT, by Oscar Hammerstein II (T. B. Harms Co.)

SKYSCRAPER, by Peter Stone (Samuel French)

SOUND OF MUSIC, THE, by Howard Lindsay and Russell Crouse (Random House)

SWEET CHARITY, by Neil Simon (Random House)

WALKING HAPPY, by Hirson and Frings (Samuel French)

WEST SIDE STORY, book by Arthur Laurents (Random House)

WHAT MAKES SAMMY RUN?, by Budd and Stuart Schulberg (Random House)

WONDERFUL TOWN, by Joseph Fields and Jerome Chodorov (Random House)

YOU'RE A GOOD MAN, CHARLIE BROWN, by Clark Gesner (Random House)

YOUR OWN THING, by Donald Driver (Dell)

ZORBA, by Joseph Stein (Random House)

APPENDIX 3

Published Vocal Scores

ALLEGRO (Richard Rodgers-Oscar Hammerstein II) 1947

ANNIE GET YOUR GUN (Irving Berlin) 1946

ANYTHING GOES (Cole Porter) 1934

APPLE BLOSSOMS (Fritz Kreisler, Victor Jacobi-William LeBaron) 1919

ARCADIANS, THE (Lionel Monckton, Howard Talbot-Arthur Wimperis) 1910

BABES IN ARMS (Richard Rodgers-Lorenz Hart) 1937

BABES IN TOYLAND (Victor Herbert-Glen MacDonough) 1903

BALLAD OF BABY DOE, THE (Douglas Moore-John Latouche)

BALLET BALLADS (Jerome Moross-John Latouche) 1948

BELLS ARE RINGING (Jule Styne-Betty Comden, Adolph Green) 1956

BLUE PARADISE, THE (Edmund Eysler, Sigmund Romberg-Herbert Reynolds) 1915

BOY FRIEND, THE (Sandy Wilson) 1954

BOYS FROM SYRACUSE, THE (Richard Rodgers-Lorenz Hart) 1938

BRIGADOON (Frederick Loewe-Alan Jay Lerner) 1947

BYE BYE BIRDIE (Charles Strouse-Lee Adams) 1960

Call Me Madam (Irving Berlin) 1950

Camelot (Frederick Loewe-Alan Jay Lerner) 1960

Can-Can (Cole Porter) 1953

Candide (Leonard Bernstein-Richard Wilbur, John Latouche, Dorothy Parker) 1956

Carousel (Richard Rodgers-Oscar Hammerstein II) 1945

Cat and the Fiddle, The (Jerome Kern-Otto Harbach) 1931

Celebration (Jones-Schmidt) 1969

Consul, The (Gian-Carlo Menotti) 1950

Damn Yankees (Richard Adler, Jerry Ross) 1955

Desert Song, The (Sigmund Romberg-Otto Harbach, Oscar Hammerstein II) 1926

Destry Rides Again (Harold Rome) 1959

Do I Hear A Waltz? (Richard Rodgers-Stephen Sondheim) 1965

Do Re Mi (Jule Styne-Betty Comden, Adolph Green) 1960

Dollar Princess, The (Leo-Fall-George Grossmith, Jr.) 1909

Eileen (Victor Herbert-Henry Blossom) 1917

Fanny (Harold Rome) 1954

Fiddler on the Roof (Jerry Bock-Sheldon Harnick) 1966

Finian's Rainbow (Burton Lane-E. Y. Harburg) 1947

Firefly, The (Rudolf Friml-Otto Harbach) 1912

Fireman's Flame, The (Richard Lewine-Ted Fetter) 1937

Floradora (Leslie Stuart-Owen Hall) 1900

Flower Drum Song (Richard Rodgers-Oscar Hammerstein II) 1958

Funny Girl (Jule Styne-Bob Merrill) 1964

Funny Thing Happened on the Way to the Forum, A (Stephen Sondheim) 1962

Gentlemen Prefer Blondes (Jule Styne-Leo Robin) 1949

Girl Crazy (George Gershwin-Ira Gershwin) 1930

GIRL ON THE FILM, THE (Walter Kollo, Willy Bredschneider, Albert Sirmay-Adrian Ross) 1913

GODSPELL (Schwartz) 1971

GOING UP (Louis A. Hirsch-Otto Harbach) 1917

GUYS AND DOLLS (Frank Loesser) 1950

GYPSY (Jule Styne-Stephen Sondheim) 1959

HAVE A HEART (Jerome Kern-Guy Bolton, P. G. Wodehouse) 1917

HELLO, DOLLY! (Jerry Herman) 1964

HIGH JINKS (Rudolf Friml-Otto Harbach) 1913

HOW TO SUCCEED IN BUSINESS WITHOUT REALLY TRYING (Frank Loesser) 1961

I CAN GET IT FOR YOU WHOLESALE (Harold Rome) 1962

IRENE (Harry Tierney-Joseph McCarthy) 1919

KATINKA (Rudolf Friml-Otto Harbach) 1915

KING AND I, THE (Richard Rodgers-Oscar Hammerstein II) 1951

KISMET (Robert Wright-George Forrest, based on Borodin) 1953

KISS ME, KATE (Cole Porter) 1948

KNICKERBOCKER HOLIDAY (Kurt Weill-Maxwell Anderson) 1938

LADY IN THE DARK (Kurt Weill-Ira Gershwin) 1941

LI'L ABNER (Gene de Paul-Johnny Mercer) 1956

LITTLE MARY SUNSHINE (Rick Besoyan) 1961

LOST IN THE STARS (Kurt Weill-Maxwell Anderson) 1949

MADAME SHERRY (Karl Hoschna-Otto Harbach) 1910

MADEMOISELLE MODISTE (Victor Herbert-Henry Blossom) 1905

MAN OF LA MANCHA (Joe Darien-Mitch Leigh) 1966

MAYTIME (Sigmund Romberg-Rida Johnson Young) 1917

ME AND JULIET (Richard Rodgers-Oscar Hammerstein II) 1953

MEDIUM, THE (Gian-Carlo Menotti) 1947

MELODY (Sigmund Romberg-Irving Caesar) 1933

MILK AND HONEY (Jerry Herman) 1961

MOST HAPPY FELLA, THE (Frank Loesser) 1956

MUSIC IN THE AIR (Jerome Kern-Oscar Hammerstein II) 1932

MUSIC MAN, THE (Meredith Willson) 1957

MY FAIR LADY (Frederick Loewe-Alan Jay Lerner) 1956

NAUGHTY MARIETTA (Victor Herbert-Rida Johnson Young) 1910

NAUGHTY-NAUGHT (Richard Lewine-Ted Fetter) 1937

NEW MOON, THE (Sigmund Romberg-Oscar Hammerstein II) 1928

NINA ROSA (Sigmund Romberg-Irving Caesar) 1930

No, No, NANETTE (Vincent Youmans-Irving Caesar, Otto Harbach) 1925

No STRINGS (Richard Rogers) 1962

OF THEE I SING (George Gershwin-Ira Gershwin) 1931

OH, BOY! (Jerome Kern-Guy Bolton, P. G. Wodehouse) 1917

OH, LADY! LADY! (Jerome Kern-Guy Bolton, P. G. Wodehouse) 1918

OKLAHOMA! (Richard Rodgers-Oscar Hammerstein II) 1943

110 IN THE SHADE (Harvey Schmidt-Tom Jones) 1963

ONLY GIRL, THE (Victor Herbert-Henry Blossom) 1914

ORANGE BLOSSOM (Victor Herbert-B. G. DeSylva) 1922

PAINT YOUR WAGON (Frederick Loewe-Alan Jay Lerner) 1951

PAJAMA GAME, THE (Richard Adler, Jerry Ross) 1954

PAL JOEY (Richard Rodgers-Lorenz Hart) 1940

PETER PAN (Mark Charlap, Jule Styne, Carolyn Leigh, Betty Comden, Adolph Green) 1954

PINK LADY, THE (Ivan Caryll-C. M. S. McLellan) 1911

PIPE DREAM (Richard Rodgers-Oscar Hammerstein II) 1955

PLAIN AND FANCY (Albert Hauge-Arnold B. Horwitt) 1955

PORGY AND BESS (George Gershwin-DuBose Heyward, Ira Gershwin) 1935

PRINCE OF PILSEN, THE (Gustav Luders-Frank Pixley) 1903

PRINCESS PAT, THE (Victor Herbert-Henry Blossom) 1915

QUAKER GIRL, THE (Lionel Monckton-Adrian Ross, Percy Greenbank) 1911

RED, HOT AND BLUE! (Cole Porter) 1936

RED MILL, THE (Victor Herbert-Henry Blossom) 1906

REDHEAD (Albert Hague-Dorothy Fields) 1959

REGINA (Marc Blitzstein) 1949

RIO RITA (Harry Tierney-Joseph McCarthy) 1926

ROBERTA (Jerome Kern-Otto Harbach) 1933

ROSE MARIE (Rudolf Friml, Herbert Stothart-Otto Harbach, Oscar Hammerstein II) 1924

SAINT OF BLEECKER STREET, THE (Gian-Carlo Menotti) 1954

SALLY (Jerome Kern-Clifford Grey, P. G. Wodehouse, B. G. DeSylva) 1920

SHINBONE ALLEY (Published as "archy and mehitabel") (George Kleinsinger-Joe Darien) 1957

SHOW BOAT (Jerome Kern-Oscar Hammerstein II) 1927

SOMETIME (Rudolf Friml-Rida Johnson Young) 1918

SONG OF NORWAY (Robert Wright-George Forrest-based on Grieg) 1944

SOUND OF MUSIC, THE (Richard Rodgers-Oscar Hammerstein II) 1959

SOUTH PACIFIC (Richard Rodgers-Oscar Hammerstein II) 1949

SPRING MAID, THE (Heinrich Reinhardt-Robert B. Smith) 1910

STEPPING STONES, THE (Jerome Kern-Anne Caldwell) 1923

STREET SCENE (Kurt Weill-Langston Hughes) 1947

STRIKE UP THE BAND (George Gershwin-Ira Gershwin) 1930

STUDENT PRINCE, THE (Sigmund Romberg-Dorothy Donnelly) 1924

SUNNY (Jerome Kern-Otto Harbach, Oscar Hammerstein II) 1925

SWEETHEARTS (Victor Herbert-Robert B. Smith) 1913

TELEPHONE, THE (Gian-Carlo Menotti) 1947

TROUBLE IN TAHITI (Leonard Bernstein) 1955

TWO GENTLEMEN OF VERONA (Guare-Shapiro-MacDermot) 1973

UNSINKABLE MOLLY BROWN, THE (Meredith Willson) 1960

VAGABOND KING, THE (Rudolf Friml-Brian Hooker) 1925

VERY GOOD EDDIE (Jerome Kern-Schuyler Greene) 1915

WEST SIDE STORY (Leonard Bernstein-Stephen Sondheim) 1957

WHERE'S CHARLEY? (Frank Loesser) 1964

WILDFLOWER (Vincent Youmans, Herbert Stothart-Otto Harbach, Oscar Hammerstein II) 1923

WISH YOU WERE HERE (Harold Rome) 1952

YOU'RE IN LOVE (Rudolf Friml-Otto Harbach) 1917

BIBLIOGRAPHY

AMERICAN DRAMA AND ITS CRITICS, by Alan S. Downer (Gemini Books)

AMERICAN MUSICAL STAGE BEFORE 1800, THE, by Julian Mate (Rutgers)

AMERICAN MUSICAL THEATRE, by David Ewen (Holt)

AMERICAN POPULAR SONG, by Alec Wilder (Oxford)

AMERICAN VAUDEVILLE, by Douglas Gilbert (Dover)

AMERICAN VAUDEVILLE AS RITUAL, by Albert F. McLean, Jr. (University of Kentucky Press)

BLUE BOOK OF BROADWAY MUSICALS, by Jack Burton (Century House)

BROADWAY, by Brooks Atkinson (Macmillan)

BURLESQUE: A PICTORIAL HISTORY OF BURLESQUE, by Bernard Sobel (Bonanza)

COLE, by Robert Kimball (Holt)

CULTURE CONSUMERS, THE, by Alvin Toffler (St. Martins)

ENCYCLOPEDIA OF THE MUSICAL THEATRE, by Richard Lewine and Alfred Simon (Random House)

GERSHWIN YEARS, THE, by Edward Jablonski and Lawrence D. Stewart (Doubleday)

JOY OF MUSIC, THE, by Leonard Bernstein (Simon & Schuster)

MAKING OF THE AMERICAN THEATRE, THE, by Howard Taubman (Coward McCann)

MERRY PARTNERS, THE, (The Age and Stage of Harrigan and Hart), by E. J. Kahn, Jr. (Random House)

MUSICAL COMEDY IN AMERICA, by Cecil Smith (Theatre Arts Book)

NEW BIOGRAPHICAL ENCYCLOPEDIA AND WHO'S WHO OF THE AMERICAN THEATRE, Walter Rigdon, editor (James H. Heineman, Inc.)

REVUE, by Robert Baral (Fleet)

RICHARD RODGERS FACT BOOK (The Lynn Farnol Group, Inc.)

SONGS OF THE AMERICAN THEATRE, by Richard Lewine and Alfred Simon (Dodd, Mead)

THEATRE IN OUR TIMES, THE, by John Gassner (Crown)

THIS BUSINESS OF MUSIC, by Shemel-Krasilovsky (Billboard)

TYNAN ON THEATRE, by Kenneth Tynan (A Pelican Book)

WORDS WITH MUSIC, by Lehman Engel (Macmillan)

WORLD OF MUSICAL COMEDY, THE, by Stanley Green (Ziff-Davis)

ZIEGFELD, by Charles Higham (Regency)

Index

258